Innovations in Peace and Security in Africa

"A great addition to the literature on peace and security. It brings a breath of fresh air to scholarship in this topical subject by including issues not usually canvassed in discussions. The coverage of leadership, alcohol abuse, gender-based violence and cybersecurity stand out. Indeed, while these are ubiquitous in security ecosystems, they are rarely brought to the fore. This is what makes for innovations as the authors and editors have ably demonstrated. The book is a gem for scholars, practitioners and policy makers in the peace and security sphere."
—Prof. Patricia Kameri-Mbote, *Director, Law Division United Nations Environment Programme*

"An accessible yet rigorous reflection by committed African scholars and practitioners on issues of peace and security. Narratives, case studies, and a careful blend of diverse theories shed more light on how to comprehend the enigmatic nexus between health and security, and to offer hope to survivors of gendered and political violence. An invaluable handbook for practitioners and theoreticians of peace and security."
—Dr. Odomaro Mubangizi, S.J., *Former Dean of the Philosophy Department at the Institute of Philosophy and Theology, Addis Ababa, Ethiopia, and Editor of Justice, Peace and Environment Bulletin*

"Brings together an impressive range of perspectives by African scholars on contemporary challenges facing African societies. The authors shine light on a range of issues often hidden in more conventional studies on peace and conflict in Africa. Each chapter is firmly based in relevant scholarly literature, thus providing solid grounding for the insights presented. This volume will provide a very useful accompanying reader for courses in regional studies, as well as peace studies and international relations more generally. But it will also be helpful to social change organizations and policy-making bodies at local, national, and international levels."
—David Atwood, Ph.D., *Former Director and Representative for Disarmament and Peace, Quaker United Nations Office, Geneva, and Consultant, Small Arms Survey, Geneva*

Joseph Adero Ngala · Rachel Julian ·
Jonathan Henriques
Editors

Innovations in Peace and Security in Africa

Editors
Joseph Adero Ngala
Nairobi, Kenya

Jonathan Henriques
South Sudan Center for Strategic
and Policy Studies
Juba, South Sudan

Rachel Julian
Leeds Beckett University
Leeds, UK

ISBN 978-3-031-39042-5   ISBN 978-3-031-39043-2   (eBook)
https://doi.org/10.1007/978-3-031-39043-2

© The Editor(s) (if applicable) and The Author(s), under exclusive license to Springer Nature Switzerland AG 2023

This work is subject to copyright. All rights are solely and exclusively licensed by the Publisher, whether the whole or part of the material is concerned, specifically the rights of translation, reprinting, reuse of illustrations, recitation, broadcasting, reproduction on microfilms or in any other physical way, and transmission or information storage and retrieval, electronic adaptation, computer software, or by similar or dissimilar methodology now known or hereafter developed.
The use of general descriptive names, registered names, trademarks, service marks, etc. in this publication does not imply, even in the absence of a specific statement, that such names are exempt from the relevant protective laws and regulations and therefore free for general use.
The publisher, the authors, and the editors are safe to assume that the advice and information in this book are believed to be true and accurate at the date of publication. Neither the publisher nor the authors or the editors give a warranty, expressed or implied, with respect to the material contained herein or for any errors or omissions that may have been made. The publisher remains neutral with regard to jurisdictional claims in published maps and institutional affiliations.

Cover design by © MC Richmond

This Palgrave Macmillan imprint is published by the registered company Springer Nature Switzerland AG
The registered company address is: Gewerbestrasse 11, 6330 Cham, Switzerland

Preface

This edited volume is the outcome of a writing workshop organized by Leeds Becket University and People for Peace in Africa. Over four days in February 2020, the workshop convened participants in Nairobi, Kenya to reflect on the state of peace and security in Africa. In attendance were African researchers, educators, practitioners, civil servants, and community organizers. Through presentations and group discussion, the participants identified key trends, challenges, and innovations in multiple areas of inquiry, including conceptual approaches to peace innovation, gender dynamics, trauma and mental health, human trafficking, and peacekeeping.

Critically, this volume spotlights local perspectives in the formulation of research and policy prescriptions. While local populations have led the struggle for sustainable peace and development in Africa, too often international influence in scholarship and policy overruns the nuances and hidden meanings that characterize local experience. This anthology attempts to cure that problem by assembling a diverse team of African researchers and practitioners dedicated to foregrounding local experience. Accordingly, the analysis and exchange of ideas captured here lend valuable insight into the African story in all of its complexities. The authors grapple with the gaps and gains in the scholarship and practice of peace and security, raising novel questions that merit more scrutiny. As such, I am confident that this volume will inspire additional research and writing.

I am very grateful to Leeds Becket University for providing the resources to make this book possible, and specifically to Prof Rachel Julian who was instrumental in seeing the project to fruition. Also, a special thanks to Dr. Jonathan Henriques who managed the editing process and helped navigate the book to publication. Finally, I would like to recognise the fine universities and other institutions represented by the contributors herein. Africa is rich in cutting edge research and practice, and that diversity in innovation is surely represented in this volume.

Nairobi, Kenya   Joseph Adero Ngala

Contents

1 Introduction: Innovations in African Research
and Writing on Peace and Security　　　　　　　　　　1
Joseph Adero Ngala, Rachel Julian, and Jonathan Henriques

2 Inculcating the Peace Innovation Approach in Shaping
the Future of Peace and Security in Africa　　　　　　7
Matilda K. Maseno

3 Community's Changing Social Structures
as an Opportunity Rather Than a Threat　　　　　　35
Patrick Mugo Mugo

4 Coping Mechanisms Employed by Survivors
of Conflict-Related Sexual Violence in the 2007/2008
Post-election Violence in Kenya　　　　　　　　　　63
Scholastica A. Marenya

5 Transcending Inward Brokenness for Growth:
A Determinant of Transformative Leadership　　　111
Nelly Jelagat Kibet

6 A Systematic Review on the Effects of PTSD Associated
Alcohol Abuse on Social Economic Status Among
Youth Living in Kiambu County, Kenya　　　　　　137
Joseph Theuri

7 The Nexus Between Peacekeeping
   and Counterterrorism: A Case of African Union
   Mission in Somalia   149
   Michelle A. Digolo Nyandong

8 Cybersecurity and Online Child Trafficking in Africa:
   A Critique of the Legal Measures Adopted by African
   Countries   201
   Mercy Mutheu Muendo

Postscript   231

Index   233

Notes on Contributors

Jonathan Henriques is a research fellow at the South Sudan Center for Strategic and Policy Studies in Juba. He holds a J.D. and Ph.D. from Indiana University. For over a decade Dr. Henriques has been focused on South Sudan in state and peacebuilding spaces, including constitution drafting, governance capacity building, and advisory support to peace negotiations. He is currently working on a book that develops bottom-up approaches to constitution-making, building from community-driven processes for peacemaking and civic education in South Sudan.

Rachel Julian is a professor of peace studies at Leeds Beckett University and has been working on peace and active nonviolence for thirty years.

Nelly Jelagat Kibet is a peace psychologist with extensive experience in diverse thematic areas such as peacebuilding and conflict management and suicide at workplace. She holds a Master of Arts in Peace Studies and International Relations (Hons.) and a Bachelor of Arts in Psychology (Hons.). Ms. Kibet previously led the Peacebuilding and Transformative Leadership project (South Sudan), Inter-Religious Dialogue in Institutions of Higher Learning project (Kenya) and supported the Senior Leadership Development Programme [Kenya]. Ms. Kibet has published on Jus Post Bellum and the Politics of Societal Reconstruction; Conflict Monitoring in Africa for strategic intervention; and Artificial Intelligence and Warfare.

Scholastica A. Marenya is a social development practitioner who has worked with various international development agencies and the United Nations. She holds a Master Degree in Development Studies and a Bachelor of Arts in Anthropology from the University of Nairobi, and is currently pursuing a Ph.D. in Social Transformation at Tangaza University College, a constituent of Catholic University of Eastern Africa. She has several qualifications in Governance, Human Rights, Gender, Peacebuilding, advocacy and Humanitarian Practice. Her research interests include Social Justice, Community organizing, Gender, Conflict Transformation and CSOs in development.

Matilda K. Maseno holds a Bachelor of Business Administration (Finance) from Kampala International University and a Master of Philosophy in Higher Education from the University of Oslo. She is currently pursuing a Ph.D. in Social Transformation, specializing in Social Entrepreneurship at the Catholic University of Eastern Africa, Tangaza University College. Matilda's areas of research interest are social entrepreneurship, social innovation, and impact. She is a champion for peace and security research as well as an advocate for social change and transformation.

Mercy Mutheu Muendo is an advocate of the High Court and Supreme Court Kenya. She holds an LL.M. from U.I.C. John Marshall Law School (Chicago, Illinois). Mercy Muendo is currently Cyber security, Information Technology, Telecommunication, Constitutional and International law lecturer at Daystar University School of Law and also the Moot Court Coordinator. She has lectured for a period of 11 years and has specialized in Information, Technology and Cyber security law. Mercy Muendo has also published widely on Cyber Security, Information Technology, and International law.

Patrick Mugo Mugo is a peace researcher with an interest in conflict transformation, media and conflict relationships, electoral violence, and complex humanitarian crisis. He has formal studies in journalism and communication, political science, sociology, and peace studies, and holds a Master of Arts in Peace, Media and Conflict from United Nation's University for Peace. Mugo's professional journalism career spans two decades, mainly focused on humanitarian crises, insecurity, peace negotiations, electoral processes, and climate change across various countries, namely—Kenya, Uganda, Tanzania, Rwanda, DR Congo, Egypt, Qatar,

Somalia, Djibouti, Ethiopia, Burkina Faso, Sudan, South Sudan, Malawi, and Mozambique. Mugo has authored more than ten publications on resource conflict, food insecurity, radicalization and terrorism, media and conflict transformation, electoral violence, sustainable development/ peace, and human rights. In 2016 his book *Violent Extremism in Kenya: Countering Al-Shabaab Threat Through "Softer-Community" Approach* was published by LAP Lambert Academic Publishing. He is currently working with Aljazeera Media Network as a television producer.

Joseph Adero Ngala is a professor of international relations and diplomacy, having taught in universities in Africa and Europe. Prof Ngala previously worked as a journalist, with his reporting appearing in Time Magazine, the National Catholic Reporter, and Our Sunday Visitor. His work has been recognized by the Maryknoll Fathers and Brothers Peace Prize (USA) and the Shalom Prize (Germany), the latter of which he shared with renowned Catholic priest and Comboni missionary, Father Sessan Kizito, for their reporting and peace mediation support during the conflicts in Rwanda and Sudan. Prof Ngala has authored five books. He is the former director of People for Peace in Africa, the oldest peace organization in Kenya.

Michelle A. Digolo Nyandong is a Programs Officer at the Life & Peace Institute (LPI), Nairobi, Kenya. She is currently engaged in youth, peace, and security; climate, peace, and security and community-based peacebuilding in six informal settlements in Nairobi. Outside her functions at the LPI, she is an independent consultant in peacebuilding and security. She also enjoys undertaking research, working on strategic security planning and serving as Lead Facilitator for the Eastern African Standby Force (Integrated Mission Planning). She has particularly strong interests in gender dimensions of conflicts, peace support operations, and post-conflict reconciliation. Michelle has contributed to several peace-related research efforts in thematic areas such as climate, peace and security, violent extremism, and ethnic-identity conflicts. She is also an accredited member of FemWise Africa (Network of African women in conflict prevention and mediation). She has a trans-disciplinary background holding a Bachelor of Arts (B.A.) in International Relations and Law (Keele University, UK) and a Master of Arts (M.A.) in International Relations and Peace Studies from the Catholic University of Eastern Africa (Hekima Institute of Peace Studies and International relations, Nairobi, Kenya).

Joseph Theuri holds a B.Com-Marketing from CUEA, an M.A. in Counselling Psychology from Africa Nazarene University, and is currently pursuing a Ph.D. in Social Transformation at Tangaza University College specializing in Organisational Management.

CHAPTER 1

Introduction: Innovations in African Research and Writing on Peace and Security

Joseph Adero Ngala, Rachel Julian, and Jonathan Henriques

Understanding peace is a complex task in any place or time, but the global challenges of technological advances and threats, climate crisis and the impact of the COVID-19 pandemic are making it hard for people to see where their work for peace is making a difference. Peace is not just an absence of war or violence; it is connected to the way our international and national institutions understand violence and the infrastructure which is created to sustain peace. Peace is not just a policy or mechanism; peace is something we experience, or hope to have, in our daily lives. The reality is that all around us people are working for and learning to

J. A. Ngala (✉)
People for Peace in Africa, Nairobi, Kenya
e-mail: ppaafrica@gmail.com

R. Julian
Peace Studies, Leeds Beckett University, Leeds, England
e-mail: R.Julian@leedsbeckett.ac.uk

J. Henriques
South Sudan Center for Strategic and Policy Studies, Juba, South Sudan
e-mail: jonathan.j.henriques@gmail.com

© The Author(s), under exclusive license to Springer Nature Switzerland AG 2023
J. Adero Ngala et al. (eds.), *Innovations in Peace and Security in Africa*, https://doi.org/10.1007/978-3-031-39043-2_1

1

understand peace. It is not a utopian dream, it is what people work for in their communities, and their analysis starts from that vantage point.

By starting with what we see and experience around us, from our work with traumatized communities or seeing innovation in our institutions, we create a powerful understanding of peace that resonates with the place and time we presently live. In this collection, the authors show that peace and security in Africa are explored and understood as diverse and vital when we start looking from African experiences. Just as there is no single way of understanding peace, the authors in this book have supported one another to explain from their viewpoint that everyday experiences of peace are connected all the way up to international mechanisms. Moreover, the authors show that the experience of survivors of violence, their communities, and their leaders are as much a part of African innovation in peace and security as are regional and international institutions like the African Union and United Nations.

In addition to multiple viewpoints on peace, the authors bring interdisciplinarity to challenge us on the nature of violence, and the source of innovation and contributions from Africa. Peace is a global goal and not one that will be achieved without the inclusion of diverse opinions and perspectives that interrogate our conventions and inspire new, creative thinking. When we think about how we overcome the challenges and threats to peace, we can easily see that peace is achieved through collaboration across communities and institutions, by those who work together in specific programmes, and by bringing together diverse perspectives.

Accordingly, this edited collection is special because it is a collaboration of African scholars and practitioners who came together in a 4-day writing workshop in Nairobi, Kenya in February 2020—just weeks before the world stopped moving in the first wave of the COVID-19 pandemic. As became clear in the participants' robust dialogue in the workshop, peace is a product of thinking about what it takes for its creation, specifically in this case through a process of listening, discussing, and sharing with one another the drafts of the chapters in this volume. All of the contributors to this collection brought their knowledge, skill, and experience with them to the workshop where everyone presented a draft paper. Although each brought different research data, there was a strong recognition and understanding that they all contribute to the way we see and think about peace. For the researcher who sits closely with affected people and communities, they see the real ways in which people cope with violence and un-peace, which shows people's resilience and the importance of institutions being able to protect people from a range of forms of violence—both direct and structural. For the researcher who brings a more global view, they do so with a lens from Africa, showing the different forms of response to violence and the ways in which African case studies or instruments are contributing to a global dialogue and understanding of peace.

As such, our aim for this book was to enable the people who live, work, and study peace in Africa to research and write on their work from local to international levels. We want to bring new voices and perspectives into peace studies, and to provide a fuller understanding of peace and security in Africa. In this way the collection is novel in its design from conception to completion, and for the range of topics it brings together. Thus, our innovation in this book project is primarily threefold—innovative in bringing African authors together to produce original research and writing on peace studies in Africa; that the topics are linked through the shared nature of the authors' discussion; and innovative in how we link aspects of peace together into a uniform book. Indeed, this approach to collaborative research and writing, and the novel analyses in this volume from an African view, will contribute to the contested meaning of peace, an ongoing discussion well established in the literature.[1]

In summary, this edited volume gave the authors an opportunity to interact through the workshop, while allowing their different knowledges to drive their research, findings, and insights. We invite readers to listen and find their own path through the chapters, as we all do through peace; but note that here, in this book, the contributions are by those who live in and bring a direct view from Africa. While the chapters represent novel approaches to peace research by the authors, their engagement in talking through ideas together is reflected in several common threads running through the book. These include—recognizing the degree to which peace settings involve complex, nested interactions; that peace research inquiries must be rooted in individual and community experiences of conflict and insecurity; which in turn can provide fertile ground

---

[1] See e.g., Galtung, J. (1969). Violence, Peace and Peace Research. Journal of Peace Research, 6(1); Wallensteen, P. (1988). The Origins of Peace Research. In P. Wallensteen (Ed.), Peace Research: Achievements and Challenges. Boulder: Westview; de la Rey, C., & McKay, S. (2002). Peace as a Gendered Process: Perspectives of Women doing Peacebuilding in South Africa. International Journal of Peace Studies, 7, 1; Albert, I. O. (2008). Understanding Peace in Africa. In D. Francis (Ed.), Peace and Conflict in Africa. London: Zed; Francis, D. (Ed.). (2008). Peace and Conflict in Africa, London: Zed; Richmond, O. P. (2020). Peace in International Relations. London: Routledge.

for innovative policy responses that are comprehensive and sustainable. Furthermore, the themes in this book span diverse aspects of interpersonal violence—from the largely hidden impact of trauma to the human impacts of cybersecurity. To that end, the path through this book is as follows.

In Chapter 2, Matilda Maseno opens the book by delineating an approach to peace that takes a holistic view of the chronic instability experienced by communities throughout the continent. Maseno's discussion is helpful in considering a conceptual frame for peace innovation and the interconnectedness of peace ecosystems, whereby collaboration between diverse stakeholders at the elite and grassroots levels is critical for effective outcomes. Maseno underscores the need for and importance of developing a state-of-the-art research agenda for peace in Africa that is rooted in community experience, in order to generate lasting solutions. These can include advances in more effective peace technologies (e.g., early warning systems and conflict mapping apps) and research findings that provide crucial agenda-setting for civic engagement and policymaking around peace and security.

Chapter 3 follows a similar vein in taking account of the complexity of conflict and instability in rural Kenya with an eye towards solutions that give space for local innovations to ripen. Patrick Mugo Mugo argues that the experience of rural communities in Central Kenya follows a pattern of disruptions and limitations to self-organization within the failures of the broader political system. Instead of policy responses that treat rural instability as an endemic threat instigating a security backlash, Mugo posits that Kenya needs peacebuilding approaches that take seriously the frustrations of local communities as key drivers of instability (e.g., dispossession and poverty). Moreover, communities should be given space to develop innovative mechanisms for conflict resolution, such as hybrid approaches that build from local community practices and social structures. Arguably, such an approach that foregrounds human dignity and empowerment can go far in ensuring peace and securing livelihoods.

Chapters 4 and 5 are useful companion pieces that explore the psychological impacts of violence from a multi-tiered view of individual, community, and leadership levels. In Chapter 4, Scholastica Marenya analyses conflict-related sexual violence (CRSV) during the 2007 postelection period in Kenya. Marenya assesses the complex impact of CRSV on victims, their families and extended social networks, with long-term consequences related to socio-economic well-being, psychological health, and community abandonment. A dimension of CRSV that is vastly understudied, Marenya examines the coping strategies utilized by victims in the aftermath of violence as a causal factor explaining the disparity of victims' trajectories post-violence. Marenya finds that the selection of coping methods may be a key variable in positive outcomes experienced by survivors of CRSV, particularly methods rooted in social support and group solidarity. In Chapter 5, Nelly Kibet moves from the individual and community levels to examine trauma experienced by leaders in Rwanda and South Sudan in the aftermath of violence. As such, Kibet provides a novel contribution to the study of trauma and the psychological impacts of conflict and war. Kibet discusses how conflict-related trauma can impact leaders and their ability to govern, either in a way that advances recovery and social cohesion or that creates further instability exacerbating social brokenness. Accordingly, Kibet argues that leaders need to develop emotional intelligence in coping with trauma, which carries important policy implications for providing requisite psychological support to leaders in post-conflict periods.

In Chapter 6, Joseph Theuri extends the discussion of psychological health to the context of PTSD-associated alcohol abuse and its impact on the socio-economic security of youth populations in Kenya. Undertaking a systematic review of the literature, Theuri finds that alcohol abuse among youth has a multi-varied impact including on transitions to post-secondary education and productivity in entrepreneurial ventures, which have knock-on effects of creating significant socio-economic insecurity among this sizable and pivotal demographic in Africa. Theuri makes a compelling case for further research on effective policy responses for rehabilitation and empowerment programmes for Kenya's youth, such as psychosocial support mechanisms implemented by NGOs and government agencies.

Finally, in the last two chapters, the authors explore the national, regional, and international tiers of peace, and the intersection of institutional and regulatory frameworks with individual and community experiences of violence and insecurity. In Chapter 7, Michelle Nyandong assesses the merger of peacekeeping and counterterrorism agendas in the African Union Mission in Somalia (AMISOM). As an international and regional response to intra-state violence, Nyandong discusses how the peacekeeping role of AMISOM morphed from observation and monitoring to securing sustainable peace. However, this paradigm shift in peacekeeping operations is not without its complications. For example, from the view of the community, the AU mission at times lost credibility in the eyes of Somali populations, as peacekeepers were viewed as an occupational force, which also instigated calculated attacks by al-Shabaab on AMISOM's military and civilian components. To that end, Nyandong argues that in order for the mission to maintain its legitimacy and effectiveness, the AU must have a clear strategy to fulfil its protection of civilians mandate, including addressing operational and logistical challenges to the mission.

In Chapter 8, Mercy Muendo analyses the endemic problem of online child trafficking and cybersecurity in Africa, with an assessment of the legal and regulatory frameworks utilized to combat this pressing security challenge. In addition to broader political and economic factors that create insecure environments where child trafficking can run rampant, Muendo identifies unresolved challenges in national legal frameworks that allow this security threat to African children to persist. These include national jurisdictions with weak or porous legal regimes which allow child traffickers and child pornographers to exploit as safe havens; as well as capacity shortcomings in judicial infrastructures which can lead to lax enforcement and prosecution. Muendo powerfully argues that African leaders and citizenries must take urgent action to protect children as the most vulnerable and valued segment of African societies.

CHAPTER 2

Inculcating the Peace Innovation Approach in Shaping the Future of Peace and Security in Africa

Matilda K. Maseno

INTRODUCTION

The African continent is conflict-prone and has experienced more than one-fourth of global violent conflicts in the past 50 years (Palik et al. 2020; Stewart 2002). These conflicts are brought about by various "drivers." "Drivers" implies the dynamic nature of the factors and processes that contribute to violent conflict (Kett and Rowson 2007). The drivers of conflict and violence include young populations, high unemployment, urbanization and poverty, the lack of equal opportunities/inequality, too many firearms, bad governance, and corruption (Palik et al. 2020). Though these worrying trends have contributed to one of the most severe crises in recent history, it is important to highlight the increasing opportunities for engagement of African actors in tackling security threats on the continent (GIZ 2018). During times of crisis and

M. K. Maseno (✉)
Tangaza University College, Nairobi, Kenya
e-mail: mmaseno@yahoo.com

© The Author(s), under exclusive license to Springer Nature Switzerland AG 2023
J. Adero Ngala et al. (eds.), *Innovations in Peace and Security in Africa*,
https://doi.org/10.1007/978-3-031-39043-2_2

instability, the support of the peace-conflict ecosystem is an efficient way to promote peace and security in all regions. From past experiences of interventions to bring peace and security to countries in Africa, scholars have realized the need for a paradigm shift towards conflict prevention. Scholars can provide methodological, theoretical, and practical guidance to innovators as they operationalize their solutions. Such innovations will have profound real-world, transformative impacts on conflict, post-conflict and fragile situations, and deepen capacity for truly responsible socially positive innovation.

Today more than ever, peace scholars understand better why conflicts start, how conditions of violence or conflict endure, and what can be done to prevent or resolve conflicts (Hoelscher and Miklian 2017). Peace Studies is a growing and vibrant academic discipline and professional field. It is entwining together the deep richness of enduring peace traditions and the fresh energy of innovation and finding new ways to link them. In this manner, tradition provides the foundation for innovation while innovation reinvigorates tradition. However, there is widespread recognition that we are only witnessing the beginning of the innovation tidal wave within Peace Studies. The field is growing rapidly, creatively, and interdisciplinarily as innovation and tradition move forward in a dynamic partnership (Amster et al. 2015). Drawing upon the traditional basis of peace advocacy, this chapter emphasizes the innovative ways in which peace studies can address cutting-edge issues, inform contemporary social and humanitarian movements, and unite the best practices of the past with the needs of the present while embracing positive visions for the future.

This book chapter identifies and holistically examines the peace innovation approach and how it can be adopted in shaping the future of peace and security in Africa. The aim of this study is to search for new and innovative ways to promote both the practice and culture of peace in a rapidly evolving continent. Social phenomena cannot be rationalized effectively without building some systematic and testable tools of explanation. Rationalization in modern society is the process where formal rationality becomes dominant in every social aspect (Jin 2016). Empiricism is thus central to building a critical theory. The ideas explored in this chapter include the innovative use of social and communications technology in the promotion of peace and the comparative accomplishments of "new" vs. "old" actors in the field. It also examines the use of unconventional or unorthodox peace promotion strategies by long-established entities and innovative applications in traditional and alternative educational settings. It further interrogates the application of foundational principles of nonviolence to cutting-edge socio-political issues.

This chapter is divided into several sections. The first section explores the background of peace and security and the peace-conflict ecosystem in Africa. The second section outlines the objectives, clarifies the term "peace innovation" and evaluates the relevance or irrelevance of the approach. The third section discusses the method and elaborates on the relevant theories of conflict for this study, as well as their claims, assumptions and possible social and innovative implications. This study concludes with recommendations about inculcating the peace innovation approach in peace initiatives in Africa.

Background

Millions of lives have been lost and violence has cost African countries billions as a result of wanton destruction and foregone economic gains, in spite of numerous attempts to foster sustainable peace (Gilpin 2016). There is a huge gap between the promise of world peace and the persistence of armed conflict (Palik et al. 2020). When dealing with conflict, the main questions are: Why does conflict occur? What are its consequences? How can it be managed? And, can it be prevented in the short and long term? Conflict-affected and high-risk areas are central to today's global development agenda with business-government-development partnerships considered as vital to sustainable peace. However, taking a step back it is important to acknowledge the macro-historical trends that have shaped a global system marked by significant inequity and predation. For example, over time, failed infrastructures and institutions built on neo-colonial values, practices related to trans-Atlantic slavery, European and American imperialist policies, post-colonial states' failures to decolonize have contributed to more conflict and instability. According to Lumumba-Kasongo (2017), conflict can also be attributed to contradictions related to expansion of monopolistic capitalism and the claims associated with struggles towards multi-polarity. It can also be brought about by consequences of intensification of illegal arms trafficking and arms race among nation-states in the name of national and regional security.

In recent years the number and intensity of armed conflicts in Africa has escalated. This is especially evidenced by the high number of civilian casualties reported (e.g., APSA 2015; IPSS 2017). As such, the engagement of African states and regional organizations in strengthening peace and security in Africa remains of great relevance. With the establishment of the African Peace and Security Architecture (APSA), the African Union (AU) has shown its commitment to finding "African solutions for peace and security" to be better prepared for the prevention, management, and resolution of conflicts on the African continent. The UN and AU also oversee the African Union Mission in Somalia (AMISOM) which is mandated to support the efforts of the Federal Government of Somalia (FGS) in ensuring the security conditions, and to create an enabling environment to facilitate political, stabilization, reconciliation, and peacebuilding processes across Somalia. Since its inception, the APSA has taken an increasingly active role in addressing conflicts in Africa (APSA 2016).

The strength of the peace studies community truly lies in its diversity (Amster et al. 2015). This is responsive to the wide range of ways in which violence—both direct and structural—manifests in the contemporary world, and the myriad paths through which peace can be promoted, nurtured, and sustained. It is not only culture, history, religion, and art that inform the traditional learning aspects of Peace Studies, but other heritages as well (McCandless 2020). The philosophical traditions related to peace and ethics are not only drawn from the ancients but are actively engaged by scholars seeking to (re)interpret and add to our understanding of human relations and to imagine anew how to understand the human dilemma of conflict. It is also important to distinguish between the types of conflicts in Africa, in order to understand how they occur and how to resolve them. In a given social and political context, we have to pose the question of whether or not what we are observing historically or empirically as relations of conflict reflect primary or secondary types of conflict (Lumumba-Kasongo 2017). Primary conflicts relate to the fundamental or a structural system of individual, societal, or state's functions, and are deeper than peripheral types of conflicts. For example, they touch on the ideology of the systems, modes of societal organizations, and governance; and they deal with individual social and political locations in a given society. Secondary conflicts generally address symptoms, behaviours, and individualistic claims. They might also be classified teleologically as significant. Nevertheless, this does not make it any less important to understand why violent conflict occurs (Kett and Rowson 2007).

THE PEACE-CONFLICT ECOSYSTEM

Peacebuilding and development intersect in scholarship and practice and also span disciplines, time and space, worldviews, policy agendas, and practice areas (McCandless 2020). During times of crisis and instability, support of the peace-conflict ecosystem is an efficient way to promote peace and security in all regions. An ecosystem refers to complex, dynamic environments in which innovative approaches are implemented (Panic 2020). Political and economic relationships between and within states clearly matter if we want to tackle violent conflict (Kett and Rowson 2007). More than 25% of the population in sub-Saharan Africa live in conflict-affected countries. There are links between the prevention of violent conflict and the alleviation of poverty, international security, and protection of basic human rights for all (Kett and Rowson 2007). For a variety of reasons, various actors make more claims and grievances within their systems today than they did half a century ago. Regardless of their origins and manifestations, grievances made by the nation-states, citizens, ethnic groups, or communities imply the existence of an adversarial relationship, social and political tensions, and agencies of protests through which grievances are organized (Lumumba-Kasongo 2017). These grievances can enhance Peacebuilding or aggravate conflict, depending on how they are handled.

The AU adopts various instruments, such as: diplomacy; mediation; peace support operation; and, Post-Conflict Reconstruction and Development (PCRD)—to a certain extent (Ntab 2018). Peacekeeping is effective in bringing armed conflicts to an end, preventing them from recurring, and protecting civilians (Hegre et al. 2015; Hultman et al. 2013). While in its infancy in comparison to its penetration in the fields of global development and humanitarian aid, social and technological innovation can contribute to peacebuilding in several ways. Technology start-ups, angel investors, and social entrepreneurs are leaping into global peacebuilding spaces, often through government and philanthropic funders who believe that cutting-edge technologies can help mitigate political evils (Hoelscher and Miklian 2017). Altogether these form the ecosystem necessary to propagate peace. Technologies are being applied in many ways to create social change. There is a great potential to further explore how technologies can best be utilized as important transformative tools for enhancing sustainable human development, including the prevention of violent conflict. Peace studies have always laboured under the label of idealism, with its recommendations dismissed as naïve and simplistic by those claiming to possess an often realist understanding of how the world works and how best to tackle its more complex problems. Tension between tradition and innovation, and between continuity and change, is central to the development of peace studies.

Breakthroughs in technological innovations, in particular, have started to influence the periphery of security and Peacebuilding (Miklian and Hoelscher 2018). Despite the fact that over the past decade, it is in fact the realist world-view that has been exposed as naïve and simplistic (most graphically by the devastation in Iraq), it's not clear that the peace studies community—as a whole—has been as effective as it might have been in terms of articulating effective alternatives to armed violence (Galtung's (1996) "peace by peaceful means") as an instrument of foreign policy (Amster et al. 2015). The diverse nature of peace studies, however, is not meant to suggest that it is merely a combination of other fields. Peace Studies possess a substantive core that emphasizes nonviolence and conflict transformation (among other values) as well as a methodological preference for direct engagement and collaborative mechanisms (Amster et al. 2015). When it comes to the issues of war and peace, international negotiation and diplomacy have generally been the most favoured means for dispute settlement at the global level since the Second World War.

Method

The qualitative research method was used to collect and analyse data for this book chapter. The secondary data was collected from publications, reports, websites, etc. This chapter draws from theoretical reflections upon which a broad framework of analysis was constructed. Peace studies are not so much interdisciplinary as post-disciplinary—in other words, they tend to refrain from discipline in favour of diversification. The most important aspect about peace research is to open new spaces for peace action, often done through reconceptualization. Research is core to evaluating processes engendered by the mainstream security discourse and the counter-trend conflict/peace discourse. This chapter refers to conflict prevention as those activities that have as their primary purpose the avoidance of—or reduction in—political violence; the resolution or peaceful management of political disputes that can lead to violent conflict; and the de-escalation of tensions within society. Trends that shape the peace-conflict ecosystem include: first, deterioration of peace, security, and human rights; and second, advancement in data science methods followed by the development of exponential technologies (Panic 2020).

The questions this study set out to address were: Why does conflict occur? What are its consequences? How can it be managed? And, can it be prevented in the short and long term? Therefore, this book chapter assessed how peace innovation can strengthen the voices and actions of stakeholders in order to prevent violent conflict. More specifically the objectives were to explore how scholarship can encourage more socially responsible pro-peace innovations that also have long-term impact; identify how stakeholders should engage innovation to prevent conflict; and, understand how to integrate local communities in peacebuilding. The data collected provided information on the following key terms; conflict, peace innovation, peace-conflict ecosystem, and Africa. From the total number of articles searched, this study selected articles either published in top journals from the Journal Quality List (2012) or articles with more than 40 citations. This approach extracted 219 articles of very good quality, which were read with an eye to their contributions related to peace innovation and peace-conflict ecosystem and the support towards peace and conflict resolution. Based on the literature, 86 articles proved relevant to this study during the first phase of the search.

The second phase adopted a snowball procedure that was used to discover articles (Wohlin 2014). Using this tactic, the initial search was complemented with papers having relevant content but where the keywords did not match the search criteria, or originating from journals and citations that did not match the high standards initially set. A total number of 113 articles were thus added. For the third and last phase the search query was run a second time through EBSCO Host, to look for new publications in the period 2015–2022. This resulted in a further 39 articles, which brought the number of articles up to 238, all of which were carefully read and analysed for this literature review. A total of 41 articles out of the 238 analysed for this literature review were related to peace innovation (17.2%), while the rest (82.8%) refer to war and conflict. As presented in the introduction, the topic of supporting peace in Africa is underdeveloped, and hence this study borrowed observations from the global peace-conflict perspective.

A Theoretical Perspective

Research on conflict and peace on the African continent has to consider historical experiences and reflect on the theories of conflict given the region's rich past (Miklian and Hoelscher 2018). For example, the fragmentation of Africa was caused by colonization which created tremendous instability and insecurity. Subsequently some parts of the region have been characterized by conflicts with devastating results, including loss of human lives, degradation of the cultures, pillage, banditry, extremism, violation of women and girls, and intense political turmoil (Palik et al. 2020). Various contemporary theories explain the many dimensions of conflict. These theories help to explain the origins, causes, manifestations, and trajectories of conflict, as well as the socio-economic and cultural impact on individuals and groups (Panic 2020). As such, by locating conflict in its complexities these analytical frameworks can inform us how conflict might be resolved and in turn how we should proceed in changing a conflict situation (Lumumba-Kasongo 2017).

Reflections on the questions indicated in the methods section, in addition to presenting a "state of the field" in terms of theory, practice, and pedagogy will enhance our understanding of this study. The complex phenomenon of peace is "unlikely to be rendered accurately through a single methodological, ontological, and epistemological lens" (Firchow and Mac Ginty 2017, p. 23). Moreover, theory must be rooted in a particular social experience. It is important to properly contextualize the approaches used to help define and examine conflict, conflict resolution, peace, and reconstruction within a historical framework. Humans embody the past and build the present on it. But the past, the present, and the future each has its own distinctive moment in space and time. The present should not sacrifice the past and vice-versa. From this perspective, a social progress agenda such as the one on peace, security, and development, is perceived as being essentially a teleological and dialectically synthesized conscious effort.

There are many theories that explain the causes of conflicts and their impact. The theories adopted for this study were conflict theory or Marx's theory of social conflict and diffusion of innovations theory. The main objective of adopting these theories was to first, explain the social, physical/economic, and political worlds—the nature of the relationship between the field of peace innovation and the actors, stakeholders, institutions, histories and behaviours and their power base. Second, theories were adopted to provide specific critical knowledge that is needed to understand the peace-conflict ecosystem from a broad to specific manner. Finally, they were employed to produce a conceptualized direction of change (Lumumba-Kasongo 2017).

Also known as the theory of social conflict, conflict theory was developed by Karl Marx (1818–1884) in order to explain the social relations of production in Western Europe. Over the decades there have been many interpretations of Marxism (Lumumba-Kasongo 2017), but there are four key assumptions espoused in this theory: competition, revolution, structural inequality, and war. Marx's conflict theory purports that society is in a state of perpetual conflict because of competition for limited resources. It holds that social order is maintained by domination and power, rather than consensus and conformity. The implication of this theory is that those in possession of wealth and resources will protect and hoard those resources, while those without will do whatever they can to obtain them. This dynamic means there is a constant struggle between the rich and the poor.

The social relations referred to in Marx's theory of social conflict mainly focus on economic aspects of society, the dynamics of which are clearly reflected on the African continent, whereby the elite wield power over the poor. Accordingly, the core propositions of Marxism deal with the contradictions of the capitalist system, capitalist conditions, and how in turn to change society. Viewing human beings essentially as economic individuals sorted into classes, Marx's theory posits that due to society's never-ending competition for finite resources it will always be in a state of conflict. Therefore, in Marxism conflict is: a social class phenomenon (social consciousness); materially defined; the outcome of unequal wealth distribution (social inequality); and, not natural or organic. Around these key tenets, Marxism serves as an umbrella for radical leftist theories containing an ideology of organizing new society and a progressive methodology.

Marx's conflict theory goes further in explaining socio-economic trends on the African continent. With enormous disparities in wealth, economic development in Africa has been below the world-recommended average, lagging behind other nations. This is significant as economic conditions determine the quality and the life of ideology, philosophy, culture, and psychology, or all that is known as the superstructures. Moreover, particularly when combined with militarism, the scramble for finite resources between wealthy and poor classes spurs conflict, even as individuals and communities work to construct new forms of engagement with the pressing issues of the day. All human and social conflicts can alienate individuals, ethnic groups, broader society, and states from their own rules and established lifestyle. They might begin to question their ways of life in a way that ultimately diminishes the social harmony of a given society (Lumumba-Kasongo 2017). Accordingly, this theory provides ideas for organizing society in a more progressive manner.

Diffusion of innovations is a theory that seeks to explain how, why, and at what rate new ideas and technology spread (Rogers 1962). Diffusion is the process by which an innovation is communicated through certain channels over time among the members of a social system (Rogers 1983). An innovation is an idea, practice, or object that is perceived as new by an individual or other unit of adoption. It matters little, so far as human behaviour is concerned, whether or not an idea is "objectively" new as measured by the lapse of time since its first use or discovery. The perceived newness of the idea for the individual determines his or her reaction to it. If the idea seems new to the individual, it is an innovation. Rogers (1983) proposes that four main elements influence the spread of a new idea: the innovation itself, communication channels, time, and a social system. This process relies heavily on human capital. In summary, diffusion is defined as the process by which "an innovation is communicated through certain channels over time and among the members of a social system" (Rogers 1962).

The diffusion of innovation can be viewed in a wider context, in that it is one part of a larger process which begins with a perceived problem or need. Indeed, the steps in the process of diffusion are observable e.g., research and development of a possible solution to a need/problem; the decision by a change agent that this innovation should be diffused; and then its diffusion, leading to certain consequences and/or outcomes. As such, taking a broader view of the innovation-development process recognizes that many decisions and activities must happen before the beginning of the diffusion of an innovation. Therefore diffusion often cannot be totally understood if the previous phases of the entire process are ignored. Scholars should provide informed guidance to innovators as they operationalize their products and services for peace innovations to deliver deeper real-world, transformative impacts on conflict, post-conflict and fragile situations.

Peace innovations, like social innovations, are creative products and changes that are motivated by social needs and bring value to society by meeting those needs (Caulier-Grice et al. 2012; Mulgan et al. 2007; Phills et al. 2008). In particular they can help manage, resolve, or transform conflict in a manner that prevents the reoccurrence of violence. According to Rogers (1983), the four main elements which influence the spread of a new idea are: the innovation itself (e.g., the CEWS Early Warning Platform), communication channels (the instruments used for dissemination of the information), time (how quickly are the warnings dispersed for preventative action), and a social system (the community, group, or region within which the conflict may arise).

Conflict Trends in Africa

Violent conflict and the power of armed non-state actors remain defining priorities in twenty-first-century Africa (Williams 2013). Since 2000, over 50 peace operations have been deployed to 18 African countries. "Partnership peacekeeping," which involves collaboration between various multilateral and bilateral actors and institutions, has become increasingly common. It is imperative to identify the violence-peace system components in the violence prevention process, and then proceed to a violence cure/solution process. Peace operations must be seen as part of an effective political strategy aimed at conflict resolution not a substitute for it. Three conflict trends worth highlighting are (a) violence in the context of elections and third-termism, i.e. attempts to pursue an unconstitutional third-term in office, (b) refugees, displaced persons, and migration, and (c) violent extremism and terrorism.

Violence in the Context of Elections and Third-Termism

2015 and 2016 were important years for elections in Africa, with voters going to the polls in fifteen countries across the continent.[1] In many cases, elections constituted a point of escalation of conflict among the voters. Key socio-economic realities can threaten to turn elections into a do-or-die affair. These include the prospect of losing power in societies

---

[1] Elections were held in Egypt, Ethiopia, Benin, Burkina Faso, Burundi, Central African Republic (CAR), Côte d'Ivoire, Guinea, Comoros, Lesotho, Nigeria, Zambia, Sudan, Tanzania, and Togo.

where almost all political power and economic resources of the state are placed in the hands of the incumbent, as well as exclusive electoral systems and weak or biased electoral institutions (Adolfo et al. 2013). In Burkina Faso and Burundi riots erupted as a result of the elections. In the CAR, elections were postponed to December 2015 due to the unstable security situation, before finally being held in a rather peaceful manner. In South Sudan, on the other hand, elections were postponed until 2017 due to continuing violence and the failure of peace talks. The social structures of legitimation and institutionalization do more than simply diffuse power away from a single source. They have also been known to create incentives for pretence from those who desire power.

Refugees, Displaced Persons, and Migration

Africa had a population of about 17.5 million (M) people in 2015 (UNHCR Global Appeal 2017). This is a 30% increase as compared to 2014 which recorded 13.5 M people (UNHCR Global Appeal 2015). By the beginning of 2015, 6 of the 10 major source countries of refugees were on the African continent—Somalia with 1.1 M, Sudan with 666,000, South Sudan with 616,000, as well as the Democratic Republic of the Congo, Central African Republic, and Eritrea. At the same time, Africa is home to 5 of the 10 countries with the highest number of internally displaced persons (IDPs), mostly located in Sudan, Democratic Republic of the Congo, South Sudan, Somalia, and Nigeria. The African refugee movement was characterized by three trends in 2015. First, mass movements of refugees arose in Central Africa due to the eruption of various conflicts (e.g., Burundi, South Sudan and CAR). Second, ongoing conflicts continued to cause protracted displacement (e.g., the civil war in Somalia produced 1.1 million refugees). Third, mixed-migration routes are playing an increasingly significant role in North Africa. According to UNHCR (2016), mixed migration refers to the phenomenon when migrants and refugees increasingly make use of the same routes and means of transport to get to a destination.

Refugee host countries and countries with a high number of IDPs in Africa face myriad challenges, as they themselves are developing countries and are often subject to violent and/or political conflict. For example, Libya is considered a hub for irregular migration towards Europe, while at the same time hosting over 400,000 IDPs (Clayton 2015) amidst broader political instability. Moreover, swelling refugee populations carry significant implications and risks for the region, particularly evident in Central Africa, northern Nigeria, northern Cameroon, and Chad. Regional destabilization is a continuously increasing threat, fundamentally because groups such as Boko Haram operate across borders and target civilians. These dynamics overburden resources and capacities, exacerbate the support-system for refugees and host populations, and potentially constitute a reason for future conflict. Consequently, the existing asylum regime in Africa is in danger of suffering lasting damage.

Violent Extremism and Terrorism

Violent extremism and terrorism have increased in North Africa, as well as in other African regions. While there is a continuous debate on the push-factors of radicalization, close connections can be seen between political, social, and other structural causes of violent extremism. Push factors or enabling circumstances include political grievances, lack of civil liberties, human rights violations, difficult economic conditions, religious and ethnic discrimination, anti-terror operations and their impact, and actual or perceived inequality and exclusion (Botha and Abdile 2014). However, research has shown that individual factors, such as poverty, are unlikely alone to cause radicalization (Botha and Abdile 2014). Additionally, in ongoing conflicts, violent extremism can be used opportunistically. Research conducted on the Horn of Africa confirms that limited development and fragility in the region have caused a number of grievances paving the way for terrorist recruitment (Global Centre for Cooperative Security 2015).

Another noticeable trend globally and in Africa is cyber security. Cyber security threats are on the rise and pose a challenge to national security, public safety, and economic welfare in the twenty-first century. Cyberspace is a defining feature of modern life and an electronic medium used to form a global computer network to facilitate online communication (Tsakanyan 2017). Individuals and communities worldwide connect, socialize, and organize themselves in and through cyberspace. The existence of numerous cyber security issues on various spheres of life naturally increases political interest in resolving them. The need for cyber security is growing, ranging from isolated cases to those of national and international concern, making cyber security a major challenge to diplomacy, peace, and world politics.

The Peace Innovation Approach

Peace Innovation (PI) is innovation that expressly aims to facilitate the prevention of conflict and/or alleviate the harmful consequences of human suffering when conflict occurs (Miklian and Hoelscher 2018). PI accepts responsibility for its own intended and unintended outcomes. Breakthroughs in technological innovations, specifically, have started to influence the periphery of security and peacebuilding. As the field of technology for peacebuilding grows, most attention is being paid to the potential of new technologies for bridging the gap between warning and response (Mancini 2013). Innovation and technology actors have begun to study peace and conflict drivers in an attempt to contribute to more peaceful societies (Larrauri and Kahl 2013; Quihuis et al. 2016). New actors are directly entering peacebuilding spaces, heavily influenced by technology but not necessarily limited to such fields. However, such interest without sufficient insight into complex conflict processes may render innovations themselves ineffective, or worse, harmful to the very societies that they propose to help (Miklian and Hoelscher 2018). With more systemic expertise and guidance there is significant potential to integrate social and technological innovation to build peace, more effectively applying new advances in technology and innovation processes to address some of our greatest global challenges.

These activities could build and promote a deeper and more socially responsible agenda for peace innovation. While the focus on the use of technology for early warning and response is important, there is more to this growing field. The empowerment of people to participate in localized conflict management efforts is one of the most significant innovations and opportunities created by new technologies. Technology can contribute to peacebuilding processes by offering tools that foster collaboration, transform attitudes, and give a stronger voice to communities. In order to better understand how new technologies can contribute to peacebuilding, it is useful to clarify the functions that new technologies can perform in conflict prevention and peacebuilding projects. This approach could help overcome four existing challenges: expanding the scholar–entrepreneur–policy triad of PI; prioritizing ethical, culturally sensitive engagement; designing innovation to more clearly deliver positive impacts in conflict environments; and, glocalizing the PI playing field (Miklian and Hoelscher 2018).

A peace innovation agenda is designed to: push peace and innovation research in radical new directions; harness the integration of social and technological innovation for peacebuilding; and, provide a framework for new innovation-driven public policy. Actors in the peace-conflict ecosystem can leverage technology to create more socially responsible and impactful pro-peace innovations. The "peace" aspect should be engaged since it includes actions and products that seek to alleviate various forms of suffering, social division, and other negative effects that arise from both violent and non-violent forms of conflict. The concept of "innovation" can be adopted to leverage technological and social innovation, align with principles of both inclusive innovations—that is, to deliver benefit to people and places where the need is greatest (Santiago 2014). Innovation is not necessarily a new creation, but could also be the discovery or development of fresh collaborations (Amster et al. 2015). By utilizing technological and social innovations, countries can achieve transformative impacts in peacebuilding processes, beyond the disciplinary silos of existing innovation networks (Welch et al. 2015).

It is both urgent and essential for innovators and peace scholars to meaningfully collaborate by incorporating contextual, area-specific and conflict-sensitive guidance. This can symbiotically create peacebuilding innovations with deeper and broader impact; and move forward the state-of-the-art in innovation and peace and conflict research fields. Such work has the potential to unite peace and innovation scholarship, create new opportunities in PI research and practice, and allow innovators and scholars to jointly activate collaborations that aim to shape peaceful societies. It is also important to examine challenges that actors in this space currently face, and show how innovator–academic partnerships can help tackle some of today's most intractable global peace and conflict issues (Miklian and Hoelscher 2018).

The Peace Innovation Process in Africa

Technological attempts to promote development and peacebuilding are numerous (Braund and Schwittay 2016). The Continental Early Warning System (CEWS) is one of the pillars of the African Peace and Security Architecture (APSA). Its main objective is to anticipate and prevent conflicts on the continent, and to provide timely information about evolving violent conflicts based on specifically developed indicators (AU 2018). In this manner, the CEWS's main task is information monitoring and data collection on simmering, potential, actual, and post-conflict initiatives and activities in Africa. The Framework for the operationalization of CEWS stresses the importance of collaboration with civil society organizations (CSOs) and stresses conflict prevention as a prerequisite to achieving peace, security, and stability in Africa. Other examples of technological peace innovations include community reconciliation tools in Rwanda, mobile early warning systems through SMS in Sudan (Larrauri 2013), and post-election violence monitoring and mapping apps in Kenya (Ríos and Espiau 2011).

Peacebuilding approaches that utilize Information and Communication Technology (ICT) to access many poor and conflict-ridden regions are showing considerable promise (Mancini 2013). ICT-led innovations have led to a number of positive outcomes, including: increased government accountability and bottom-up civic engagement in politics (Breuer and Welp 2014); enabled community mediation in conflict (Bailey and Ngwenyama 2016); empowered local conflict victims to pursue peace and state-building (Karlsrud 2014; Tellidis and Kappler 2016); reduced socio-political instability (Groshek and Bachman 2014); safeguarded indigenous social memory (De Ville et al. 2015); enabled indigenous communities to bridge "digital divides" (Salazar 2008); and, reversed cultural erosion within disadvantaged communities (Ashraf et al. 2015). Researchers should interrogate other innovative ways in which peace studies address cutting-edge issues through technological approaches to peace and conflict resolution.

New technologies have great potential but do not always result in positive change. Employing new technologies for conflict prevention can produce very different results depending on the context in which they are applied and whether those using the technology take that context into account. The same technologies that foster social change and political activism can also be used by a government to control its people, enhance surveillance, and aid groups that promote violent action to achieve their ends (Morozov 2011). Technologies are not neutral; much depends on the governance mechanisms in place that allow for (or hinder) the widespread use and diffusion of technologies (Larrauri and Kahl 2013). Networks, apps, and tools can also adversely be used to track down and punish activists and dissidents who have used these services through their digital footprints (Comninos 2013). Further, the use of technology has been adopted based on existing protocols, particularly the

Protocol Relating to the Mechanism for Conflict Prevention, Management, Resolution, Peacekeeping and Security of 1999 (also known as the Mechanism) and the Supplementary Protocol on Democracy and Good Governance of 2001. ECOWAS and its partners have deployed efforts aimed at operationalising the Early Warning System in accordance with Chapter IV of this Mechanism. Emphasis on early warning and early response was intended to underscore the importance of prevention of violent conflicts both at the structural and operational levels, and the adoption of the ECOWAS Conflict Prevention Framework in January 2008 is proof of the determination of West African leaders to work proactively to avert or prevent violent conflicts (Chambas 2015).

The following discussion of cases in Kenya and Sudan illustrates the promise of utilizing new technologies for conflict prevention. The National Cohesion and Integration Commission in Kenya, which monitors hate speech, is a partner in a conflict-prevention initiative called the "Uwiano Platform for Peace." This initiative includes a web-based data collection and analysis system and a short messaging service (SMS) system. The Uwiano Platform for Peace is a unique partnership between the National Steering Committee, the civil society organization PeaceNet Kenya, the National Cohesion and Integration Commission, and UNDP. It was established in the lead-up to the historic referendum on the constitution in August 2010 (National Cohesion and Integration Commission 2012). Kenya's National Conflict Early Warning and Early Response System are pioneering the use of crowdsourcing to gather peace and conflict information through two main media. The first is through SMS using a 108 SMS short code (Musila 2013) and the other is web-based data collection. New technology does not necessarily create local capacities for peace but can increase existing local capacities. Specifically, the Participatory Digital Mapping project in Kenya suggests that new technology in areas with a history of violent conflict can be an effective tool in bolstering community capacity for conflict prevention by building on existing mechanisms and combining analogue and digital technology.

Since 2007, UNDP Sudan's Crisis and Recovery Mapping and Analysis project (CRMA) has carried out community-level mapping of threats and risks affecting communities in six states of Sudan and ten states of South Sudan, in collaboration with the respective state governments (Larrauri 2013). In 2011, UNDP Sudan identified that the work of the CRMA project provided an entry point for setting up a state-level conflict early warning system that drew on grassroots information and utilized new technologies. Such an early warning system would use the community-level mapping exercise as a baseline, and then update in real time a set of minimum indicators drawn from this baseline. New technologies for conflict prevention are more likely to be adopted when capacity building includes training in the use of technology (Lindberg and Torjesen 2013). Given the importance of government buy-in demonstrated in the case studies, international actors should invest in building government capacities to use new technology. The success of investing in training as a path to sustainable use of new technologies for conflict prevention is demonstrated by the Uwiano Platform for Peace in Kenya and the CRMA in Sudan.

Finally, integrating advances in technology with aspects of social innovation is central to deliver meaningful technology-based peacebuilding. "Social innovation" is a broad term and can refer to any attempt to offer "a novel solution to a social problem that is more effective, efficient, sustainable, or just than current solutions. The value created accrues primarily to society rather than to private individuals" (Stanford 2017). While the idea of social innovation may be conceptually ambiguous (van der Have and Rubalcaba 2016), creating innovation for social or inclusive purposes holds considerable promise (Moulaert 2013). José Manuel Barroso, Former President of the European Commission declared that "if encouraged and valued, social innovation can bring immediate solutions to the pressing social issues citizens are confronted with" (Hubert 2012).

Challenges for Peace Innovation

The economic, political, and demographic consequences of armed conflict are profound and far-reaching (World Bank 2011). War is fundamentally a development concern. Intricately tied to poverty (Fearon and Laitin 2003), war is both a consequence and cause of underdevelopment (Collier et al. 2003), increasing malnourishment and infant mortality and lowering life expectancy (Gates et al. 2012; Braithwaite et al. 2016). Peace Innovation is a powerful approach to addressing social suffering and crisis. Therefore, as the integration of social innovation and advances in ICT holds promise in addressing complex social problems (Misuraca et al. 2016), this integration has the potential to generate new advances in violence prevention and peacebuilding tools. PI propagates the ideology of carefully negotiated and continually renegotiated peaceful coexistence, and encourages learning the past in the present while striving for a peaceful future. Technological and social innovations can have transformative impacts in peacebuilding processes (Welch et al. 2015). Instead of focusing on supply-driven technical fixes, those undertaking prevention initiatives should let the context inform what kind of technology is needed and what kind of approach will work best (Mancini 2013).

In 2015, APSA reported that the AU and REC had become effective, indispensable actors in maintaining peace and security in Africa but that there were still significant challenges (APSA Impact Report 2015). Addressing 28 out of 67 conflicts in Africa, the APSA report showed that the African Union and Regional Economic Communities (REC) were more likely to intervene in high-intensity conflicts. 78% of interventions were deemed successful or partly successful. For example, in the Sahel the fallout of the 2011 Libyan crisis and the subsequent spill-over of the conflict continued to have a devastating impact on neighbouring countries (Chambas 2015). After the massive support and engagement of the international community, which led to the stabilization of the situation in Mali, the country remains fragile in the face of numerous security challenges. Indeed, security in Mali remains of critical concern, with unprecedented incidents of communal violence and increasingly deadly terror attacks (UN News 2019).

Innovations should be designed to deliver specific positive peace impacts and accordingly PI actors must take steps to avert unintended outcomes. While innovative tools are designed to improve peacebuilding outcomes, their blind adoption without accounting for local context can make conflicts worse. This can manifest as intensifying inter-group inequalities, allowing authorities to pinpoint vulnerable groups, promoting misinformation, or being used in ways not intended by the developers who are otherwise promoting conflict (Morrison 2015). Proponents may also over-promise on the humanitarian impacts of innovative technologies (Read et al. 2016) and underplay how innovation "failures" in conflict settings can have grave human consequences (Chandler 2016). Peace innovation actors can take steps to address these unintended outcomes. Multi-stakeholder integration is crucial for peace innovation, since providing innovators with context-specific, conflict-sensitive guidance helps innovations have greater impact and ultimately provide greater peace dividends for affected communities. More tangible links between peace and conflict experts and entrepreneurs would better focus innovation activity as a legitimate and important part of peacebuilding (Hoelscher and Miklian 2017). When developing innovations for life-or-death situations, actors should adhere to ethical considerations (e.g., informed purpose is interlinked with ethics under a PI approach).

Finally, PIs can reduce the likelihood that unintended consequences will exacerbate conflict by incorporating the interconnectedness of global and local issues. Given the challenges of building peace in complex crisis environments where political actors may have more to gain from conflict, glocal-oriented PIs can improve accountability and efficiency in conflict reduction and peace promotion. As glocalization is necessary to improve local ownership, key actors in the peace-conflict ecosystem should devise glocal-oriented community engagement. For example, firms are encouraged to pursue "corporate diplomacy" in conflict-prone or fragile areas of operation, leveraging local influence to support peacebuilding (Miklian 2017). Thinking in terms of the "glocal" is an instructive paradigm which incorporates both global and local considerations, and adapts international products and ideas to local cultures (Gilboa et al. 2016). Glocalized peace innovations carry additional benefits such as reducing response timeframes, providing contextualized understandings, and enabling more rapid engagement of PIs. For example, conflicts in remote settings do considerable damage to lives and livelihoods before the international community or even national actors can respond. While there are nearly always early warning signs of conflict, securing this information in a timely, actionable manner remains a major hurdle. In the design and implementation of Glocalized PIs, there is a strong need for greater inclusion of civil society, especially youth and women, to have a comprehensive approach. Additionally, it is important to focus on the strengthening of regional integration and a clear division of roles and responsibilities.

Conclusion

As shown in this chapter, there is much to be researched in the study of peace and innovation processes. Scholars and advocates can shape development in the field of peace and security while considering its historical roots. Pushing research frontiers forward will help innovators develop better tools that prevent violence and promote peace in crisis and conflict environments. State-of-the-art peace research will maximize chances to develop new technologies that support human security and peacebuilding. By creating conditions to formalize collaboration between stakeholders, a PI approach and agenda can design new solutions to complex conflict problems. The field of Peace Studies is more than a set of theories, it strives to promote action that yields a more just and peaceful world.

Major proponents in today's conflict situations have demonstrated a greater propensity to come to the negotiating table to address their differences. This inclination has been affected by many factors. The abundance of third parties of the intergovernmental, state, and non-state variety who are willing to support peace settlements means that warring parties do not have to struggle to reach a negotiated compromise on their own. Improvements in scholarly work have also come a long way in exposing the complexities of peace and conflict and allowing a better understanding of the field. The onslaught of technological advances has allowed scholars and innovators to view peace from a different lens and try to devise ways in which peace and conflict can be mitigated with a long-term focus on how to create solutions. The use of early warning systems, SMS texts, and conflict mapping apps has enabled the prevention of some of the conflicts that could have taken place and worsened the devastation in Africa. The strategic incentives to look for solutions are however adversely affected by several factors, including acute security dilemmas, communities and their leaders' experience in civil conflict situations and pressuring tactics. Accordingly, security guarantees and other kinds of positive and negative inducement are often necessary to instigate, manage, and sustain the peace innovation process.

Peace innovation processes must engage diverse groups at the grassroots and elite levels; this is critical for building trust and laying the foundations for the kinds of social and political relationships that will sustain civil society. Furthermore, maintaining legitimacy among international and local stakeholders is a crucial part of achieving sustainable peace. While conflict parties increasingly turn to third parties to support peace settlements, the reality is that there is no one-size-fits-all approach to negotiation and conflict management. It is imperative to strengthen the exchange between different international, government agencies and peace stakeholders and monitor outputs for adaptive learning. It is critical to synergize peace innovations and collaborate with peacebuilding agencies for effective interventions and actions to respond to the nexus between human rights, governance and peace and security. Peace innovations can easily build on already existing mechanisms which emphasize civilian protection mandates and activate policing and civilian dimensions of peace support operations (PSOs). The diffusion of the peace innovation approach can further strengthen the link between (micro) realities and decisions, and between primary stakeholders and decision makers.

Conflict is a problem that transcends economic, social, and political boundaries. As such, identifying the predictors of conflict should be an important focus for social innovators, political leaders, policymakers, and researchers alike. More must be done to engage with local voices in African societies and to help build and improve civil society-driven conflict prevention and resolution mechanisms throughout the region. Inculcating modern technology in the process enables not only conflict resolution but also long-term prevention. To prevent a relapse into conflict and disorder in countries that are still in fragile recovery, we as a region must not lose sight of providing the necessary support to diplomatic and political mediation. This includes embracing the diffusion of peace innovation, ensuring free and fair elections, implementing security sector reform, and combating terrorism, cyber-crime and transnational crime. We cannot allow ourselves to forget that prevention of conflict remains a pressing priority in Africa. Ultimately, this chapter captures both the ambition and the breadth of the contemporary peace studies agenda. It also illustrates both the opportunities and the challenges faced by a maturing field at a historical moment marked by profound uncertainty.

References

Adolfo, E. V., Kovacs, M. S., Nyström, D. & Utas, M. (2013). Electoral Violence in Africa. Policy Notes 2012/3. Nordic Africa Institute.

African Peace and Security Architecture. (2015). APSA Roadmap: 2016-2020, African Union Commission. Peace and Security Department. Addis Ababa, December 2015.

African Union. (2018). Conflict Prevention and Early Warning. Division of the AU Peace and Security Department. 13 February 2018. https://www.peaceau.org/uploads/conflict-prevention-and-early-warning-booklet-13feb18-approved.pdf.

Amster, R., Finley, L., Pries, E., & McCutcheon, R. (2015). Peace Studies Between Tradition and Innovation. From the Series Peace Studies: Edges and Innovations. Cambridge Scholars Publishing.

Ashraf, M., Grunfeld, H., & Quazi, A. (2015). Impact of ICT Usage on Indigenous Quality of Life. Australasian Journal of Information Systems, 19(1), 1–16.

Bailey, A., & Ngwenyama, O. (2016). Community Bridging Through ICTs: Seeking to Overcome Digital and Community Divides. Journal of Community Informatics, 12(1), 69–89.
Botha, A., & Abdile, M. (2014). Radicalisation and Al-Shabaab Recruitment in Somalia. Institute for Security Studies Papers, 266, 20.
Braithwaite, A., Dasandi, N., & Hudson, D. (2016). Does Poverty Cause Conflict? Isolating the Causal Origins of the Conflict Trap. Conflict Management and Peace Science, 33(1), 45–66.
Braund, P., & Schwittay, A. (2016). Scaling Inclusive Digital Innovation Successfully: The Case of Crowdfunding Social Enterprises. Innovation and Development, 6(1), 15–29.
Breuer, A., & Welp, Y. (Eds.). (2014). Digital Technologies for Democratic Governance in Latin America. London: Routledge.
Caulier-Grice, J., Davies, A., Patrick, R., & Norman, W. (2012). Defining Social Innovation. A Deliverable of the Project: "The Theoretical, Empirical and Policy Foundations for Building Social Innovation in Europe" (TEPSIE), European Commission 7th Framework Programme. Brussels, Belgium: European Commission, DG Research.
Chambas, M. I. (2015). The Growing Challenges of Peace and Security in Africa: A West African Perspective. 2015 Kofi Annan/Dag Hammarskjöld Annual Lecture. By Special Representative of the Secretary-General-United Nations Office for West Africa (UNOWA).
Chandler, D. (2016). How the World Stopped Worrying and Learned to Love Failure: Big Data, Resilience and Emergent Causality. Millennium, 44(1), 1–20.
Clayton, J. (2015). Numbers of Internally Displaced in Libya Double since September. UNHCR. Available at: http://www.unhcr.org/news/latest/2015/6/5592a8286/numbers-internally-displaced-libya-double-since-september-unhcr.html.
Collier, P., Elliott, V. L., Hegre, H., Hoeffler, A., Reynal-Querol, M., & Sambanis, N. (2003). Breaking the Conflict Trap: Civil War and Development Policy. Washington, DC: World Bank.
Comninos, A. (2013). The role of social media and user-generated content in post-conflict peace building. The World Bank.
De Ville, G., Albert, G., Buckley, A., & Butler. B. (2015). Pantani Blog: Using ICT for Safeguarding and Sharing Indigenous Social Memory. Journal of Research and Didactics in Geography, 2(4), 97–102.
Fearon, J., & Laitin, D. (2003). Ethnicity, Insurgency, and Civil War. American Political Science Review, 97(1): 75–90.
Firchow, P., & Mac Ginty, R. (2017). Measuring Peace: Comparability, Commensurability, and Complementarity Using Bottom-Up Indicators. International Studies Review, 19(1), 6–27.

Galtung, J. (1996). Peace by Peaceful Means: Peace and Conflict, Development and Civilization. International Peace Research Institute, Oslo (PRIO). Sage.

Gates, S., Hegre, H., Nygård, H., & Strand, H. (2012). Development Consequences of Armed Conflict. World Development, 40(9), 1713–1722.

Gilboa, E., Jumbert, M. Miklian, J., & Robinson, P. (2016). Reaching Beyond the CNN Effect to Study New Media and Conflict. Review of International Studies, 26(4): 1–19.

Gilpin, R. (2016). Understanding the Nature and Origins of Violent Conflict in Africa. Minding the Gap: African Conflict Management in a Time of Change, 21.

GIZ. (2018). The State of Peace and Security in Africa: Successes and Challenges in Tackling Violent Conflicts. Capacity4Change (C4C) Event on 21 March 2018. Brussels. Available at: https://www.giz.de/en/worldwide/63606.html.

Global Centre for Cooperative Security. (2015). Countering Violent Extremism and Promoting Community Resilience in the Greater Horn of Africa: An Action Agenda. May 2015.

Groshek, J., & Bachman, I. (2014). Examining Digital Diffusion and Youth Bulges in Forecasting Political Change in Latin America. In Y. Welp & A. Breuer (Eds.), Digital Opportunities for Democratic Governance in Latin America (pp. 17–32). London: Routledge.

Harzing, A.W.K. (2012). Journal Quality List. Google Scholar.

Hoelscher, K., & Miklian, J. (2017). Can Innovators Be Peacebuilders? A Peace Innovation Action Plan. Available at: https://www.globalpolicyjournal.com/blog/01/08/2017/can-innovators-be-peacebuilders-peace-innovation-action-plan.

Hubert, A. (2012). Foreword: Challenge Social Innovation. In H. W. Franz, J. Hochgerner, & J. Howaldt (Eds.), Challenge Social Innovation: Potentials for Business, Social Entrepreneurship, Welfare and Civil Society (pp. v–x). Berlin: Springer.

Hultman, Lisa, Jacob Kathman, and Megan Shannon. (2013). United Nations Peacekeeping and Civilian Protection in Civil War. American Journal of Political Science. 57(4), 875–891.

IPSS, A. (2017). Impact Report 2016: Assessment of the Impacts of Intervention by the African Union and Regional Economic Communities in 2016 in the Frame of the African Peace and Security Architecture (APSA).

Jin, D. (2016). The Partial Transcendence of the Axial Age. In The Great Knowledge Transcendence (pp. 85–105). Palgrave Macmillan, New York.

Karlsrud, J. (2014). Peacekeeping 4.0: Harnessing the Potential of Big Data, Social Media and Cyber Technologies. In B. Kremer & A. R. Mueller (Eds.), Cyberspace and International Relations, 141–160. New York: Springer.

Kett, M., & Rowson, M. (2007). Drivers of Violent Conflict. Journal of the Royal Society of Medicine, 100, 403–406. Available at: http://www.ncbi.nlm.nih.gov/pmc/articles/PMC1963391/pdf/0403.pdf.

Larrauri, H. P. (2013). New Technologies and Conflict Prevention in Sudan and South Sudan. In F. Mancini (Ed.), New Technology and the Prevention of Violence and Conflict. New York: International Peace Institute.

Larrauri, H. P., & Kahl, A. (2013). Technology for Peacebuilding Stability. International Journal of Security and Development, 2(3). https://doi.org/10.5334/sta.cv.

Lindberg, Y., & Torjesen, S. (2013). Mobile Phones Build Peace. Stanford Social Innovation Review. Available at: https://ssir.org/articles/entry/mobile_phones_build_peace.

Lumumba-Kasongo, T. (2017). Contemporary Theories of Conflict and their Social and Political Implications. Peace, Security and Post-Conflict Reconstruction in the Great Lakes Region of Africa (pp. 29–48). Oxford: African Book Collective.

Mancini, F. (Ed). (2013). New Technology and the Prevention of Violence and Conflict. New York: International Peace Institute.

McCandless, E. (2020). Peacebuilding-Development Nexus. Palgrave Encyclopaedia of Peace and Conflict Studies, 82–97.

Miklian, J. (2017). How Businesses Can Be Effective Local Peacebuilders—Evidence from Colombia. PRIO Policy Brief 27.

Miklian, J., & Hoelscher, K. (2018). A New Research Approach for Peace Innovation. Innovation and Development, 8(2), 189–207. Available at: https://doi.org/10.1080/2157930X.2017.1349580.

Misuraca, G., Kucsera, C., Lipparini, F., Voigt, C., & Radescu, R. (2016). ICT-Enabled Social Innovation to Support the Implementation of the Social Investment Package. EUR 27838 EN. https://doi.org/10.2791/743181.

Morozov, E. (2011). The Net Delusion: The Dark Side of Internet Freedom. New York: Public Affairs.

Morrison, C. (2015). Engaging with Local Communities to Prevent Violence: What Role for ICTs? Brighton: IDS.

Moulaert, F. (Ed). (2013). The International Handbook on Social Innovation. London: Edward Elgar.

Mulgan, G., Tucker, S., Ali, R., & Sanders, B. (2007). Social Innovation: What It Is, Why It Matters and How It Can Be Accelerated. Skoll Center for Social Entrepreneurship, Oxford, England: University of Oxford.

Musila, G. M. (2013). Early Warning and the Role of New Technologies in Kenya. In F. Mancini (Ed.), New Technology and the Prevention of Violence and Conflict. New York: International Peace Institute.

National Cohesion and Integration Commission. (2012). Milestones of the National Cohesion and Integration Commission. The Star, September 10, 2012.

Ntab, M. N. (2018). APSA Impact Report 2016: Assessment of the Impact of Interventions by the AU and RECs in 2016 in the frame of APSA Trends and core findings. Presentation on 21 March 2018, GIZ—Addis Peace and Security Group, Brussels.

Palik, Júlia; Siri Aas Rustad & Fredrik Methi (2020) Conflict Trends: A Global Overview, 1946–2019. PRIO Paper. Oslo: PRIO

Panic, Branka. (2020). Data for Peacebuilding and Prevention Ecosystem Mapping: The State of Play and the Path to Creating a Community of Practice. New York: NYU Center on International Cooperation.https://cic.nyu.edu/wp-content/uploads/1662/65/data_for_peacebuilding_and_prevention_-_ecosystem_mapping_-_october_2020.pdf.

Phills, J. A., Deiglmeier, K., & Miller, D. T. (2008). Rediscovering Social Innovation. Stanford Social Innovation Review, 6, 34–43.

Quihuis, M., Nelson, M., & Guttieri K. (2016). Peace Technology: Scope, Scale and Cautions. Washington, DC: Building Peace.

Read, R., Taithe, B., & MacGinty, R. (2016). Humanitarian Information Systems and the Mirage of Technology. Third World Quarterly, 37(8): 1314–1331.

Ríos, P., & Espiau, G. (2011). New Trends in Peace-Building: Another Form of Social Innovation. Barcelona: Institut Català Internacional per la Pau.

Rogers, E. M. (1962). Diffusion of Innovations. First Edition. The Free Press. Macmillan Publishing Co., Inc.

Rogers, E. M. (1983). Diffusion of Innovations. Third Edition. The Free Press. Macmillan Publishing Co., Inc.

Salazar, J. F. (2008). Indigenous Peoples and the Cultural Constructions of Information and Communication Technology (ICT) in Latin America. In C. van Slyke (Ed.). Information Communication Technologies: Concepts, Methodologies, Tools, and Applications. Hershey, PA: IGI Global.

Santiago, F. (2014). Innovation for Inclusive Development. Innovation and Development, 4(1), 1–4.

Stanford Graduate School of Business. (2017). Defining Social Innovation. Available at: https://www.gsb.stanford.edu/faculty-research/centers-initiatives/csi/defining-social-innovation.

Stewart, F. (2002). Root Causes of Violent Conflict in Developing Countries. BMJ, 324(7333), 342–345.

Tellidis, I., & Kappler, S. (2016). ICT in Peacebuilding: Implications, Opportunities and Challenges. Cooperation and Conflict, 51(1): 75–93.

Tsakanyan, V. T. (2017). The Role of Cybersecurity in World Politics. Vestnik RUDN. International Relations, 17(2), 339–348.

UN News. (2019). 'Continuing Deterioration' Leaves Mali Facing Critical Security Level: UN Expert. Available at: https://news.un.org/en/story/2019/12/1052531.
UNHCR. (2015). UNHCR Global Appeal 2015 Update. Available at: https://www.unhcr.org/528a0a190.pdf.
UNHCR. (2016). 'Refugees' and 'Migrants' – Frequently Asked Questions (FAQs). United Nations Higher Commissioner on Refugees, 16 March 2016, https://www.unhcr.org/news/stories/refugees-and-migrants-frequently-asked-questions-faqs
UNHCR. (2017). Global Appeal 2016–2017. Available at: https://www.unhcr.org/publications/fundraising/564da0df0/unhcr-global-appeal-2016-2017-global-appeal-2016-2017.html.
Van der Have, R. P., & Rubalcaba, L. (2016). Social Innovation Research: An Emerging Area of Innovation Studies? Research Policy, 45(9), 1923–1935.
Welch, J., Halford, S., & Weal, M. (2015). ICTs and Peacebuilding: A Conceptual Framework. ACM Web Science Conference No. 4.
Williams, P. D. (2013). Peace Operations in Africa: Lessons Learned Since 2000. Africa Security Brief. A Publication of the Africa Center for Strategic Studies #25.
Wohlin, Claes. (2014). Guidelines for Snowballing in Systematic Literature Studies and a Replication in Software Engineering. EASE '14: Proceedings of the 18th International Conference on Evaluation and Assessment in Software Engineering, 38, 1–10. https://doi.org/10.1145/2601248.2601268.
World Bank. (2011). World Development Report 2011. Washington, DC: World Bank.

CHAPTER 3

Community's Changing Social Structures as an Opportunity Rather Than a Threat

Patrick Mugo Mugo

INTRODUCTION: AUTHOR'S PERSPECTIVE—CONVERSATION WITH MY GRANDFATHER

It is mid-2004, I am visiting my grandparents' upcountry at a time when Kenya's economic growth is at 2.3%[1]; and yet within the Central region of Kenya, the story in the minds of many in the village is about insecurity and violence. With my grandfather—Joseph Kiragu Mugo alias "Githu," aged 82 years old (deceased September 2017)—we are seated outside his small shop having our occasional conversations and interactions about the state of affairs of the village and the country. By then I was 27 years old.

---

[1] In 2004 Kenya's GDP growth picked up to 2.3% in early 2004, compared with a sluggish 1.4% in 2003. Agriculture remains the population's main occupation and source of income with almost 75% in agriculture. 15% of the labour force is officially classified as unemployed; other estimates place Kenya's unemployment much higher, even up to 40% (Library-of-Congress, June 2007).

P. M. Mugo (✉)
Al Jazeera Media Network, Narobi, Kenya
e-mail: patrickmaragi@gmail.com

© The Author(s), under exclusive license to Springer Nature Switzerland AG 2023
J. Adero Ngala et al. (eds.), *Innovations in Peace and Security in Africa*,
https://doi.org/10.1007/978-3-031-39043-2_3

35

My grandfather decides to share with me startling details about the state of affairs in our village. Below is our conversation:

Grandfather: Mugo, I think it is wise if you would contemplate not ever settling within this village. The insecurity that will prevail in the future, as you can witness at this moment in time, due to poverty and unemployment among the youth will not allow you to live in peace.[2] Its better if you acquire a plot in the city (Nairobi, Kenyas capital), and settle there.

Grandson: Grandfather, are you telling us (second generation) that we have no future in this village?

Grandfather: Mugo, your mother, your uncle and even some of our family members and friends no longer reside here; there is nothing of value in this village. Your only connection with this village for now is just me and your grandmother (deceased August, 2012), when we are long gone, there will be loose ties. Should you opt to settle within this village, the economically dispossessed plus those who cannot find a source of income will try to steal from you. There is no meaningful way of making a living in this village, and those who could have created an enabling environment, have migrated and settled in the city in search of a better life and familys security. Unlike in the past, the land is no longer productive, even the little that is left has been subdivided among family members and exploited and it is now barren.

Fast forward to mid-2007, another memorable conversation and interaction with my grandfather takes place. A time when the Kenyan government is carrying out a crackdown on the Mungiki gangs/militias,[3]

---

[2] Thayu: Is a Kikuyu word meaning peace. Kikuyu ethnic group is one of the 42 ethnic groups in Kenya, constituting 22% of the population, mainly inhabiting Central region. According to the 2009 census there are 6,622,576 Kikuyus in Kenya.

[3] Mungiki is a militia/terrorist group/pseudo-criminal gang and banned in Kenya. Its name means "A united people" or "multitude" in the Kikuyu language and arguably has its roots in discontent arising from severe unemployment and landlessness resulting from

accusing them of involvement in beheadings, extortion rackets, and protection racketeering within the rural areas of the Central region of Kenya and other parts of the country. It is a very insecure moment for the unemployed youth within the upcountry:

> *Grandson*: Grandfather, I know you have heard of the on-going crackdown of suspected Mungiki gangs' adherents? ... (He didnt let me finish my question)
> *Grandfather*: What the Government is doing is terrible, if any of those Mungiki gangs' adherents come along seeking help or protection, I would host them without making the police aware. During the emergency[4] that is how Mau Mau[5] managed to survive. That is why I would protect the Mungiki suspects.
> *Grandson*: Why then would a government that has Kikuyus[6] as President and as Minister for Internal Security turn around and seek to kill Kikuyus. Yet, they are all from the same ethnic affiliation.
> *Grandfather*: During the emergency it is the Kikuyu Home Guards[7] and collaborating chiefs who were selling out the Mau Mau to colonialist. Even when we attained independence, it was the children of the same collaborators who benefited... (he poses). Mugo... people are cannibalistic[8]... (he laughs) ... I know... (loud laughter). Most of us, who were

Kenya's rapid population growth. Many disaffected unemployed youth are attracted to an organization, giving them a sense of purpose and cultural and political identity, as well as income. The founders supposedly modelled Mungiki on the Mau Mau fighters (Brief gathered from my interview with Dr. Mutuma Ruteere, Human Rights Researcher on 11 October 2012.).

[4] Reference to the period between 1952 and 1960 when the British colonial Government placed the Kenyan colonial territory under a state of emergency due to the Mau Mau rebellion.

[5] Mau Mau Uprising/Revolt: Kenyan freedom fighters who back in 1952–1960 waged a guerilla warfare; their main aim was to end the British's colonial rule and reclaim land forcibly acquired by European settlers.

[6] The Kikuyu ethnic group are a Bantu people found in Kenya, mainly inhabiting the Central region, the largest ethnic group in Kenya; 7 million in number by estimates (Lewis 2009).

[7] Kikuyu Home Guards: existed from early 1953 until January 1955. Formed in response to Mau Mau attacks by loyalist leaders, an extremely divisive development within Kikuyu society. At its peak it number 25,000 men, and thought to have been instrumental in the capture of Mau Mau leader Dedan Kimathi.

[8] Cannibalism is when people eat people, or animal eats another animal. In the context of my grandfather it implies that, politically speaking, the survival of colonial rule and subsequent defeat of Kenya's fight for independence was enabled or facilitated by local

not educated by then had to look for menial work. I had to work for an Italian family as a cook; as to educate your mum and your uncle. The constitution that people are trying to review now (2007) is not the one that the Mau Mau wanted... and you think... they (those in power) will ever allow it to be changed, never... (laughing as he sits up to stress a point) never. Since independence we have had the wrong leaders. (Raises his voice, with his eyes on me now) It's then that I made a commitment of educating my children, so that together with their generations they won't have to go through what I went through. I would hate to see my children's generation doing menial work. Without an education... one is nothing. As I have told you before, there is nothing in this village of value and for those who refused to educate their children, things are bad for them, and the coming days might even be worse.

...It did not matter if anyone died poor provided, he or she could one day say, "look, I've a son as good and as well-educated as any of you can find in the land". You did not need to be educated to know this... a lot of motives had indeed combined into one desire, the desire to have a son who had acquired all the learning that there was. (Thiong'o 1987, p. 16)

Research Problem: Grandfather's Conversations Implications

This was not a message one would anticipate to come from a grandfather, least of all from a man who had made his contribution during the violent struggle for Kenya's independence from the British colonial rule back in the 1950s. It is often argued in Kenya that Kenya's freedom fighters—the "Mau Mau"—might have "lost the war" for Kenya's independence to the British colonial government, and subsequently the control of power in post-independent Kenya to British government local loyalist. In other views, however, the Mau Mau *did not* lose "the argument" that forcibly

collaborators. In view of most freedom fighters like my grandfather, it was the colonial collaborator and their children that have benefited in post-colonial Kenya at the expense of wider society; and that those who have tried to offset the balance of order have been targeted or "sold." Thus his reason to call his fellow community members—Cannibalist— and thereby leading him to acquire a nickname—Githu—which means "The Cannibalist."

acquired land[9] and other subjugated rights of indigenous communities needed to revert back to the rightful owners. Among Kenya's founding fathers, Bildad Kaggia[10] remained true to his ideals and can be taken as the moral compass of what has been wrong and right about post-independence Kenya. Bildad Kaggia had to resign from government in 1964, just after one year in the post-independence government. While resigning, Bildad Kaggia argued that "as a representative, I found it difficult to forget the people who elected me on the basis of definite pledges, or forget freedom fighters who gave their all, for the independence we are enjoying" (1975). My grandfather and Bildad Kaggia never had the benefit of meeting to my knowledge, but Kaggia's concerns in 1964 have been vindicated by the reality my grandfather was warning me about—the tragic transformation of rural community social structures.

Stemming from my conversations and interactions with my late grandfather about human insecurity in the rural Central region and the rest of Kenya, the bottom stratum of the rural community is still not at peace with itself. Indeed, the rural Kenya community still remains highly unequal, fearful, insecure, and uncertain about their future. Even without a definitive cut-off date, Kenya's post-independence high economic growth, and not sustainable development, has been marked by rising cases of violence and insecurity. This could be explained by the tragic changes to the rural community's social structures, namely diminishing land productivity, dispossession inequality, and drastic demographic changes, which have resulted in human insecurity. As the third generation, after the death of our grandparents, we are less and less connected to the village; we only go to the village either during special ceremonies or to check on the status of what we inherited from them. These conversations have had a lasting impact on my life, giving me a critical point of view about

---

[9] Land in the context of most Kenyan communities is a factor of production and a community's survival/continuity.

[10] Bildad Mwaganu Kaggia (1921–7 March 2005) was a Kenyan nationalist, activist, politician, and member of the Mau Mau Central Committee. In 1953 Kagia and others were sentenced to seven years hard labour for managing Mau Mau. Subsequently, he was imprisoned at Lokitaung, together with Jomo Kenyatta, Paul Ngei, Kungu Karumba, and Fred Kubai. Later, Achieng' Oneko won his appeal but was not left free but detained in camps all over Kenya. After Kenya gained independence, Kaggia became a Member of Parliament, establishing himself as a militant, fiery nationalist who wanted to serve the poor and landless people (Sources: The Life of Bildaa Kaggia—Bildad M. Kaggia Foundation).

violence and insecurity in Kenya, and the need to perceive them as an opportunity by the bottom stratum in search of human security. This chapter aims to bring forth the notion that there is a correlation between the tragic changes to the social structure of the rural economy and the prevailing violence and insecurity. These phenomena within the rural region of Central Kenya can be attributed to the national government's failure to ensure protection to citizens, as well as a failed socio-economic project.

According to Briggs and David (1998), violence and insecurity may "appear incredibly complicated with a simple origin," but this is just the "surface that might be concealing something stunningly complex at the bottom," which needs to be understood. Beneath the surface, at the bottom stratum of the society, there is the feeling among youth of exclusion from power structures, in addition to the absence of legitimate channels of expression for grievances. This has made rural violence a ventilation through which frustrations are voiced, due to individual vulnerability and dispossession. However, Kaplinsky (2001) reminds us that "although the perception of insecurity is not always borne out of statistical evidence, it fundamentally affects the well-being" of an individual and community (cited in Moser and Rodgers 2005, p. 4).

In this regard, the community in discussion is a "grouping of people who reside in a specific locality and who exercise some degree of local autonomy in organising their social life in such a way that they can, from that locality, satisfy the full range of their daily needs" (Edward and Jones 1976, p. 12). Beyond concurring with this definition, some authors add ingredients like group structure, integration around specific goals, local autonomy and responsibility. However, others challenge the "local autonomy" notion arguing that "external forces will exert influence over its form," adding that it's "too idealistic to expect a community to be absolutely self-contained, in the supply of all its needs" (see discussion in Mulwa 2010, p. 39).

Additionally, when looking at community survival, McIlwaine and Moser (2003) opine that "livelihood security" does imply the "ability to access resources to ensure survival," which is connected to a "series of structural factors underpinning violence," with "citizen insecurity" being "closely linked with failure of government public security" (cited in Moser and Rodgers 2005, p. 4). According to Keane (1996, p. 67), when one does look at the issue of violence it applies to the use or application of "physical interference" by state institutions or "groups and/or individuals with the bodies of others." In a broader sense, in view of Galtung (1985 and 1991), Schroder and Schmidt (2001) also capture "psychological hurt, material deprivation and symbolic disadvantage" (cited in Moser and Rodgers 2005, p. 4). Ultimately, a through-line is the recognition that the application of violence through power has been "invariably used to legitimise the use of force for specific terms" (Moser and Rodgers 2005, p. 4)—as witnessed in independent and post-independence Kenya's rural areas, particularly in the Central region.

Over time, interweaving peace and development has not lifted the rural resident out of poverty as "poverty and development have proved far more difficult and challenging to achieve." This goes against what had been "envisaged in the immediate post-independence period" in Africa due to a "range of domestic and external factors" (Francis 2008, p. 3). Therefore, it is not surprising that rural Kenya seems to be the last place any poor or rich, educated or uneducated, employed or unemployed person wants to live at any given time, unless there is no alternative. In other words, the future of rural areas in Central Kenya, and rest of the country, will be characterized by violence and insecurity, unless a sustainable and peaceful development paradigm is put into practice. Thus, the prevailing phenomena of rural violence and insecurity in question could be due to internal and external dynamics that have made Kenya's rural livelihood and intra-community coexistence unattainable, if not unsustainable.

Dismantling and Devaluation of Community's Social Structures

Prior to colonization, people in the rural region of Central Kenya, and the rest of the country, lived their entire lives isolated from the global economy. By then a majority of the people enjoyed a quality of life whereby challenges like violence or conflict were resolved through traditional conflict resolution mechanisms. While resources were hard to come by, all communal needs were produced and distributed within a structured and favourable trading system. Within community social structures, those who had fallen into extreme poverty were either assisted or protected from being dispossessed or exploited. The colonization that came into effect at the beginning of the nineteenth century brought about the re-organization of rural community social structures and with disastrous effect:

> ...*colonialism did not only destroy the basis upon which Africans could define themselves, but where it could, it also co-opted the indigenous structures and mechanisms of governance and dispute resolution to serve the interests of the colonial administration. Indigenous traditions with regard to governing and resolving disputes in African societies were therefore corrupted by the centralising power of colonialism.* (Murithi 2006, p. 14)

Through his anthropological work on the Kikuyu people, Kenyatta's view was that the interaction with British colonial rule (1920–1940) had negative impacts. This included "reducing the African to a state of serfdom" by being "denied social, economic and political rights," and being "subjected to the most inferior positions in human society." Moreover, tribal democratic institutions were "suppressed" and replaced by "oppressive laws and ordinance, engrossing the monopoly of thought and judgement" being "imposed on the African" (Kenyatta 1965, p. 190). After Kenyatta became the first post-independence president of Kenya, however, he notably continued with the same policies while paradoxically fashioning his governance as having brought political independence to Kenya. A majority of those who controlled the instruments of power in the new Kenyan state ended up appropriating much of the land that was supposed to be returned to dispossessed community members. This was particularly prevalent in the rural communities of Central Kenya which had suffered great loss of land and other rights during colonization. This complicated the ability of the rural community to reset its social structures and instead propagated the continued dismantling and devaluation of the community's social structures.

Arguably, land is central to the survival and sustainability of any African community's social and economic way of life. Therefore, those who interfere with the way land is exploited, administered, and distributed effectively disrupt the community's way of life. In short, from past to present, land has been, and continues to be, a factor of production, communal survival, and continuity. The case of the Kikuyu is an example:

> ...*land being the foundation rock on which the Gikuyu (Kikuyu) economy stands, and the only effective mode of production that the people have, the result is that there is a great desire in the heart of every Gikuyu man to*

own a piece of land on which he can build his home, and from which he and his family can get the means of livelihood. A family group with land to cultivate is considered as a self-supporting economic unit. The group work harmoniously with a view to satisfying their immediate needs, and with the desire to accumulate wealth in the form of cattle, sheep and goats. (Kenyatta 1965, p. 54)

The colonialist and subsequent post-colonial ruling elites misappropriated as much land as they could by displacing thousands, and thereby disorganizing community social structures and way of life. The misappropriation of land later triggered a chain of events leading to the war for Kenya's independence, driven by aspirations to reclaim land and human freedom more broadly. As traditional and indigenous conflict resolution systems were devalued and dismantled, they were replaced by very intrusive and dehumanizing national state-driven policies aimed at achieving compliance and silence, against a backdrop of violence and insecurity. Any effort by the generation of rural community youth to seek redress, or to express their resentment through violence, has over time been met with national state monopolization of violence. This has neither resolved the simmering problem of insecurity nor provided a channel for the rural community to reset its social structures through sustainable peace and development.

But, even if given a chance, many rural community members at the bottom stratum were not willing to buy into sustainable development as a route out of their predicament. The rural population in question, including my grandfather and his peers, by then were hooked into a modernization[11] concept that over the decades has dehumanized the community. Additionally, in the process, modernization cemented dispossession and propagated a climate of violence and insecurity at the bottom stratum of the rural community. For example, the shift in emphasis away from food or subsistence farming to cash crop farming, while not entirely wrong, devalued food or subsistence farming and in turn

---

[11] Modernisation—A process through which a community transitions from traditional farming practices to modern practices, driven by long distance market needs rather than local food needs. Further, development and modernisation are two concepts concerned with the processes of social change of a society. However, we can very well say that development is related to planned change, and modernization is related to the entire process of change. Modernization refers to how a society transforms from one stage to another. https://shodhganga.inflibnet.ac.in/bitstream/10603/29119/11/11_chapter%202.pdf.

increased dependency and dispossession. This triggered the crumbling of the rural standard of living, marking the clear onset of income disparity and rising insecurity within the rural community:

> ...*violence has led to the breakdown of societies. The ties that link people together have been broken, social solidarity has collapsed and political tension has been generated. In addition, socio-economic development has also been severely retarded as a result of the carnage and destruction caused by conflicts.* (Murithi 2006, p. 11)

Notably, agriculture has been adversely affected by diminishing land returns, with knock-on effects to household income, a factor that determines a family's sense of security. For example, in the Murang'a region the top 10 percent of the household commands about 39% of the total income, while those at the "bottom" stratum or the bottom 10 percent command less than 1.1 percent (SID 2004, p. 4), with a poverty rate of 29.9% (CRA, December, 2011, p. 45, quoted in KNBS 2010). This begs the question—what are the consequences of primitive wealth accumulation by political elites to the unemployed and dispossessed youth who have no means of meeting basic needs? As Oucho notes:

> ...*in a society like Kenya where newspaper reading, radio listening to television watching have become the rule rather than exception, it is then a matter of time before the publics digest and make rational conclusion about being duped by their leaders.* (2010, p. 512)

The Central region of Kenya registers one of the highest crime rates in the country, a glaring disparity where crime acts as either a multiplier or a parameter. On average, between "2000 to 2002, Central Kenya level of crime rate was 14,000 cases annually" (SID 2004, p. 16), compared to a national average of 10,000 cases. Yet, available research has paid less attention to the youth who are starting to understand the contradictions within their society, the consequence of which can only be deep-seated anger. Osaghae (2001, p. 14) argues that "radical economists who dominated the thinking on the continent from the 1960s to 1980s contributed to a disabling environment for the study of conflict—in particular ethnic conflict." Others have argued that "it has often turned out that a conflict apparently caused by ethnicity or triggered by election rigging has been nothing more than a conflict between competing élites for the control of state power and consequent access to certain material resources" (Hansen 1987, p. 13, cited in Bangura and McCandless 2007, p. 44). This adds weight to the hesitation to blame ethnicity, and instead highlights the need to interrogate the role of the changing structure of the rural economy. However, Bangura and McCandless (2007, p. 44) note that "radical economic scholars in Africa" presently accept "ethnicity as a factor, interpreting it as a weapon of struggle from below rather than as a mask for class privilege or false consciousness."

On the other hand, due to drastic changes to the rural social structure, education was perceived as a viable way of empowering generations, premised on the possibility of employment in urban centres and as a viable alternative to agriculture. But, as Oucho (2010) notes, "indiscriminate expansion of secondary and tertiary education without concomitant creation of employment opportunities has in time defeated the very purpose of education in the country," resulting in a large pool of unemployed youth. Alternative approaches are needed for a lasting solution against decades of the "modernisation development paradigm."[12] It has dominated the development scene for about half a century now, and "sought to maximize on the immediate concerns" around "accumulation of commodities and financial wealth" (Mulwa 2010, p. 18). Mulwa further observes:

> ...it was not in the interest of development planners to consider any possibilities of adverse social implications of the development strategies they adopted, as long as "growth" indices were appreciating. Such "development" had a debilitating effect on the social-cultural fabric of the traditional rural communities...disintegration of traditional institutions, community kinship, extended family bonds...cultural values begun to erode...this reduced people's potential for self-sufficiency. (Mulwa 2010, pp. 19–20)

According to Todaro, the "question to ask" in such predicaments is: "what has been happening to poverty, unemployment and inequality? If the answer to these issues" is that either—or all—of them has "been growing worse, it would be strange to call the result 'development' even

---

[12] Modernization: an approach to social development that has dominated the scene for decades; inspired by economic growth and accumulation of wealth, and characterized by heavy investment in physical structures and technology (Mulwa 2010, p. 37).

if per capita income doubled" (2000, 15, cited in Mulwa 2010, p. 21). This is an argument vindicated by Escobar:

> ...*social structure change is a process rooted in the interpretation of each society's history, cultural tradition and any attempt to make societies fit in pre-existing models that embodies structures and functions of modernity has negative consequences.* (1995, p. 52)

The end result of Escobar's argument is that underdevelopment, or distorted development, has made substantial parts of the population in Kenya poor or dispossessed.

Poverty has four[13] dimensions, as argued by Swedish International Development Cooperation: "poverty is not only about the lack of materials resources, but also other poverty dimensions such as lack of power and voice." More than that, the majority of the individuals within the Kenyan rural setting is perpetually "resource-poor" (SIDA 2017a cited in SIDA 2018, p. 9). Furthermore, this context limits the ability to define a sustainable future, and thereby subjects the rural population in question to living within an environment in which peace is constrained. In this context, poverty is a "complicating factor" that limits the achievement of "the noble attributes of human security," while not forgetting that "human security can coexist with poverty" even though "poverty in itself is not always associated with the negation of peace and abuse of human rights" (Salih 2008, p. 171). Indeed, this was witnessed in the rural region of Central Kenya during the 2007 crackdown of suspected criminal gangs labelled as Mungiki. In the view of Salih:

> ...*many poor societies enjoy peace, as much as poverty may undermine peace by creating situations that contribute to the abuse of human rights as a results*

---

[13] First, being poor in terms of resources means not having access to or power over resources that can be used to sustain a decent living standard and improve one's life (where resources can be both materials and non-materials). Second, being poor in terms of opportunities and choice concerning what possibility you have to develop and/or use your resources so as to move out of poverty—namely access to capital, land, and choices. Third, being poor through lack of power and voice relates to the ability of people to articulate their concern, needs and rights in an informed way, and to take part in decision-making that relates to these concerns. Fourth, being poor in terms of human security implies that violence and insecurity are constraints on different groups' and individual possibilities to exercise their human rights and to find paths out of poverty (SIDA 2017a cited in SIDA 2018, p. 9).

of horizontal (such as ethnic, religious, regional, etc) or vertical (such as class and elite) inequality and inequitable distribution of resources. (2008, p. 171)

The consequence of the above has been the prevalence of rural poverty and inequality, and in turn the onset of intra-community violence. When a population's ability to access or own factors of productions is curtailed, then "poverty is widespread." This reproduces or increases "tension within society, generates mistrust, and fosters crime, which further weakens the social fabric of society" and undermines the community's ability to redefine a prosperous and sustainable future (Murithi 2006, p. 12).

In this regard, key ingredients of violence and insecurity have been ubiquitous—diminishing land returns, food insecurity, land dispossessions, a widening gap between the rich and poor, and high levels of youth unemployment, resulting in episodic cases of extortionist acts, racketeering, and killing. These factors have triggered or accelerated rural–urban migration, in search of livelihoods by the have-nots and security by the haves. The consequence of this has been a rise in cases of inter and intra-community violence, with the disposed and frustrated youth turning against those perceived to be well-to-do within the rural areas. In summary, one can attribute these dynamics to simmering greed and grievance contestation.

Regarding the insecurity and violence phenomena, if one pushes aside the ethnic equation, the demographic and poverty factors cannot be ignored. According to the Kenya National Bureau of Statistics (KNBS) the country's population in 2019 was at 47.6 million, up from a record low of 8 million in 1960. In view of KNBS, while the average household size declined from 4.2 in 2009 to 3.9 in 2019, within the same decade Kenya's population increased from 37.7 million in 2009 to 47.6 million in 2019 (KNBS 2019). Population conflict scholars remind us that such drastic changes in population can have implications:

...population issues feature in conflict as 'parameters' that shape the situation itself, as 'multipliers' by aggravating the underlying or existing hostilities, and as 'variables' by serving as critical factors in conflict that shape the unfolding and/or determine the outcome of conflict. (Choucri 1974, 1984, quoted in Oucho 2002)

Yet, in Kenya the demographic equation has been looked into in the "context of violence, largely as an ethnic composition, size and growth to spatial distribution" (Oucho 2002). This means that the demographic equation acted as a "parameter" to the insecurity and violence situation. In other instances, however, demographics acted as a "multiplier" by aggravating the exploitation of land; and, as a multiplier of "existing" family tension regarding inheritance matters, and village tension between those with large but idle land and the landless or disinherited. Furthermore, the demographic factor acted as a "variable" in mobilization patterns that trigger violence due to vulnerability and dispossession of segments of the populations. This could mean that variable factors influenced the "unfolding" pattern of inter and intra-communal violence, which resulted in rural–urban migration of elite members of the community. In light of these factors, Tirtosudarmo's question of "why demographic and population studies seem unmoved on issues and consequences of conflict" (2006) is of great interest to this chapter.

According to the World Bank, in Kenya "the proportion of the population living below the national poverty line fell from 46.8 percent in 2005/06 to 36.1 in 2015/16." This is attributed to "progress in rural areas, where poverty declined from around 50 percent in 2005/06 to 38.8 percent" within ten years, begging the question—why is the rural region in Kenya still insecure? The above changes have been used to denote progress within the national government development paradigm; however, when one looks at the poverty question through the lens of Todaro's argument, Mulwa and Escobar surface. That is, progress against poverty is underdevelopment, or distorted development, falling short of offsetting rural violence and insecurity. In other words, the absolute number of poorer rural Kenyans has been increasing. As the Kenya Institute of Public Policy Research and Analysis (KIPPRA) noted, "the figures increased from 13.4 million in 1997 to 16.6 million in 2006 (KIPPRA 2009, cited at NCPD 2013, p. 12). Additionally, the "10 percent poorest household in Kenya" controls "only 1.63 percent of total expenditure, while the richest 10 percent control nearly 36 percent of expenditure" (NCPD 2013, p. 12). In short, "poverty levels are higher in rural areas, 50 percent, compared to urban areas, 34 percent," thereby making the feeling of dispossession and exclusion more pronounced in rural areas than urban centres. As regards urban centres, the "absolute number of people living below the poverty line increased from 2.3 million in 2005/06 to 3.8 million in 2015/16." This negative development is attributed to the failure of urban areas to provide "enough economic opportunities for urban households to improve their income levels and obtain adequate standards of living" (World Bank Group, April, 2020).

The patterns of disruption and underdevelopment have proven difficult to predict or resolve, making the future of the rural community gloomy. The heart of the matter is the politics of patronage and clientelism—a hallmark of Kenya's post-independence governance system and the anchor by which political elites maintain political authority. The system of "patrimony (public resources)" found in Kenya and other African states has been "used to serve the private and vested interest of the state power-holders, including the ruling and governing elites" (Francis 2008, p. 10). In short:

> ...There is no distinction between the public (res publica) and the private realm of governance, and political ascendancy as well as individual preferment is based on loyalty to the power-holder. Within this system, the power-holder emerges not only as a personalised ruler and prime purveyor of patrimonial resources but also commands monopoly over all formal political activity, whereby the formal state and governmental institutions are subordinated to the leader's vested and strategic interest. (Yates 1996, p. 5; Weber 1958, cited in Francis 2008, p. 10)

The patrimonial system has significantly impacted governance in Kenya. Over time institutions have been captured, exploited, diverted, and turned into personal property to serve and enrich those in power, and their collaborators, at the expense of the wider population, and more so in the rural region. In this regard, one can argue that the prevailing fear of insecurity and violence could be a result of dysfunctional relations within a system and/or incongruent communication styles of one or more parties. In essence, Kenya's political elites, irrespective of ethnicity and/or geographical origin, have gestured to reform as long as such notions do not threaten their interest and existence. That is, they "happily" accepted but not embraced any extensive tackling of the elements and structures that continue to make rural life insecure and violent. This explains their reluctance or delaying tactics when it comes to support for implementation of human security ideas. Perceptively, "there is no national policy on conflict resolution and peacebuilding in Kenya," despite the prevailing violence and insecurity in rural areas. Indeed, "fragmented and uncoordinated policy statements" have been "implemented with no regard for community local knowledge, indigenous systems of governance and natural resource management" (Adan and Pkalya 2006, p. 1).

While Kenya's 2008 Peace and National Reconciliation Accord could have tackled some of the insecurity and violence in the rural areas through its Long-Term Agenda[14] for reforms, its implementation has failed to meet such potential. Twelve years on, it has only benefitted the ruling class; and the reforms that could have brought sustainable peace have been implemented piecemeal while others are frozen. This is what Osaghae refers to as "unrealistic goals, reactive and emergency rather than proactive and comprehensive objectives, expertise and poor implementation" (2001, p. 25, cited in Bangura and McCandless 2007, p. 46). Moreover, according to Conteh-Morgan's critique, some peacebuilding efforts in Africa "are largely characterized by a language of power, exclusion, or defense of an international order that does not adequately address issues of emancipation and inappropriate impositions" (2005, p. 71). In essence, "political liberalisation did not substantially transform the institutional bases of African states," but on the contrary "engendered regime insecurity" (Kanyinga et al. 2010, p. 2). This makes the state a very paranoid creature, preoccupied with its own survival and less about the peaceful survival of the individual and the rural community at large.

The consequences of this have been the continued prevalence of injustices, unrest, crime, frustrations, and aggression among and across rural community members, whereby violence and insecurity are common features. What ought to have been done over time, and has not been properly done, is social engineering through sustainable development within the bottom stratum of the rural community; which would chart a path towards the removal of conditions causing violence and insecurity. Kenya's 2008 peace accord, the 2010 constitution, and subsequent peacebuilding efforts were premised on power sharing or the devolution concept, ostensibly the greatest strength of these initiatives. With time, however, this has not helped and instead created a new lower level of

---

[14] Long-Term Agenda: Kenya's current political problems demand taking a new look at the Long-Term Agenda. In particular, addressing long standing injustices in regional development, including resource allocation, the land question, historical injustices and widespread ethnic chauvinism, which tends to undermine national solidarity (Oucho 2010, p. 492). The OHCHR (2008) identified four main causes of Kenya's post-election violence: long standing disputes over land rights; recurrent violence and persistent impunity; pre-existing violence to economic and social rights; and vigilant groups (cited in Oucho 2010, p. 494).

corrupt officials with the same appetite as those at the national level. Fuelled by the primitive accumulation of wealth mentality, they have misappropriated resources that belong to the rural communities.

When it comes to resolving violence, it's not those who are pulled out of poverty that matter most, but the few or many left behind or made absolutely poor by distorted development. Rural underdevelopment, or distorted development, has turned into a heart-rending affair that gives insight into the prevailing insecurity and violence within the rural region. This implies that social structural change is a process rooted in the interpretation of each society's history and cultural tradition. Furthermore, failure to take this into account implies that the quest for human security remains a luxury among affected populations.

Sustainable Peace Through Chaos as an Opportunity

In the last few decades, some research on possible solutions to the violence phenomenon has been preoccupied with whether to give priority to tackling ethnicity or election violence. However, the focus instead should be on re-engineering the rural community so that it can be at peace with itself. This necessitates a peacebuilding approach that captures the aspirations and frustrations of the most fortunate, and the dispossessed, implying that one aspect of peacebuilding should not be prioritized to the point of compromising another. For example, it does not pay any benefit to have a national state that is fearful of the rural community's quest for justice and equality, and therefore applies force as a way of achieving silence and consent. Such a response by the state only reproduces resentment, anger, hatred, violence, and rural–urban migration. In essence, the path to attaining peace within the rural community is not through silence and consent but the "transformation of the extant social systems" that are critical to the survival and continuity of individuals, family, and community at large (Hansen 1987, cited in McCandless and Karbo 2011). Indeed, the search for peace cannot be "separated from the struggle for social and democratic rights, and human dignity" (Hansen 1987). Hansen further elaborates:

> ...*peace and development are inextricably intertwined; removal of conflict is only the minimalist condition for the attainment of peace. For a lasting and reliable peace [its] important to fashion economic systems [that] generate sustain economic growth [but this won't] remove all conflict but it would eliminate some of the causes of tension which lead to conflict.* (cited in McCandless 2011, p. 42)

When one contemplates how to achieve sustainable peace within a rural community, the salient challenge is how to tackle pre-existing injustices—such as, widespread youth dislocation, unemployment, and rapid demographic changes in land's diminishing returns. Accordingly, the sustainable peace and development approach dwells on the root causes of why the rural community is not at peace with itself. As these problems can vary from one village to another, or from one individual to another, sustainable peace responses must consider current local realities and long-term consequences. Indeed, peace is a form of investment that is anchored in the sustainable balance between production and consumption in the present, without compromising the livelihoods of generations in the future. In essence, when groups of people self-organize, they are able to create highly adaptable and resilient forms, through which a few individuals can help others rethink their path towards self-reliance. A search for self-reliance must not be rooted in diminishing land availability, but rather anchored in farming practices that enrich the individual, the community, and the soil. This will ensure that exploitation of the land is sustainable and productive. In other words, an "individual cannot live well, if the community as whole is not well"; and, community development should not be premised on "material wealth" but rather on the "well-being of persons and communities" within their context (Harthaway and Boff 2009, p. 353). Moreover, as climate change cannot be ignored in the present times, a community cannot live well in a degraded environment. As such, the peacebuilding approach needs to incorporate farming practices within conflict transformation that are sustainable and add value to the community as a living organism. Tackling these root causes through "sustainable" thinking implies re-education of the rural community on the need to "embrace limits" and exploit their already degraded environment, while also revitalizing it. Consequently, a rural economy that "reuses and recycles materials wisely," anchored in conflict transformation, aims to be "frugal with resources but generous in creativity" (Harthaway and Boff 2009, p. 354).

In reality, the violence that is bleeding into periodic insecurity within the rural community is not a regular condition that a community is supposed to be accustomed to. Rather, it is a condition that a nation can halt if there is political will to accept and incorporate human security thinking by action and not by statements. In Briggs and David's (1998) perspective, violence may "appear incredibly complicated with a simple origin," but this is just the "surface that might be concealing something stunningly complex at the bottom," which needs to be understood. Critically, in order to understand what has been concealed one should not look to the flow of information from those seeking to help, namely the peacebuilders, but instead to the flow of information from the bottom stratum of the rural community towards those seeking to help. This could signal respect of the wisdom of those in need—a welcome departure from decades of being targeted by the nation state as criminals. Additionally, the state's willingness to listen to those in need can in the process strengthen the rural community's inherent knowledge systems. Crucially, peacebuilding that directs the flow of information from the bottom stratum of the community towards those seeking to help is best anchored in the system theory, which brings to the table a broader, participatory strategy.

Through system theory, the route to sustainable peace is accorded a broader perspective, which creates a path for the affected community to start a journey towards sustainable development. In essence, "the alteration of any element in a system affects all the others" (Satir 2016), implying that one issue cannot be resolved in a sustainable manner if all other issues at play are not also given the attention they deserve. It is worth noting that the rural population at the bottom stratum of society has been on a continuous search for new patterns to function, a process marked by expressions and experiences of violence that periodically result in insecurity. If one was to take the rural community in question as a living organism, then "living systems are self-organised and self-regenerating [;] and if inputs and outputs cannot be matched" through the process of development, then a "system must keep constantly searching for a new pattern through which to function" (2009, p. 198). If achieved or supported, a new pattern can help resolve violence within the rural community context. In the view of Harthaway and Boff, the "whole is always greater than the mere sum of its parts, and the parts can be understood only in the context and function of the whole system." In a sense, the "pattern, rather than individual parts, is the essence of a living system" (2009, p. 198), implying that there is a need for re-engineering the various patterns for possible solutions. For example, considering what has worked or failed before, community-driven conflict resolution practices, along with the propagation of new ideas to farming practise, could bring life to the rural social structures. In perspective, a broader peacebuilding process is plausible—one that is based in respect of ethics and a caring and right relationship within the community of interest.

Moreover, any envisaged peacebuilding approach ought to be aimed at the re-creation of the rural community's sustainable and harmonious way of life—one that is functional and enriching, and that draws from the idea that the community, first and foremost, is a living self-organism like the natural environment it seeks to exploit for survival.

The gender dynamics in the rural community place women at a comparative disadvantage to men. Affected the most by dispossession, women assume the burden of family and community, while men have given up on trying. Therefore, it is necessary to give women more attention through peace and development strategies, as such approaches in communities across Africa have been noted for "transforming the socio-economic and political spheres" (Karbo 2008, pp. 131–132). However, there is still much work to do for the empowerment of women. For example, increasing the number of women in political positions remains a challenge; and, the socio-economic outlook in Central Kenya communities, and its impact on women, hasn't changed as much compared to improvements seen elsewhere. Women are central to any sustainable development, as they are pillars of economically disadvantaged families, including under circumstances whereby men are prisoners to frustrations and alcoholism.

In other words, it has been the "overall structures, patterns and cycles," rather than isolated events, that have undermined the rural social structures to the detriment of the wider population. This needs resetting through a broadened peacebuilding approach:

> ...*broad view does help a peacebuilding person or a peace researcher to identify the real causes of insecurity and violence at the rural level and know how and where to work from and through towards addressing them. System theory does help in the understanding of how changes in the negative or tragic changes in the rural community social structures have been influenced by multiple factors triggering the prevalence of insecurity and violence.* (Manamara 2006)

Through system thinking, one has a broadened perspective of the various factors, patterns, cycles, and elements, rather than focusing on single events or decisions that have conspired to make the rural area prone to violence. System theory also brings forth the notion of chaos theory. Along this line of thought, the question at the bottom stratum of the rural setting is not confusion, but a continuous attempt by the disrupted community social structures to reset itself and find a new paradigm by which to operate.

In other words, this broad view helps peacebuilders or peace researchers to identify the real causes of violence at the rural level, and to know how and where to work to address them. System theory helps in understanding how negative changes in the rural community's social structures have been influenced by multiple factors. Along this thinking, one can conceive of the idea that the chaos brought by negative development is an opportunity rather than an obstacle towards possible solutions; and, that these solutions need to be employed in resolving rural violence.

There are those who will argue that accepting chaos as an opportunity in some aspects could also re-open old wounds. Indeed, over the years such grievances have been subjected to the "politics of applying bandages" on the rural social structures problem, aimed at merely stopping the "bleeding" rather than surgically looking at the problems in question (Mugo 2011). However, "opening of the wounds" and "surgically cleansing" them, despite the pain or disruptions that might come forth, can help in understanding the patterns causing the violence. Such an approach would not be supported by those controlling the instruments of power and resources of the nation. Rather, they have argued for decades that there are insufficient national resources to implement sustainable peace and development at the rural level. Accordingly, the approach put forth here could trigger upheavals, if not chaos, however such a chaotic process doesn't foretell death and destruction. Instead, the process is an opportunity that needs to be harnessed—a disruption and breakdown of old systems towards new forms. The renewed approach in reviving the challenges in rural Kenya towards a sustainable peace is based on values of what matters in life; like a development approach that adds value to the diminishing land returns to a constantly increasing rural population.

While resources are vital to any peacebuilding effort, they are of limited supply. Those in decision-making positions always take possession of public resources for their own benefit to prevent an approach that seeks to reset the rural social structures. In this regard, a viable route for any sustainable peace and development plan is to partner with civil society, philanthropists, and private sector entities. Such partnerships would ensure a sustained plan towards the empowerment of the bottom stratum of rural community. This will depend on an apparent randomness of chaotic complex systems, which have underlying patterns, interconnections, and constant feedback loops in search for self-organization. In view of Colin (1999), "chaos theory provides a metaphorical language" that helps in prescribing people's networks of "social groups and the contemporary world"; and, in the end, it will bring up a "new paradigm for understanding changing processes."

In reality, the rural community in the Central region of Kenya, and rest of the country, has been continuously operating through some form of disruption and chaos, which needs harnessing for constructive and revitalizing outcomes. This entails the application of traditional conflict resolution mechanisms, instead of the use of security agencies to root out violence or to compel the rural community into silence. The 2007 security operation to root out suspected "criminal gangs," like Mungiki, had a negative outcome. The operation spread fear and resentment within the Central Kenya community, and it didn't solve the underlying issues that triggered the dispossessed youths at the bottom stratum of the rural community. Instead, resentment, anger, and mistrust were further cemented, bleeding into insecurity among and between those who have and those who don't. In an effort to find a sustainable way for rural Kenya to be at peace with itself, there is a need to conceptualize the violence that bleeds into insecurity as an opportunity. That is, instead of condemning such violence, what is needed is a critical assessment and understanding of the pre-existing patterns of resentment, dispossession, and violence that created insecurity in the first instance.

What is missing in rural Kenya is the notion that "peace is not just the absence of violence, but the presence of social solidarity." This entails "confronting corruption and promoting power sharing, inclusive governance and the equitable distribution of resources among all members of society" (Murithi 2006, pp. 30–31). This not only implies that all must have the same status of living or income, but also that the gap between the rich and the poor is tackled so as to not "manifest a fundamental lack of fairness that can lead to resentment," escalating up to violence. Closely tied to the equity issue is the need for climate "justice"; and, therefore, the need to tackle inequality and the "needs of humanity," without "compromising the well-being of other species" or future generations (Harthaway and Boff 2009, p. 354).

This brings forth the notion of having the human security perspective anchored in rural community interpretations of possible solutions out of their predicament. In other words, the exploration of a "framework that is a hybrid" of indigenous peace processes and modern technology solutions will "ensure human dignity and inclusion of all members of society," including "women, men, girls and boys" (Murithi 2006). The human security approach aims at "protecting and empowering citizens to obtain vital freedom from wants, fear and hunger," and more than that the "freedom to take action on one's behalf." This will result in the creation of "building blocks" for the flourishing of the rural community "peace and dignity and a secure livelihood" within their context (Salih 2008, p. 171).

In essence, when seeking to "transform social, economic, and cultural systems – including common paradigms" by way of conflict transformation, there must be a keen understanding of the relevant context. One needs to have in mind that any rural community is "most sensitive in those places where it is subjected to the greatest pressure," often the youth and dispossessed. A segment of the community has been rebelling, and therefore a peacebuilding approach is needed that redirects their frustrations into creative and constructive forms. This entails seeking out "creativity on the periphery of our social, economic, and cultural systems," as it might be along those areas, "where structures and paradigms are beginning to break through." In such cases the dispossessed youth, if perceived positively, can contribute to "new forms" (Harthaway and Boff 2009, p. 214). However, as already witnessed, dispossessed youth can be a threat when perceived negatively and not well harnessed through conflict transformation. Indeed, such an approach to development has made rural livelihoods and survival uncertain. The challenge for peacebuilders using the human security approach is to come up with strategies that are appropriate to rural communities' harmony and survival.

One of the greatest human achievements of the last half century has been technological advancements, that if properly exploited by peacebuilders can work towards a transformed society as envisioned. Such a vision is what the rural area ought to be—communities not compelled into silence or compliance, and with minimal or free of violence. The challenges encountered along the way will refine the vision of the rural community. This calls for a fundamental change, in scale and purpose, in the way modern technology—whether agribusiness or communication platforms—is intertwined with peacebuilding efforts. We need to understand that a rural community afflicted with violence, periodically bleeding into insecurity, could take different paths during conflict transformation.

REFERENCES

Adan, M., & Pkalya, R. (2006). Conflict Management in Kenya Towards Policy and Strategy Formulation. Nairobi: Practical Action.
Briggs, J., & David, F. (1998). Seven Life Lesson of Chaos: Spiritual Wisdom from the Science of Change. New York: HarperCollins.
Colin, C. (1999). Addressing Complexity: Exploring Social Change Through Chaos and Complexity Theory. Ottawa, National Library of Canada.
Choucri, N. (1974). Population Dynamics and International Violence: Propositions, Insights and Evidence. Lexington, MA: Lexington Books.
Chourci, N. (1984). Multidisciplinary Perspective of Population and Conflict. Syracuse: Syracuse University Press.
Conteh-Morgan, Earl. (2005). Peacebuilding and Human Security: A Constructivist Perspective. International Journal of Peace Studies, 10(1), 69-86.
CRA. (2011, December). Kenya County Fact Sheets. Nairobi: Commission on Revenue Allocation (CRA).
Edwards, Allan D. and Dorothy G. Jones. (1976). Community and Community Development. Volume 23 of New Babylon. Mouton De Gruyter.
Escobar, Arturo. (1995). 'The Problematisation of Poverty: The Tale of Three Worlds and Development'; 'Power and Visibility: Tales of Peasants, Women, and the Environment'. In Encountering Development: The Making and Unmaking of the Third World (Chapter 2, pp. 21–54 and Chapter 5, pp. 155–171). Princeton: Princeton University Press.
Francis, D. J. (2008). Introduction: Understanding the Context of Peace and Conflict in Africa. In The Book-Peace and Conflict in Africa. New York: Zed Books Ltd.
Galtung, J. (1985). Twenty-five Years of Peace Research: Ten Challenges and Some Responses. Journal of Peace Research, 22(2), 145–46.
Galtung, J. (1991). Peace by Peaceful Means: Peace and Conflict, Development and Civilization. Oslo: International Peace Research Institute.
Hansen, Emmanuel (ed.). (1987). Africa: Perspectives on Peace and Development. London: Zed Press.
Harthaway, M., & Boff, L. (2009). The Tao of Liberation: Exploring the Ecology of Transformation. Maryknoll, New York: Orbis Books.

Kaggia, Bildad. (1975). Roots of Freedom, 1921–1963: The Autobiography of Bildad Kaggia. Nairobi: East African Pub. House.
Kanyinga, K., Okello, D., & Akech, A. (2010). Contradictions of Transition to Democracy in Fragmented Societies: The Kenya 2007 General Elections in Perspective. In U. o. Society for International Development (SID) and Institute for Development Studies (IDS), Tensions and Reversals in Democratic Transitions: The Kenya 2007 General Elections (pp. 1–30). Nairobi: Society for International Development (SID)-East Africa Regional Office.
Kaplinsky. R. (2001). Globalisation and economic insecurity. IDS Bulletin, 32(2), 13–24.
Karbo. T. (2008). Peace-Building in Africa. In the Book-Peace and Conflict in Africa. New York: Zed Books Ltd.
Keane. J. (1996). Reflections on Violence. London: Verso.
Kenyatta. J. (1965). Facing Mount Kenya. New York: Vintage Books.
KNBS. (2010). 2009 Kenya Population and Housing Census Report. Nairobi: Kenya National Bureau of Statistics.
KNBS. (2019). 2019 Kenya Population and Housing Census Report. Nairobi: National Bureau of Statistics.
Library of Congress. (2007). Country Profile: Kenya. Federal Research Division. https://tile.loc.gov/storage-services/master/frd/copr/Kenya.pdf.
Manamara, C. (2006, March). Field Guide to Consulting and Organizational Development: A Collaborative and Systems Approach to Performance, Change and Learning (for Working with For-Profit Businesses and Government Agencies). Independent Publisher.
McCandless, Erin and Abdul Karim Bangura. (2007). Peace Research for Africa: Critical Essays on Methodology. Switzerland: University for Peace.
McCandless, Erin and Tony Karbo. (2011). Peace, Conflict, and Development in Africa: A Reader. Switzerland: University of Peace.
McIlwaine, C and C Moser. (2003). Poverty, Violence and Livelihood Security in Urban Colombia and Guatemala. Progress in Development Studies, 3(2), 113–130.
Moser, C. O. N., & Rodgers, D. (2005). Change, Violence and Insecurity in Non-Conflict Situations. London: Overseas Development Institute.
Mugo, P. (2011). Horn of Africa Hunger Crisis: Why the Politics of Applying Bandages Hasn't Stopped the Bleeding. Peace and Conflict Monitor Journal, 12.
Mulwa, F. W. (2010). Demystifying Participatory Community Development. Nairobi: Paulines Publications Africa.
Murithi, T. (2006). African Approaches to Building Peace and Social Solidarity. International Conference on Strategies for Peace with Development in Africa:

The Role of Education, Training and Research, hosted by the University for Peace and the African Union, 12–14 June 2006 (p. 27). Addis Ababa, Ethiopia: African Journal on Conflict Resolution, 6(2), 2006.

NCPD. (2013). Kenya Population Situation Analysis. Nairobi: National Council for Population and Development.

OHCHR. (2008). Report from OHCHR Fact-finding Mission to Kenya, 6-28 February 2008. United Nations High Commissioner for Human Rights, 18 March 2008. https://www.ohchr.org/sites/default/files/Documents/Press/OHCHRKenyareport.pdf.

Osaghae, Eghosa E. (2001). The Role and Function of Research in Divided Societies: the Case of Africa. In Researching Violently Divided Societies: Ethical and Methodological Issues, ed. Marie Smyth and Gillian Robinson. London: Pluto Press.

Oucho, J. O. (2000). Consequences of Rapid Population Growth for Conflict: A Case Study of Kenya. In J. Oucho, A. Ocholla-Ayayo, & L. Omwanda (Eds.), Population and Development in Kenya. Nairobi: School of Journalism Press.

Oucho, John. (2002). Undercurrents of Ethnic Conflict in Kenya. Leiden: Brill.

Oucho, J. O. (2010). Undercurrents of Post-Election Violence in Kenya: Issues in the Long-Term Agenda. In SID-IDS, Tension and Reversals in Democratic Transitions: The Kenya 2007 General Elections (pp. 491–564). Nairobi: Society for International Development (SID) and Institute for Development Studies (IDS), University of Nairobi.

Ruteere, M. (2008). Dilemmas of Crime, Human Rights and the Politics of Mungiki Violence in Kenya. Nairobi: Kenya Human Rights Institute.

Salih, M. A. M. (2008). Poverty and Human Security in Africa: The Liberal Peace Debate. In The Book-Peace and Conflict in Africa. New York: Zed Books Ltd.

Satir, V. (2016). Satir Transformational Systemic Therapy. https://www.goodtherapy.org/learn-about-therapy/types/satir-transformational-systemic-therapy.

Schröder, I W and Schmidt, B E. (2001). 'Introduction: Violent Imaginaries and Violent Practices', in B E Schmidt and I W Schröder (eds), Anthropology of Violence and Conflict. London: Routledge.

SID. (2004). Pulling Apart—Figures and Figures on Inequality in Kenya. Nairobi: Society for International Development Eastern Africa Regional Office.

SIDA. (2018) Understanding Poverty in Kenya, A multidimensional analysis report. Nairobi: Swedish International Development Cooperation-Kenya.

Thiong'o, N. W. (1987). Weep Not, Child. Nairobi: Heinemann Publishers.

Tirtosudarmo, R. (2006). Population, Ethnicity and Violent Conflict. Population Journal, 45.

Turner, T. E., & Brownhill, L. (2001). African Jubilee. Mau Mau Resurgence and the Fight for Fertility in Kenya, 1986–2002.
World Bank Group. (2020). Poverty and Equality Brief, Sub-Saharan Africa, Kenya, April 2020. World Bank Group.

CHAPTER 4

Coping Mechanisms Employed by Survivors of Conflict-Related Sexual Violence in the 2007/2008 Post-election Violence in Kenya

Scholastica A. Marenya

Introduction

Conflict-related sexual violence (CRSV) has persisted globally in past and current conflicts despite its horrific consequences. CRSV comprises any form of sexual violence associated with conflict, directly or indirectly, including rape, sexual assault, forced marriage, and prostitution. Global awareness of CRSV has risen over the past decade due to several factors, such as its recognition as an international crime, United Nations policy responses to end it, and the award of the Nobel Peace Prize in 2018 to two CRSV advocates.

In addition, various studies have tried to shed light on the causes, trends, and consequences of CRSV, which is a welcome development in

S. A. Marenya (✉)
Tangaza University College, Nairobi, Kenya
e-mail: marenya.schola@gmail.com

© The Author(s), under exclusive license to Springer Nature Switzerland AG 2023
J. Adero Ngala et al. (eds.), *Innovations in Peace and Security in Africa*,
https://doi.org/10.1007/978-3-031-39043-2_4

order to better understand its occurrence and devise solutions. However, there has been limited focus on how survivors cope with the consequences of CRSV and are restored to healthy functioning as individuals and community members. This chapter addresses this gap by conducting a literature review on the long-term consequences of CRSV and investigating the coping strategies adopted by survivors of the 2007/2008 post-election violence in Kenya.

The chapter is organized as follows. Section one gives a general overview of CRSV, in terms of its nature, trends, and consequences. This is followed by a discussion of coping mechanisms employed by survivors, with reference to relevant theories and empirical literature. Lastly, CRSV is discussed as it pertains to the 2007/2008 post-election violence in Kenya, its long-term consequences and the coping strategies adopted by survivors. The chapter concludes with recommendations for enhancing the management of survivors.

Background

Sexual violence during conflict, also referred to as CRSV, is as old as war itself. Prior to the horrific sexual violence in Rwanda and the Balkan conflicts, CRSV was ignored and trivialized, occasionally dismissed as "the spoils of war." This changed when CRSV was recognized as an international crime. The International Criminal Tribunals for the former Yugoslavia (ICTY) and Rwanda (ICTR), which were set up to address war crimes committed in the Balkans and Rwanda, respectively, both identified the systematic use of rape and other forms of sexual violence during armed conflict as war crimes and crimes against humanity.[1]

In 2000, the United Nations (UN) increased its global response to CRSV by adopting UN resolution 1325, with key elements for combatting its incidence. It called on parties in armed conflict to protect women and girls from gender-based violence, particularly rape and other forms of sexual abuse; and on states to put an end to and prosecute all cases of sexual and other violence against women and girls, excluding perpetrators from amnesty. Since then, the UN has adopted several other resolutions to prevent, respond to, and ensure accountability for CSRV, including

---

[1] Bergoffen, D. (2013). Ungendering Justice: Constituting a Court, Securing a Conviction, Creating a Human Right. Transitional Justice Review, 1(2), 3.

1820 (2008), 1888 (2009), 1960 (2010), 2106 (2013), 2331 (2016), 2447 (2018), and 2467 (2019). The UN and other international bodies also set up various teams of experts and task forces to prevent, respond to, and combat CRSV. This has improved the security of women and girls in conflict situations, and strengthened the medical, judicial, and psychosocial response to CRSV. However, these efforts have neither deterred CRSV in subsequent conflicts nor improved the reporting of CRSV cases.

CRSV is defined as "rape, sexual slavery, forced prostitution, forced pregnancy, enforced sterilization and other forms of sexual violence of comparable gravity perpetrated against women, men, girls or boys that is linked, directly or indirectly to a conflict."[2] Historically, CRSV is perpetrated by state military personnel, armed rebels and militias, and non-combatants against women and girls, with fewer incidents against men and boys.

The causes of CRSV are complex and unique to each conflict. For example, it may be a deliberate tactic of war, an opportunistic act due to lawlessness related to the conflict, a result of intra-group dynamics, or even due to socio-cultural norms such as attempts of men to exert control over women, gender inequalities, or the breakdown of social norms.[3]

CRSV has profound medical, psychological, social, and economic consequences. It leads to psychosocial trauma that affects survivors, and extends to families and communities for many generations. The intersectionality of sexual violence, serious injury and threat, and actual death leads survivors to experience complex traumatic stress disorders.[4] This is manifested as alterations to emotional regulation, somatic experiences, relationships, perceptions of the perpetrator, consciousness, and

---

[2] United Nations. (2019). Secretary General Report on Conflict Related Sexual Violence 2018. New York.

[3] Cohen, D. K., & Nordås, R. (2014). Sexual Violence in Armed Conflict Introducing Critical Explanation and the Study of Wartime Sexual Violence. European Journal of International Relations, 19(4), 797–7821. https://doi.org/10.1177/1354066111427614; Koos, C. (2017). Sexual Violence in Armed Conflicts: Research Progress and Remaining Gaps. Third World Quarterly, 38(9), 1935–1951; van Dijkhorst, H., & Vonhof, S. (2005). Gender and Humanitarian Aid: A Literature Review of Policy and Practice Wagenenin: Wageninen University, 43 p.

[4] Koos, C. (2018). Decay or Resilience?: The Long-Term Social Consequences of Conflict-Related Sexual Violence in Sierra Leone. World Politics, 70(2), 194–238.

systems of meaning.[5] Survivors employ internal and external resources to manage this complex trauma and be restored to a pre-trauma state. These resources include legal and medical responses, as well as key coping mechanisms including problem focused, emotional focused, social, and meaning making (to be discussed further below). The coping mechanisms utilized are dependent on the survivor and the environment in which they find themselves,[6] each with varying outcomes/results.

Such coping mechanisms have varying outcomes that enable survivors to survive, recover, or thrive.[7] Those who survive never regain previous levels of well-being and functioning, while those recovering return to their status of health prior to the event. Thrivers on the other hand gain enhanced levels of well-being, functioning, and capacities beyond the pre-trauma state—which is referred to as post-traumatic growth (PTG). Thrivers exhibit prosocial behaviour such as cooperation, altruism, and helping. As there are ongoing debates on the reasons for these varied outcomes, a deeper understanding is needed of how different coping mechanisms shape the long-term consequences of conflict-related sexual violence.[8]

Problem Statement

The enormity of CRSV for women and girls and its consequences cannot be underestimated. Communal and electoral conflicts in Kenya since 2007 have resulted in many cases of CRSV. In the 2007/2008 post-election violence over 900 cases of CRSV were reported. States' obligations to prevent, protect, and provide reparations have largely remained unfulfilled. While non-state actors have provided some kind of response this is

---

[5] Courtois, C. A., & Ford, J. D. (2013). Treatment of Complex Trauma: A Sequenced, Relationship-Based Approach. Guilford Press.

[6] Moskowitz, J. T., Shmueli-Blumberg, D., Acree, M., & Folkman, S. (2012). Positive Affect in the Midst of Distress: Implications for Role Functioning. Journal of Community & Applied Social Psychology, 22(6), 502–518.

[7] Thomas, K. (2017). Women and Sexual Violence, Paths to Healing: Resistance, Rebellion, Resilience and Recovery (Doctoral Dissertation, Middlesex University).

[8] Koos, C. (2018). Decay or Resilience?: The Long-Term Social Consequences of Conflict-Related Sexual Violence in Sierra Leone. World Politics, 70(2), 194–238; Thomas, K. (2017). Women and Sexual Violence, Paths to Healing: Resistance, Rebellion, Resilience and Recovery (Doctoral Dissertation, Middlesex University).

often short lived and reliant on donor funding.[9] Societies on the other hand rarely offer supportive social acknowledgement, often stigmatizing and rejecting survivors.[10] This leaves survivors of CRSV to develop their own coping mechanism to survive such ordeals. Studies done in Kenya have majorly focused on the trends, nature, consequences, and effectiveness of strategies employed by state and non-state actors to assist survivors.[11] However, there has been very limited focus on the coping mechanisms employed by survivors and their effectiveness in restoring their well-being at individual, family, and community levels. This study aims to fill this gap.

OBJECTIVES

The objective of this study is to examine the coping strategies adopted by survivors of the 2007/2008 post-election violence in Kenya.

Specific Objectives

1. To explore causes of CRSV in 2007/2008 violence in Kenya
2. To investigate the impact of CRSV on individuals, families, and society
3. To document the various coping mechanism employed by women in responding to CRSV

---

[9] UNOHCHR, UNwomen, Physicians for Human. (2019). Breaking Cycles of Violence Gaps in Prevention of and Response to Electoral Related Sexual Violence.

[10] Makau, E. M. (2018). Exploring the Intervention Efforts in Helping Women Survivors of Sexual Violence in the Aftermath of the 2007/2008 Post-Election Violence in Kisumu County, Kenya (Doctoral Dissertation); Ryanga, H. (2013). Women and Conflict in Mt. Elgon: Assessing Rape as a Weapon in Armed Conflict, 1991–2008 (Doctoral dissertation, University of Nairobi).

[11] Thomas, K., Masinjila, M., & Bere, E. (2013). Political Transition and Sexual and Gender-Based Violence in South Africa, Kenya, and Zimbabwe: A Comparative Analysis. Gender & Development, 21(3), 519–532; Makau, E. M. (2018). Exploring the Intervention Efforts in Helping Women Survivors of Sexual Violence in the Aftermath of the 2007/2008 Post-Election Violence in Kisumu County, Kenya (Doctoral dissertation); Human Rights Watch (New York, NY). (2016). "I Just Sit and Wait to Die" Reparations for Survivors of Kenya's 2007–2008 Post-Election Sexual Violence. Human Rights Watch; UNOHCHR, UNwomen, Physicians for Human (2019) Breaking Cycles of Violence Gaps in Prevention of and Response to Electoral Related Sexual Violence.

LITERATURE REVIEW

This section will situate the study of CRSV and coping mechanism by discussing the nature, trends, causes, and consequences of CRSV as well as exploring various coping strategies and empirical studies that have been undertaken to determine the effectiveness of such coping strategies in assisting CRSV survivors to thrive.

Conflict-Related Sexual Violence

CRSV is contested in its meaning and manifestations,[12] which has implications for the various actors involved and the responses employed. Elisabeth Jean Wood[13] defines CRSV as "sexual violence by armed organisations during armed conflict" thus focusing on perpetrators and forms of sexual violence. Dara Kay Cohen et al.[14] on the other hand, focus on various aspects of CRSV such as the location of incident (private or public); number of perpetrators (single or multiple); target group (men or women); perpetrators (combatant or non-combatants); and determinants (deliberate or opportunistic). This study adopts the UN definition, which focuses on sexual violence forms, gravity, target groups, and context and its association with the conflict. According to the UN Secretary General's report in 2019,[15] CRSV refers to rape sexual slavery, forced prostitution, forced pregnancy, enforced sterilization, and other forms of sexual violence of comparable gravity perpetrated against women, men, girls, or boys; and such acts that are linked, directly or indirectly to a conflict. To understand CRSV and how survivors cope, there is a need to go beyond conceptualization to an examination of its causes, trends, and consequences.

---

[12] Koos, C. (2018). Decay or Resilience?: The Long-Term Social Consequences of Conflict-Related Sexual Violence in Sierra Leone. World Politics, 70(2), 194–238.

[13] Wood, E. J. (2014). Conflict-Related Sexual Violence and the Policy Implications of Recent Research. International Review of the Red Cross, 96(894), 457–478.

[14] Cohen, D. K., & Nordås, R. (2014). Sexual Violence in Armed Conflict: Introducing the SVAC Dataset, 1989–2009. Journal of Peace Research, 51(3). https://journals.sag epub.com/doi/10.1177/0022343314523028.

[15] United Nations. (2019). Secretary General Report on Conflict Related Sexual Violence 2018; New York.

Global Trends on Conflict-Related Sexual Violence
Global sexual violence has been a feature of many civil wars and political strife. It was largely ignored and only gained attention in the 1990s after being declared a crime against humanity and war crime. Some of the wars with a high number of reported incidents of sexual violence include between 20,000 and 50,000 in Bosnia and Herzegovina (1992–1995)[16]; between 250,000 and 500,000 in Rwanda (1994),[17] over 1.5 million in the Democratic Republic of the Congo (1996–present)[18]; between 215,000 and 257,000 in Sierra Leone (1991–2002)[19]; and in Northern Uganda (1986–2006) 25% of women report having experienced a form of CRSV.[20] According to Palermo and Peterman,[21] most of these are estimates way below the actual figures, due to lack of accountability and rigour surrounding citation of estimates of sexual violence during conflict; hence, there is the need to strengthen systems of reporting and collecting data.

The incidence of CRSV persists in various theatres of war. According to the UN, in 2018 there were nineteen countries of concern. These include 13 conflict countries—Afghanistan, Colombia, Yemen, Democratic Republic of the Congo, Somalia, Syria, Iraq, South Sudan, Sudan, Mali, Central Africa Republic, Libya, and Myanmar; and four post-conflict countries—Bosnia and Herzegovina, Nepal, Cote de Voire, and Sri Lanka; as well as Nigeria and Burundi.[22] Africa has the highest number of countries at ten.

[16] Palermo, T., & Peterman, A. (2011). Undercounting, Overcounting and the Longevity of Flawed Estimates: Statistics on Sexual Violence in Conflict. Bulletin of the World Health Organization, 89(12), 924–925. World Health Organization. http://dx.doi.org/10.2471/BLT.11.089888.

[17] Nowrojee, B. (1996). Shattered Lives: Sexual Violence during the Rwandan Genocide and Its Aftermath. United States: Human Rights Watch.

[18] Palermo and Peterman (2011).

[19] Physicians for Human Rights (US), & United Nations Assistance Mission in Sierra Leone. (2002). War-related sexual violence in Sierra Leone: A Population-based Assessment: A Report. Physicians for Human Rights.

[20] Kinyanda, E., et al. (2010, November 10). War Related Sexual Violence and It's Medical and Psychological Consequences as Seen in Kitgum, Northern Uganda: A Cross-Sectional Study. BMC Int Health Hum Rights, 10, 28.

[21] Palermo and Peterman (2011).

[22] United Nations. (2018): Secretary General Report on the Protection of Civilians in Armed Conflict (S/2018/462); For an overview of the report see Peace Women:

Conflict-related sexual violence, while persistent, doesn't occur in all conflicts. In a study of 177 conflicts in 20 African countries, there were no reports of sexual violence in 59% of the conflicts and varying degrees of incidence in the others (11% reporting massive, 16% numerous, and 11% isolated).[23] Nonetheless, 41% prevalence is still quite high, thus a need to understand the causes of CRSV and the circumstances in which it happens.

Causes of CRSV

Variations in prevalence, form, and severity of CRSV indicate that there may be different causes of CRSV including its use as a military strategy, individual or opportunistic motives, and intra-group dynamics. There may also be differences in the cause of CRSV, depending on whether the perpetrators are combatants and non-combatants, as discussed below.

Some studies argue that sexual violence is often utilized as a military strategy whereby combatants inflict bodily harm to humiliate, terrorize, and control survivors, their families, and communities.[24] This is common among armed groups, unlike non-combatants. In such circumstances, CRSV is commonly meted out to women to wound the opponents "masculine pride," as they are unable to protect the women in their communities. Acts of sexual violence in these cases are mostly committed in public, in front of family members, or even between family members in incidents where they are forced to rape one another to maximize humiliation. This has been common in conflicts in Central African Republic, Democratic Republic of the Congo, Mali, Myanmar, and South Sudan, among others.[25] This school of thought however is critiqued by studies demonstrating the absence of military documentation regarding the use

Women's International League of Peace and Freedom, United Nations Office, May 2018, https://www.peacewomen.org/node/102054#top.

[23] Nordås, R. (2011). Sexual Violence in African Countries. CSCW Policy Brief 01 | 2011. Center for the Study of Civil War (CSCW). Peace Research Institute (PRIO). https://www.usip.org/sites/default/files/missing-peace/Ragnhild-Nordas.pdf.

[24] Boesten, J. (2014). Sexual Violence During War and Peace: Gender, Power, and Post-Conflict Justicein Peru. New York: Palgrave Macmillan; Domingo, P., et al. (2013). Assessment of the Evidence of Links between Gender Equality, Peacebuilding and Statebuilding: Literature Review. London: Overseas Development Institute.

[25] Boesten (2014); Cohen, D. K. et al. (2013). Wartime Sexual Violence: Misconceptions, Implications, and Ways Forward. United States Institute of Peace. https://wcfia.harvard.edu/sites/projects.iq.harvard.edu/files/wcfia/files/dcohen_usip2013.pdf.

of sexual violence as a strategy.[26] Therefore, it's an assumption that sexual violence would be a strategy especially where there is systematic sexual violence such as in Rwanda or the former Yugoslavia.

Certain contextual conditions increase the likelihood of sexual violence in conflicts. These include the absence of the rule of law, impunity, weakened state institutions, and gender inequalities.[27] Perpetrators take advantage of such opportunities to commit sexual violence; and, where gender inequalities are ingrained in society, combatants and non-combatants alike reproduce such structural inequalities through sexual violence.[28] While contextual conditions are exploited by combatants, it is quite common with non-combatants as well, as they take advantage of such scenarios knowing they will not be held accountable for their actions.

Individual motives have also been suggested as a cause of sexual violence in conflict. For example, a study of 200 combatants in the Democratic Republic of the Congo found that victims' suffering, the infliction of physical wounds, and the aggression of the sexual act itself have the potential to be a highly rewarding experience for some combatants.[29] Further, perpetrators attributed CRSV to personal frustration and the absence of a wife with whom they could be sexually intimate, and to avenge the rapes their families and communities had experienced.[30] As such, these individuals are driven by lust, bloodthirstiness, frustrations, absence of spouses or female company, anger, peer pressure,

[26] Koos, C. (2017). Sexual Violence in Armed Conflicts: Research Progress and Remaining Gaps. Third World Quarterly, 38(9), 1935–1951; Wood, E. J. (2018). Rape as a Practice of War: Toward a Typology of Political Violence. Politics & Society, 46(4), 513–537.

[27] Cohen, D. K., et al. (2013). Wartime Sexual Violence: Misconceptions, Implications, and Ways Forward. United States Institute of Peace. https://wcfia.harvard.edu/sites/projects.iq.harvard.edu/files/wcfia/files/dcohen_usip2013.pdf; Dijkman, N. E. J., et al. (2014). Sexual Violence in Burundi: Victims, Perpetrators, and the Role of Conflict. HiCN Working Paper 172, Institute of Development Studies, University of Sussex, Brighton.

[28] Dijkman et al. (2014).

[29] Hecker, T., et al. (2013, February). Does Perpetrating Violence Damage Mental Health? Differences between Forcibly Recruited and Voluntary Combatants in DR Congo. Journal of Traumatic Stress, 26(1), 142–148.

[30] Hecker et al. (2013).

substance abuse, and sometimes witchcraft, among others, to commit sexual violence.[31]

Another theory proposed to explain the cause of CRSV is intra-group dynamics. Tobias Hecker et al.[32] found that collective rape increases cohesion between members of an armed group by generating collective feelings of superiority, power, and brotherliness. In circumstances whereby rebels are forcefully recruited, sexual violence is used to enhance group cohesion, boost group morale, and as a reward for victory.[33] Loss of control over troops, and lack of penalties and norms prohibiting CRSV, also increase the likelihood of committing CRSV.[34] However, when groups are fighting primarily for control of the state, they rarely engage in CRSV as this could lead to retaliation against them by victims and their communities.

CRSV is also perpetrated by non-combatants who may include neighbours, friends, and community members. This has been attributed to, among other reasons—taking advantage of the weak security apparatus and lawlessness to commit crimes, boredom, stress, trauma, lack of work (especially in refugee and IDP camps), substance abuse, and sometimes just for pleasure and to punish women.[35] Thus determinants for CRSV may include military purpose or strategy, genocide, revenge, opportunism, revenge, boredom, and lust, among others.[36]

---

[31] Baaz, M. E., & Stern, M. (2009). Why Do Soldiers Rape? Masculinity, Violence, and Sexuality in the Armed Forces in the Congo (DRC). International Studies Quarterly, 53(2), 495–518; Cohen, D. K., et al. (2013); Wood, E. J. (2014). Conflict-Related Sexual Violence and the Policy Implications of Recent Research. International Review of the Red Cross, 96(894), 457–478.

[32] Hecker, T., et al. (2013).

[33] Cohen, D. K., & Nordås, R. (2014). Sexual Violence in Armed Conflict: Introducing the SVAC Dataset, 1989–2009. Journal of Peace Research, 51 (3). https://journals.sagepub.com/doi/10.1177/0022343314523028; Koos, C. (2017). Sexual Violence in Armed Conflicts: Research Progress and Remaining Gaps. Third World Quarterly, 38(9), 1935–1951.

[34] Wood, E. J. (2014). Conflict-Related Sexual Violence and the Policy Implications of Recent Research. International Review of the Red Cross, 96(894), 457–478.

[35] Ceelen, I. (2016). Conflict-Related Sexual Violence and the Prevention of it. Royal Tropical Institute. Master Thesis. Available at: https://bibalex.org/baifa/Attachment/Documents/pauwGznix7_20170424145031723.pdf.

[36] Ibid., p. 20. See venn diagram of the determinants that influence CRSV by combatants and non-combatants.

Consequences of Conflict-Related Sexual Violence
CRSV is not only an indignity to the survivors but also results in complex and long-lasting health, social, and economic consequences. Firstly, CRSV leads to a myriad of health problems, both mental and physiological. Physically, survivors suffer bodily injuries and chronic pain, which affect their ability to maintain social and economic well-being. Reproductive health effects carry medical and social consequences for survivors. In such instances, fistula, sexually transmitted disease, HIV/AIDS, infertility, and spousal and community rejection are common. Additionally, survivors have reported mental health problems, such as anxiety disorders, loss of self-esteem, post-traumatic stress disorder (PTSD), suicidality, and delusions.[37] Health consequences tend to be costly, long term, and affect social relations, especially with male members of the society; hence, long-term medical and social interventions are needed to alleviate the toll on survivors.

Secondly, CRSV has social ramifications that may last for several generations. Communities may marginalize, stigmatize, and reject survivors of CRSV due to the dishonour and shame associated with sexual violence. For example, a study conducted in Eastern Democratic Republic of the Congo found that 29% of rape victims were rejected by their families and 6.2% by their community.[38] Rejection by survivors' partners can be associated with cultural practices, the stigma of rape (which is intensified in cases of gang rape), and fear of contamination and contraction of disease.[39] Spousal rejection follows patterns of blame, anger, domestic violence, neglect, and divorce.[40] Community rejection, on the other hand, stems largely from cultural norms and practices around rape, which

---

[37] Koos, C. (2017). Sexual Violence in Armed Conflicts: Research Progress and Remaining Gaps. Third World Quarterly, 38(9), 1935–1951; Wood, E. J. (2018). Rape as a Practice of War: Toward a Typology of Political Violence. Politics & Society, 46(4), 513–537.

[38] Kelly, J., et al. (2012). 'If Your Husband Doesn't Humiliate You, Other People Won't': Gendered Attitudes Towards Sexual Violence In Eastern Democratic Republic of Congo. Global Public Health, 7(3), 285–298.

[39] Makau, E. M. (2018). Exploring the Intervention Efforts in Helping Women Survivors of Sexual Violence in the Aftermath of the 2007/2008 Post-election Violence in Kisumu County, Kenya (Doctoral Dissertation).

[40] Hecker, T., et al. (2013, February). Does Perpetrating Violence Damage Mental Health? Differences Between Forcibly Recruited and Voluntary Combatants in DR Congo. Journal of Traumatic Stress, 26(1), 142–148.

stigmatize survivors by blaming them for the act as payment for ancestral sins, or blaming them for dishonouring the community. Rejected survivors lose their dignity and self-respect, as well as their means of economic survival, and often fall into abject poverty.[41]

Thirdly, CRSV may result in pregnancies and children. Children born of rape were a common phenomenon in conflicts in Northern Uganda involving the Lords Resistance Army, the Democratic Republic of the Congo, and the post-election violence in Kenya. Mothers of such children face isolation and negative reactions by both family and community. The children are often neglected by the families and become the sole responsibility of their mothers. Furthermore, children of rape face generational stigmatization as they are branded as bad omens throughout their lives.

Finally, CRSV may result in intra-communal cleavages, especially where such violence was committed by fellow community members or opposing groups residing in one locality. This leads to the erosion of trust and tensions between the groups, which may lead to revenge if not well managed.

CRSV also leads to increase in domestic violence in post-conflict scenarios due to the trauma in the population, reversed gender roles, and normalization of CRSV as a result of the conflict. This calls for renegotiation of roles as well as developing new ways to ensure trauma experienced in the community doesn't tip over to cause harm to the already overwhelmed survivors.

Coping Strategies

Coping is defined as thoughts and behaviours that people use to manage the internal and external demands of situations that they appraise as stressful.[42] It's a dynamic process that involves the individual, their environment, and the relationship between them. To cope with the consequences of CRSV, survivors employ various mechanisms. The coping strategies adopted depend on the following factors: characteristics of the event, such as severity, intensity, and duration of exposure to a perceived

---

[41] Makau (2018).

[42] Lazarus, R. S., & Folkman, S. (1986). Cognitive Theories of Stress and the Issue of Circularity. In M. H. Appley, & R. Trumbull (Eds.), Dynamics of Stress. Physiological, Psychologcal, and Social Perspectives (pp. 63–80). New York: Plenum.

threat; psychosocial dimensions, such as personality, social support, and access to services; and pre-event circumstances, such as socio-economic status, family stability, and history of the victim.

Coping has been studied since the early 1920s, beginning with Sigmund Freud (1856–1939). Freud described several defence mechanisms that the ego uses to protect itself against unpleasant internal ideas and feelings and to maintain mental balance. Other psychologists explain coping as a defence against external threats[43] and as an adaptation to difficult conditions.[44] Viktor Frankl shed further light on how individuals cope with trauma by focusing on finding meaning to a problem and moving forward with renewed purpose.[45] He proposed the theory of logotherapy as a way of finding meaning to life when faced with adversity.[46]

Scholars have further advanced a range of coping mechanisms including problem-focused and emotional-focused mechanisms[47]; active behavioural, active cognitive, and avoidance mechanisms[48]; meaning focused[49]; and social coping.[50]

In recent literature, coping mechanisms are grouped in a four-factor solution that includes problem/active focused, emotion focused, social

---

[43] Adler, A. (1930). Individual Psychology. In C. Murchison (Ed.), *Psychologies of 1930* (pp. 395–405). Clark University Press; White, R. W. (1974). Strategies of Adaptation: An Attempt at Systematic Description. In G. V. Coelho, D. A. Hamburg, & J. E. Adams (Eds.), Coping and Adaptation. New York: Basic Books.

[44] White, R. W. (1974). Strategies of Adaptation: An Attempt at Systematic Description. In G. V. Coelho, D. A. Hamburg, & J. E. Adams (Eds.), Coping and Adaptation. New York: Basic Books.

[45] Frankl, V. E. (1985). Man's Search for Meaning. Simon and Schuster.

[46] Costello, S. J. (2019). Applied Logotherapy: Viktor Frankl's Philosophical Psychology. Cambridge Scholars Publishing.

[47] Lazarus, R. S., & Folkman, S. (1986). Cognitive Theories of Stress and the Issue of Circularity. In M. H. Appley, & R. Trumbull (Eds.), Dynamics of Stress. Physiological, Psychologcal, and Social Perspectives (pp. 63–80). New York: Plenum.

[48] Billings, A. G., & Moos, R. H. (1981, June). The Role of Coping Responses and Social Resources in Attenuating the Stress of Life Events. Journal of Behavioral Medicine, 4(2), 139–157.

[49] Park, C. L., & Folkman, S. (1997). Meaning in the Context of Stress and Coping. Review of General Psychology, 1(2), 115–144.

[50] Zautra, A. J., Sheets, V. L., & Sandler, I. N. (1996). An Examination of the Construct Validity of Coping Dispositions for a Sample of Recently Divorced Mothers. Psychological Assessment, 8(3), 256–264.

coping, and meaning focused.[51] Coping outcomes are dependent on the qualities of the traumatic event itself as well as personal reactions to the event. Personal reactions include primary cognitive appraisals (i.e., "What are the potential consequences of this event? Is it a challenge, a threat, or a loss?") and secondary cognitive appraisals of a stressful event (i.e., "Do I have the resources necessary to successfully handle this stressor?").[52] This is accompanied by an assortment of cognitive, behavioural, and relational coping strategies employed to deal with the stressor. These include acceptance, active coping, denial, disengagement, humour, planning, positive reframing, religion, restraint, social support, self-distraction, and suppression of competing activities. The four-factor coping theories are further discussed below.

Problem-Focused Coping
Problem-focused coping involves addressing the problem causing distress through adaptation and managing the stressful situation. It includes strategies like active coping, planning, and restraint. It utilizes the following steps—defining the problem, searching for alternative solutions to the problem, evaluating the pros and cons of the alternatives, and choosing among those solutions for the best approach to take (Lazarus & Folkman, 1984). While most efforts linked to problem-focused coping tend to be successful and permanent, it mostly applies to stressful circumstances that are controllable by the individual. CRSV however is not in the survivors' control and as such it's difficult to apply this strategy. For prevention of CRSV, at risk groups in hotspot areas can be trained in preventive measures that they can use to prevent and mitigate consequences of CRSV, such as settings up early warning systems, safe houses, provision and use of post-exposure prophylaxis, and awareness creation on effects of CRSV and its management. These proactive steps go a long way in preventing and mitigating the effects of CRSV.

Emotion-Focused Coping
Emotion-focused coping mechanisms deal with ameliorating emotions associated with a problem. It functions to manage (i.e., tolerate, reduce,

---

[51] Moskowitz, J. T. (2011). Coping Interventions and the Regulation of Positive Affect. In S. Folkman (Ed.), The Oxford Handbook of Stress, Health, and Coping (pp. 407–427). Oxford University Press.

[52] Moskowitz (2011).

or eliminate) the physiological, emotional, cognitive, and behavioural reactions that accompany the experience of a stressful situation[53]; that is, it involves altering the way one thinks or feels about a situation or an event. This may involve denying the existence of the stressful situation, freely expressing or venting emotions, or the positive reinterpretation or avoidance of stressful situations that remind one of the events. In emotion-focused CRSV scenarios, the survivors commonly employ negative emotional coping methods such as disassociation, avoidance and denial, silence, and drugs and alcohol abuse in order to forget about the violations.[54] Through counselling and employing emotional-approach coping—which entails identifying, processing, and expressing one's emotion towards a certain goal—survivors may go through various emotion regulation therapies, enabling them to deal with triggers that recall the traumatic event, and thus control such emotions with time.[55]

Social Coping
Social coping involves the interactions between the survivor and the social environment they find themselves in. Coping doesn't occur in a vacuum and involves one's engagement with the social environment. The social environment comprises social structures and relationships.[56] It involves seeking support from a spouse, family, friend, and community who offer not only emotional social support but also instrumental (i.e., offering assistance in tangible manner), informational (i.e., providing advice, suggestions, and general information), and appraisal (i.e., providing information for self-evaluation) social support. Studies have indicated that social support goes a long way in helping survivors gain effective functioning in the society.[57] However, the cultures and norms in social

---

[53] Ben-Zur, H. (2020). Emotion-Focused Coping. In V. Zeigler-Hill & T. K. Shackelford (Eds.), Encyclopedia of Personality and Individual Differences. Cham: Springer.

[54] Thomas, K. (2017). Women and Sexual Violence, Paths to Healing: Resistance, Rebellion, Resilience and Recovery (Doctoral Dissertation, Middlesex University).

[55] Baker, J. P., & Berenbaum, H. (2007). Emotional Approach and Problem-Focused Coping: A Comparison of Potentially Adaptive Strategies. Cognition and Emotion, 21(1), 95–118.

[56] Moskowitz, J. T., Shmueli-Blumberg, D., Acree, M., & Folkman, S. (2012). Positive Affect in the Midst of Distress: Implications for Role Functioning. Journal of Community & Applied Social Psychology, 22(6), 502–518.

[57] Koos, C. (2018). Decay or Resilience?: The Long-Term Social Consequences of Conflict-Related Sexual Violence in Sierra Leone. World Politics, 70(2), 194–238.

structures can shape community perceptions of the sexual incident, and in turn influence the kind of support the community gives to the survivor.[58]

Meaning-Focused Coping
Meaning-focused coping is an appraisal-based coping in which the person draws on his or her beliefs (e.g., religious, spiritual, or beliefs about justice), values (e.g., "mattering"), and existential goals (e.g., purpose in life or guiding principles) to motivate and sustain coping and well-being during a difficult time.[59] Such approaches include positive reinterpretation, spiritualism, humour, and acceptance. While meaning-focused coping approaches may lead to positive changes it may also lead to spiritual crises which may cause additional distress. Negative spiritual coping can occur when a survivor who has been a very good devotee of a higher power undergoes a traumatic experience. The survivor in this case would ask "Why me?" questions, doubt their life philosophies, and totally lose interest in spirituality. This can lead to further distress and unhealthy behaviour like self-harm.

All these coping mechanisms lead to various outcomes that can be considered adaptive or maladaptive. The selection and effectiveness of coping mechanisms are dependent on one's personality, the continuum of a stressful situation, and the context under which a violation occurs. For instance, in dealing with a sexual violation, it may be prudent to first seek psychological support in order to attain emotional balance, after which the survivor can engage in more problem-focused mechanisms that deal with future plans and restoring one's social and economic well-being. Furthermore, an individual's use of coping flexibility (i.e., utilizing various strategies rather than only one) may also assist in dealing with such violations. Under such circumstances, survivors move from one coping mechanism to another in the healing process.

Post-Traumatic Growth and Conflict-Related Sexual Violence
Recent studies of CRSV recognize that while all survivors of sexual violence suffer different degrees of post-traumatic stress there are some

---

[58] Makau, E. M. (2018). Exploring the Intervention Efforts in Helping Women Survivors of Sexual Violence in the Aftermath of the 2007/2008 Post-Election Violence in Kisumu county, Kenya (Doctoral dissertation).

[59] Folkman, S. (2008). The Case for Positive Emotions in the Stress Process, Anxiety, Stress & Coping, 21(1), 3–14.

who outgrow PTSD. Posttraumatic growth (PTG) is defined as beneficial change in cognitive and emotional capacities beyond previous levels of adaptation, psychological functioning, or life awareness.[60] PTG results in genuine and transformative positive changes to an individual's identity, relationships, and worldviews. PTG measures growth in five domains—relationships with others, new possibilities, personal strength, spiritual change, and appreciation for life. However, the growth in these domains by survivors of CRSV differ from person to person, ranging from greater relationship with family,[61] greater appreciation of life,[62] greater personal strength, and spiritual change.[63]

The theory of PTG argues that a traumatic experience such as sexual violence has the potential to severely challenge (or even shatter) an individual's prior beliefs and assumptions about the world, and cause them to question their philosophies of life. For PTG to occur, the individual needs to take a series of steps—disengage from prior beliefs and goals that no longer make sense in their current situation, search for meaning in their experience, and rebuild their identities in a manner that incorporates these lessons. The results of such cognitive processing can either lead to post-traumatic growth, or sometimes more distress and hopelessness. In addition, post-trauma adjustment is differentiated from

---

[60] Cann, A., Calhoun, L. G., Tedeschi, R. G., Triplett, K. N., Vishnevsky, T., & Lindstrom, C. M. (2011). Assessing Posttraumatic Cognitive Processes: The Event Related Rumination Inventory. Anxiety, Stress, & Coping, 24(2), 137–156; Jayawickreme, E., & Blackie, L. E. R. (2014). Post-Traumatic Growth as Positive Personality Change: Evidence, Controversies and Future Directions. European Journal of Personality, 28(4), 312–331.

[61] Anderson, K., et al. (2019). Predictors of Posttraumatic Growth among Conflict-Related Sexual Violence Survivors from Bosnia and Herzegovina. Conflict and Health, 13(1), 23. Assessment of 2007–2008 election-related violence in Kenya. Conflict and Health, 8(2), 1–12.

[62] Koos, C. (2018). Decay or Resilience?: The Long-Term Social Consequences of Conflict-Related Sexual Violence in Sierra Leone. World Politics, 70(2), 194–238; Gillihan, S. J., et al. (2012, October 1). Common Pitfalls in Exposure and Response Prevention (EX/RP) for OCD. Journal of Obsessive–Compulsive and Related Disorders, 1(4): 251–257.

[63] Van Hook, M. P. (2016). Spirituality as a Potential Resource for Coping with Trauma. Social Work and Christianity, 43(1), 7.

post-trauma growth, often in important ways.[64] While PTG focuses on lifelong changes that enable the survivor to thrive, and may encompass empathy, wisdom, and forgiveness, post-trauma adjustment is temporary and focuses on what resources are needed to survive the threat at a specific time (e.g., acceptance, hope, and responsibility to live).

Coping mechanisms, context, and personalities impact cognitive processing that leads to either PTG or distress and hopelessness. Survivors who employ active coping mechanisms such as planning and positive reinterpretation of the sexual violence experience tend to recover faster than those who adopt avoidance mechanisms (Anderson 2019). In addition, the survivors who demonstrate growth relocate to conflict free and economically stable environments where they are not stigmatized based on their cultures or experiences. In this new environment, they feel in control of their recovery process and can plan and seize new opportunities.[65] Personality types also influence growth.[66] People who have tendencies of pessimism and negative perceptions of themselves respond more intensely to sexual trauma than others, and may even be psychotic if the distress period is prolonged.

Unlike other forms of violence, the shame, embarrassment, and stigma associated with sexual violence may also affect the healing process and trajectory of post-traumatic growth.[67] Lack of social support and stigma leads to self-blame and isolation of survivors. This has a negative influence on survivors' attempts to build resources and capacities to cope with the sexual trauma. Hence, survivor-centred approaches are needed that promote acceptance of the survivors so that they can transition to a better life.

---

[64] Blackie, L. E. R., Jayawickreme, E., Hitchcott, N., & Joseph, S. (2017). Distinguishing Post-Traumatic Growth from Psychological Adjustment among Rwandan Genocide Survivors. In D. Carr, J. Arthur & K. Kristjánsson (Eds.), Varieties of Virtue Ethics. Palgrave Macmillan, pp. 299–317.

[65] Thomas, K. (2017). Women and Sexual Violence, Paths to Healing: Resistance, Rebellion, Resilience and Recovery (Doctoral Dissertation, Middlesex University).

[66] Thomas (2017).

[67] Koos, C. (2017). Sexual Violence in Armed Conflicts: Research Progress and Remaining Gaps. Third World Quarterly, 38(9), 1935–1951; Spangaro, J., et al. (2013). What Evidence Exists for Initiatives to Reduce Risk and Incidence of Sexual Violence in Armed Conflict and Other Humanitarian Crises? A Systematic Review. PLoS ONE, 8(5), e62600.

Empirical Literature Review

The devastating nature and consequences of conflict-related sexual violence has been widely documented.[68] The consequences coupled with other forms of violence meted out to survivors during such events leads to extreme trauma to the survivors, their families, and community at large.[69] To restore their physical, psychological, and social well-being, survivors utilize the interventions provided by various organizations, as well as adopt various coping strategies.

The main interventions provided for CRSV survivors include medical, legal, and psychosocial services, as well as economic support.[70] For such services to be effective they need to be accessible, responsive, and protect the dignity of the survivor. In the Kenyan case, however, there were various challenges to the access of these services. These include the road closures during periods of violence; the irresponsiveness of the security apparatus and health professionals; delayed justice; and cultural and social

---

[68] United Nations. (2019). Secretary General Report on Conflict Related Sexual Violence 2018; New York; Koos, C. (2017). Sexual Violence in Armed Conflicts: Research Progress and Remaining Gaps. Third World Quarterly, 38(9), 1935–1951; Wood, E. J. (2014). Conflict-Related Sexual Violence and the Policy Implications of Recent Research. International Review of the Red Cross, 96(894), 457–478; Cohen, D. K., & Nordås, R. 2014. Sexual Violence in Armed Conflict: Introducing the SVAC Dataset, 1989–2009. Journal of Peace Research, 51 (3); Koegler, E., et al. (2019). Understanding How Solidarity Groups—A Community-Based Economic and Psychosocial Support Intervention—Can Affect Mental Health for Survivors of Conflict-Related Sexual Violence in Democratic Republic of the Congo. Violence against Women, 25(3), 359–374; Albutt, K., et al. (2017). Stigmatisation and Rejection of Survivors of Sexual Violence in Eastern Democratic Republic of the Congo. Disasters, 41(2), 211–227; Human Rights Watch (New York, NY). (2016). "I Just Sit and Wait to Die" Reparations for Survivors of Kenya's 2007–2008 Post-Election Sexual Violence. Human Rights Watch; Makau, E. M. (2018). Exploring the Intervention Efforts in Helping Women Survivors of Sexual Violence in the Aftermath of the 2007/2008 Post-Election Violence in Kisumu County, Kenya (Doctoral dissertation).

[69] Friedman, M. J., Resick, P. A., Bryant, R. A., & Brewin, C. R. (2011). Considering Ptsd for Dsm-5. Depression and Anxiety, 28(9), 750–769.

[70] Makau, E. M. (2018). Exploring the Intervention Efforts in Helping Women Survivors of Sexual Violence in the Aftermath of the 2007/2008 Post-Election Violence in Kisumu county, Kenya (Doctoral dissertation); Koos, C. (2017). Sexual Violence in Armed Conflicts: Research Progress and Remaining Gaps. Third World Quarterly, 38(9), 1935–1951.

norms that promoted stigmatization and dishonouring of survivors.[71] To cope with these challenges, as well as the effects of CRSV, survivors adopt various coping mechanisms that enable them to survive, recover, or thrive.[72]

Silence is one of the coping mechanisms adopted by CRSV survivors.[73] The horrific nature of CRSV, manifested by shock, unconsciousness, distress, and humiliation, may lead to disassociation, silence, and isolation. When survivors anticipate rejection, they will not disclose what they have experienced and may resort to silence both privately and publicly.[74] According to Johanna Selimovic,[75] silence can be enabling and disabling, and used to forget or remember the traumatic sexual event. As a coping mechanism, it is useful in protecting survivors from social rejection, stigma, and perpetrators if they still live in conflict contexts. Thus, silence acts as a survival mechanism to maintain one's dignity and rebuild a sense of normality. Further, it can be used to protect children born out of sexual violence until such a time that they are accepted in the community.[76] However, if survivors are not healing over time, silence as a coping strategy can lead to self-destructive behaviour, such as suicide attempts,

---

[71] Makau (2018); Human Rights Watch (New York, NY). (2016). "I Just Sit and Wait to Die" Reparations for Survivors of Kenya's 2007–2008 Post-Election Sexual Violence. Human Rights Watch; Masinjila, M. (2013) in Thomas, K., Masinjila, M., & Bere, E. (2013). Political Transition and Sexual and Gender-Based Violence in South Africa, Kenya, and Zimbabwe: A Comparative Analysis. Gender & Development, 21(3), 519–532.

[72] Thomas, K. (2017). Women and Sexual Violence, Paths to Healing: Resistance, Rebellion, Resilience and Recovery (Doctoral Dissertation, Middlesex University).

[73] Johanna Mannergren Selimovic. (2020). Gendered Silences in Post-Conflict Societies: A Typology. Peacebuilding 8(1), 1–15.

[74] Makau (2018); Selimovic (2020); Kohli, A., et al. (2014). Risk for Family Rejection and Associated Mental Health Outcomes among Conflict-Affected Adult Women Living in Rural Eastern Democratic Republic of the Congo. Health Care for Women International, 35(7–9), 789–807; Albutt, K., et al. (2017). Stigmatisation and Rejection of Survivors of Sexual Violence in Eastern Democratic Republic of the Congo. Disasters, 41(2), 211–227; Amone-P'Olak, K., et al. (2015). War Experiences and Psychotic Symptoms among Former Child Soldiers in Northern Uganda: The Mediating Role of Post-War Hardships—The WAYS Study. South African Journal of Psychology, 45(2), 155–167.

[75] Selimovic (2020).

[76] Carpenter, C. (2007). Gender, Ethnicity, and Children's Human Rights: Theorizing Babies Born of Wartime Rape and Sexual Exploitation. In C. Carpenter (Ed.), Born of War: Protecting Children of Sexual Violence Survivors in Conflict Zones. Bloomfield: Kumarian Press.

nightmares, isolation, depression, sexual problems, low self-esteem, and mental disorder.[77]

Passive/avoidance coping (e.g., denial and emotional avoidance) is also a common coping mechanism adopted by survivors. Survivors who feel they have insufficient resources to manage or change the stressor will adopt avoidance coping. Studies indicate that while it is one of the most commonly used strategies, survivors only get a temporary reprieve and they are prone to suffer heightened anxiety–depression.[78] A study conducted in the Democratic Republic of the Congo found that survivors who adopted avoidance mechanisms experienced social isolation. While avoidance enabled them to survive in the period after the traumatic experience they became anti-social, after losing empathy from the community and being unable to maintain relationships or seek services.[79]

Spirituality is another coping strategy employed by people suffering from various forms of trauma.[80] Spiritual coping involves dealing with stressful life events through beliefs and practices that are based around religion or worldviews that are spiritual in nature. Studies indicate that spirituality can both contribute to resiliency (i.e., the ability to bounce back or thrive after hardship) and intensify pain and distress. To achieve resilience, survivors employ spirituality in many ways, including seeking spiritual connection to a higher being; seeking spiritual support; seeking grace and forgiveness between the perpetrator and survivor; collaborative religious coping; and benevolent religious appraisal.[81] This elicits common phrases like "God hasn't brought me this far to let me die" or "So long as I got God on my side I can't give up." Spiritual coping can also develop a new meaning of and role for faith in one's new life

---

[77] Ramírez, H. (2014). Psychological Effects on Children and Adolescents Exposed to Armed Conflict in a Rural Area of Colombia. Acta Colombiana De Psicología, 17(1), 79–89.

[78] Leiner, A. S., et al. (2012). Avoidant Coping and Treatment Outcome in Rape-Related Posttraumatic Stress Disorder. Journal of Consulting and Clinical Psychology, 80(2), 317.

[79] Albutt et al. (2017), Koegler (2018).

[80] Adedoyin, A. C., et al. (2016). Religious Coping Strategies among Traumatized African Refugees in the United States: A Systematic Review. Social Work and Christianity, 43(1), 95; Van Hook, M. P. (2016). Spirituality as a Potential Resource for Coping with Trauma. Social Work and Christianity, 43(1), 7.

[81] Van Hook, M. P. (2016). Spirituality as a Potential Resource for Coping with Trauma. Social Work and Christianity, 43(1), 7.

experiences.[82] For example, Jessica Gladden[83] suggests that spirituality is a powerful coping mechanism used by African immigrants to overcome the countless struggles they face in being merged into American culture. Religious coping was used in the aftermath of the 2007/2008 post-election violence in Kenya. In a study on the association between trauma exposure, religious coping, and psychiatric distress in a community in Nairobi, Kenya, 90% of 708 witnesses to the violence indicated that they belonged to a religion and had used various religious coping mechanisms.[84] Spirituality is commonly used because of accessibility and ready support received from church leaders and groups. Where churches are not accessible it is not a common coping strategy. Spirituality can also lead to negative coping emotions, such as feelings of being abandoned by God, self-blame for a perceived punishment from God, or losing trust and loss of confidence in ones' beliefs in a higher being.[85] In such instances survivors may totally disengage from attending church functions.

Emotional regulation is also used as a coping mechanism. This is the process by which an individual exerts influence over what emotions they feel, when they feel them, and how they are experienced and expressed.[86] In Colombia, for example, NGOs have used various therapies to manipulate triggers that elicit certain emotional responses in sexual survivors. This therapeutic approach has enabled survivors to better manage their emotions stemming from the trauma and eventually recover from the

---

[82] Simmelink, J., et al. (2013). Understanding the Health Beliefs and Practices of East African Refugees. American Journal of Health Behavior, 37(2), 155–161. Cohen, D. K., & Nordås, R. (2014). Sexual Violence in Armed Conflict: Introducing the SVAC Dataset, 1989–2009. Journal of Peace Research, 51(3), 418–428. https://journals.sagepub.com/doi/10.1177/0022343314523028.

[83] Gladden, J. (2013). Coping Strategies of Sudanese Refugee Women in Kakuma Refugee Camp, Kenya. Refugee Survey Quarterly 32(4), 66–89.

[84] Shin, H. J., et al. (2017). Associations between Trauma Exposure, Religious Coping, and Psychiatric Distress in a Community Sample in Nairobi, Kenya. Journal of Prevention & Intervention in the Community, 45(4), 250–260.

[85] Adedoyin, A. C., et al. (2016). Religious Coping Strategies Among Traumatized African Refugees in the United States: A Systematic Review. Social Work and Christianity, 43(1), 95; Makau, E. M. (2018). Exploring the Intervention Efforts in Helping Women Survivors of Sexual Violence in the Aftermath of the 2007/2008 Post-Election Violence in Kisumu County, Kenya (Doctoral dissertation).

[86] Gross, J. J. (2015). Emotion Regulation: Current Status and Future Prospects. Psychological Inquiry, 26(1), 1–26.

ordeal.[87] This is however not common in Africa due to lack of trained personnel.

Coping strategies have also been found to change during conflict periods. In a study conducted among 434 youths in Eastern Democratic Republic of the Congo, who were exposed to traumatic experiences related to sexual violence, a majority indicated that they preferred emotional- focused coping to problem-focused coping mechanisms.[88] As youths are unable to control stressors unlike during peacetime they tend to resort to emotion-focused coping strategies, such as disengaging from emotions, distraction, and seeking emotional support from peers, family, and external actors. Problem-focused coping as a strategy used alone may worsen internalizing and externalizing problems and reduce self-esteem and prosocial behaviour, as the youth cannot fix the problem during this period. Greater emotional-focused coping, especially using social support, provided enhanced social relationships and greater closeness with family and community, and thus reduced PSTD and increased healthy living and growth.

Coping strategies have also been used as identifiers as to who may be at greater risk of poor outcomes in the long term and who will thrive. A study by Kimberly Anderson et al.[89] on sexual violence survivors from Bosnia and Herzegovina found that adoption of the positive problem-focused coping mechanism led to enhanced emotional and cognitive capacities of CRSV survivors as compared to avoidance mechanisms. As such, planning and positive reinterpretation of the sexual violence was more effective than isolation, disassociation, and substance abuse in coping with trauma. By reframing their experiences, learning lessons, and applying them to their new lives, survivors were better prepared to seize new opportunities. They also related better with others, sought new possibilities, and had new perceptions of life; in stark contrast to those

---

[87] Ubillos-Landa, S., et al. (2019). Coping Strategies Used by Female Victims of the Colombian Armed Conflict: The Women in the Colombian Conflict (Mucoco) Program. Sage Open, 9(4), 2158244019894072.

[88] Cherewick, M., et al. (2016). Potentially Traumatic Events, Coping Strategies and Associations with Mental Health and Well-Being Measures among Conflict-Affected Youth in Eastern Democratic Republic of Congo. Global Health Research and Policy, 1(1), 8.

[89] Anderson, K., et al. (2019). Predictors of Posttraumatic Growth among Conflict-Related Sexual Violence Survivors from Bosnia and Herzegovina. Conflict and Health, 13(1), 23.

adopting avoidance mechanisms who remained distressed, hopeless, and had suicidal tendencies.

Social coping also leads to the enhancement of healthy functioning after sexual trauma. It is considered a moderating factor for negative consequences of sexual violence. While there are still questions on how social support works, scholars argue that actual or perceived social support results in decreased levels of depression and life stress.[90] For example, Verelst et al.[91] conducted a study among adolescent girls in the Democratic Republic of the Congo who experienced sexual violence. They found that stigmatization related to sexual violence had a greater intervening impact on mental health outcomes than the act itself. Over one-third of the girls in a population of 1305 had experienced sexual violence and showed signs of anxiety, depression and post-traumatic stress, with worse results for those who indicated rejection and stigma by family and community. Verelst et al. thus call for family therapy, community interventions, and sensitization activities to support victims.

Social support from fellow survivors also helps in enhancing individuals' lives. In a study on group therapy for sexually violated women in the 1994 Rwandan genocide, Jeanne Marie Ntete[92] found that belonging to the group, and being taken through an integrated group therapy model, improved their lives in notable ways. Particularly, the survivors reported the following: 80.4% regained their freedom; 76.3% experienced autonomy; 75.1% were coping well with their environment; 87.5% experienced personal growth; 82.9% improved their relationship with others; and, 84.4% had a new purpose in life and were making plans for their future. While this was a study limited in scope and number or participants, it's a good pointer that group therapy can lead to the adoption of adaptive coping mechanisms that are essential in helping survivors of CRSV to survive and thrive beyond the sexual trauma. The group sessions can give them a sense of belonging, support, and self-value. Similar findings

---

[90] Koos, C. (2017). Sexual Violence in Armed Conflicts: Research Progress and Remaining Gaps. Third World Quarterly, 38(9), 1935–1951.

[91] Verelst, A., et al. (2014). The Mediating Role of Stigmatization in the Mental Health of Adolescent Victims of Sexual Violence in Eastern Congo. Child Abuse & Neglect, 38(7), 1139–1146.

[92] Ntete, J. M. (2017). Effect of Group Therapy in Restoring Psychological Wellbeing of Sexually Violated Women of 1994 Tutsi Genocide In Rwanda (Doctoral Dissertation, Kenyatta University).

were also reported in a study in Kenya where CRSV survivors in Kisumu reported that social support from their peers helped them in improving their self-esteem and gave them a new sense of belonging and direction.[93]

Relocation of survivors to more peaceful settings has also been found to improve chances of growth and restoration to pre-war situations. Studies of CRSV survivors who have been relocated to more peaceful and economically stable countries have demonstrated greater growth than those who remained behind or were relocated to less stable regions.[94] Those who remain in the same contexts do not cope well, due to continuing relief of the traumatic experiences, social economic hardships, fear or retribution for perpetrators if they still live in the area, and societal instability.

Thus, the various coping mechanisms can either lead to survival, recovery, or growth. When one adopts avoidance and silence as coping mechanisms they tend to remain at the survival stage and find it very challenging to reintegrate into the society or flourish as they were prior to the CRSV incident. For one to recover and thrive, there is a need to find new meaning beyond what they have experienced. Through adopting spiritual, problem-solving, and social coping mechanisms one can find new meaning in life. These strategies enable survivors to reconfigure their global goals that have been violated by the traumatic event, and in most case they develop better goals and philosophies of life and tend to be more resilient.[95] While much has been studied on CRSV in Kenya—the trends, causes, consequences, and responses[96]—there is very limited data pertaining to coping strategies. This study aims to fill this gap by exploring the limited literature to consolidate what has been researched

---

[93] Makau, E. M. (2018). Exploring the Intervention Efforts in Helping Women Survivors of Sexual Violence in the Aftermath of the 2007/2008 Post-Election Violence in Kisumu County, Kenya (Doctoral dissertation).

[94] Gladden, J. (2013). Coping Strategies of Sudanese Refugee Women in Kakuma Refugee Camp, Kenya. Refugee Survey Quarterly, 32, 4, 66–89.

[95] Park, C. L., & Ai, A. L. (2006). Meaning Making and Growth: New Directions for Research on Survivors of Trauma. Journal of Loss and Trauma, 11(5), 389–407.

[96] Human Rights Watch (New York, NY). (2016). "I Just Sit and Wait to Die" Reparations for Survivors of Kenya's 2007–2008 Post-Election Sexual Violence. Human Rights Watch; Masinjila, M. (2013) in Thomas, K., Masinjila, M., & Bere, E. (2013). Political Transition and Sexual and Gender-Based Violence in South Africa, Kenya, and Zimbabwe: A Comparative Analysis. Gender & Development, 21(3), 519–532; Makau (2018).

so far. Accordingly, the section below focuses on the CRSV survivors of the 2007/2008 post-election violence.

CONFLICT-RELATED SEXUAL VIOLENCE IN KENYA

Like other multi-ethnic societies, Kenya has endured many conflicts. According to the Armed Conflict Location and Event Data Project, Kenya recorded over 3500 violent events between 1997 and 2013.[97] Woven through this violence are key drivers, such as ethnic intolerance, politics, border disputes, competition over natural resources, proliferation of arms, political rivalry, land zoning, weak security apparatus, socio-economic inequality, poverty, and marginalization. The main actors culpable for the violence include government security, political and community militias, and sometimes civilians.[98] The conflicts represent cycles of election-related violence, inter-communal violence over water, pasture, and land, and terrorist attacks, which have increased in incidence, gravity, and intensity in the recent past.[99] These forms of violence have an array of consequences, such as population displacement, sexual violence, livelihood insecurity, destruction of social services, weakened infrastructure, and fatalities.

Sexual violence occurs in these conflicts but is grossly underreported. For example, in the case of land conflicts between a local rebel group, The Kenya Defence Forces, and the community in Mount Elgon region of Western Kenya, reported cases of sexual violence (especially rape and forced marriages) were estimated to be only 18% of the actual cases and were never verified.[100] Kylie Thomas et al.[101] further contend that during electoral periods in Kenya cases of sexual violence are higher as compared

---

[97] Raleigh, C., & Dowd, C. (2013). Governance and Conflict in the Sahel's 'Ungoverned Space'. Stability: International Journal of Security and Development, 2(2), p. Art. 32.

[98] Makau (2018), HRW (2016).

[99] Rohwerder, B. Conflict Analysis of Kenya. Birmingham, UK: Gsdrc, University of Birmingham (2015).

[100] Thomas, K., Masinjila, M., & Bere, E. (2013). Political Transition and Sexual and Gender-Based Violence in South Africa, Kenya, and Zimbabwe: A Comparative Analysis. Gender & Development, 21(3), 519–532; Truth, J., & Reconciliation Commission. (2013). TJRC Report Volume 1.

[101] Thomas, K., et al. (2013).

to other periods. For example, in the aftermath of the 2007/2008 elections, Nairobi Women Hospital Gender Recovery Centre attended to over 650 cases of sexual and gender-based violence, three times its normal intake. This was the period when over 900 cases of rape and other forms of sexual violence were reported across the country.[102] The major sexual violence incidents experienced include—single and multiple perpetrated rape, genital mutilation, circumcision, and forced marriages.

While Kenya has a robust legal system to prosecute generalized sexual violence there has been a delay of justice for CRSV survivors due to lack of proper planning; poor documentation and collection of evidence; limited resources to provide post-rape care, train doctors, and provide safe houses; as well as poor prosecution of CRSV cases.[103]

Conflict-Related Sexual Violence During the 2007/2008 Post-Election Violence in Kenya

Background
CRSV in Kenya has been associated significantly with general elections, even though it also occurs in other forms of violent conflict. Since the 1990s, general elections have witnessed various levels of CRSV mostly in the period following the announcement of presidential election results. The worst cases were experienced after the 2007 general elections which recorded more than 900 cases of sexual violence, 1000 fatalities, 350,000 internally displaced people (IDP), and some refugee populations in Uganda.[104] The conflicts took place in most regions of the country including Nairobi, Central and North Rift, Nyanza, Coastal, Central, and Western.

While appearing to pit minority voters against majority voters of one political party in a region, the post-election violence was interwoven with a constellation of factors, including land ownership challenges; patrimonialism; a culture of impunity; state-sanctioned violence; strongly ethicized political discourse; weak institutions; and dissatisfaction with the

---

[102] HRW (2016).

[103] UNOHCHR, UNwomen, Physicians for Human. (2019). Breaking Cycles of Violence Gaps in Prevention of and Response to Electoral Related Sexual Violence

[104] Truth, Justice, and Reconciliation Commission, "Commissions of Inquiry—CIPEV Report (Waki Report)" (2008). IX. Government Documents and Regulations. 5.

results.[105] Acts of sexual violence in the 2007/2008 post-election period included rape, gang rape, forced circumcisions, assault, and genital mutilation[106] carried against women, girls, and men. The perpetrators included members of warring militias or gangs supporting various political parties, the security apparatus, and sometimes other community members. Gang rape and female genital mutilation, which are not common in generalized violence in Kenya, also featured in the post-election violence.[107] In Nairobi's informal settlements, women and children were particularly targeted for rape on account of their ethnicity, although some men and boys were also raped. Circumcision of Luo men and boys was reported in Nairobi and Naivasha to punish them for supporting the Orange Democratic Party.[108]

The aftermath of this post-election violence led to the establishment of various commissions, including the Commission of Inquiry into Post-Election Violence (CIPEV), the Truth Justice and Reconciliation Commission (TJRC), and the Constitution of Kenya Review Commission. These commissions developed several laws (e.g., Constitution of Kenya 2010) and policies and recommendations to deter future electoral violence. Despite these reforms, implementation was very weak with no judicial rulings on any CRSV cases to date. A similar situation was witnessed in the 2017 elections where 201 electoral conflict-related sexual violence cases were again reported from 11 counties.[109]

Causes

There are various explanations advanced regarding the causes of sexual violence during the 2007/2008 election period. Firstly, CRSV was explained as a strategy by militias and other perpetrators to humiliate,

---

[105] Mueller, S. (2012). The Political Economy of Kenya's Crisis. In D. Bekoe (Ed.), Voting in Fear. Washington, DC: U.S. Institute of Peace; Somerville, K. (2011). Violence, Hate Speech and Inflammatory Broadcasting in Kenya: The Problems of Definition and Identification, Ecquid Novi: African Journalism Studies, 32(1), 82–101; Brown, S., & Sriram, C. L. (2012). The Big Fish Won't Fry Themselves: Criminal Accountability for Post-Election Violence in Kenya. African Affairs, 111(443), 244–260.

[106] Auchter, J. (2017). Forced Male Circumcision: Gender-Based Violence in Kenya. International Affairs, 93(6), 1339–1356.

[107] HRW (2016).

[108] KNCHR. (2018). Silhouettes of Brutality: An Account of Sexual Violence During and After the 2017 General Elections (2018). 5, ibid., p. 6.

[109] KNCHR (2018).

terrorize, and displace their victims. In the 2007/2008 post-election period, sexual violence was strategically used by various militias to pressure people to leave their homes, to retaliate against them for having voted for the wrong candidate, tribe, or party, and to dominate, humiliate, and degrade them and their community into a pit of powerlessness.[110] Thus, sexual violence essentially was used to repress or punish political participation.

In other instances, individuals took advantage of the general backdrop of lawlessness, disorder, and chaos to commit sexual violence during the elections and in IDP camps. Such perpetrators included neighbours, community members, security personnel, and humanitarian workers, and generally were motivated by sexual gratification and control of women.[111] Thus, it can be argued that the crisis provided an enabling environment for offenders to perpetuate sexual crimes, while warring groups used it as a tactic to harm, punish, and displace communities.[112]

Consequences of CRSV on Survivors in Kenya
CRSV during the 2007/2008 post-election period resulted in physical, psychological, health, social, and economic impacts to the victims, families, and communities at large, which have persisted to date[113] as discussed below.

One of the main consequences of CRSV to survivors is poor health. Survivors in Kenya demonstrated declines in both physical and psychological health. Acts of bodily harm against survivors included stabbing, kicking, cutting with machetes, beatings with heavy objects, and penetration with sticks, bottles, and guns. There were documented cases of grievous bodily harm to women and men, who after being raped and

---

[110] Truth, Justice, and Reconciliation Commission, "Commissions of Inquiry—CIPEV Report (Waki Report)" (2008). IX. Government Documents and Regulations. 5.

[111] CIPEV Report (Waki Report) (2008); Kuria, M. et al. (2013). Is Sexual Abuse a Part of War? A 4-year Retrospective Study on Cases of Sexual Abuse at the Kenyatta National Hospital, Kenya. Journal of Public Health in Africa, 4(1).

[112] Makau (2018).

[113] HRW (2016) and CIPEV (2008).

circumcized were left to bleed to death.[114] According to Michael P. Anastario, et al.[115] evidence from medical records of sexually assaulted patients from three hospitals in the Rift Valley region showed that most victims of sexual violence also exhibited abdominal injuries, indicating other forms of physical assault in addition to sexual violence. These physical injuries led to various disabilities with ongoing pain in limbs, as described by one survivor:

> *I don't know what they did to my left leg because it has never stopped paining from that day. I have problems walking for long distances or standing for some time. This has affected my ability to work. If I look for a washing job, I have to do it while seated and people are not very accommodating of such behaviour because they think you are lazy. I cannot work.*[116]

Sexual violence alone is a big stressor, but when coupled with associated trauma from other forms of violence it may lead to post-traumatic stress disorder (PTSD). Survivors showed symptoms of PTSD, including anxiety, headaches, palpitations, depression, and suicidality. In a study conducted among 209 female survivors of rape in Nairobi, Kenya, the respondents exhibited signs of PTSD and related psychological trauma as follows: PTSD (90.4%); depressive disorder (70.8%); panic disorder (55.1%); suicidal ideation (9.6%); suicidal plans (28.2%); and suicidal attempts (2.4%).[117] This post-traumatic stress has persisted, as conveyed below:

> *The man was so violent with my sister because she was screaming. He hit her on the head with his fists and she fainted. She was in a coma for six months. She is not okay mentally. She does not know how to use a toilet. She faints often. Sometimes she gets violent and breaks things in the house.*[118]

---

[114] Auchter, J. (2017). Forced Male Circumcision: Gender-Based Violence in Kenya. International Affairs, 93(6), 1339–1356.

[115] Anastario, M. P., et al. (2014). Time Series Analysis of Sexual Assault Case Characteristics and the 2007–2008 Period of Post-Election Violence in Kenya. PLoS ONE 9(8): e106443.

[116] HRW (2016).

[117] Nyaga, I. M. (2010). Prevalence of PTSD, Depression and Anxiety among Female Survivors of Rape Following Post Election Violence 2007 December Nairobi-Kenya (Doctoral Dissertation, University of Nairobi, Kenya).

[118] HRW (2016, p. 36).

In addition, survivors also suffered various reproductive health concerns, including traumatic fistula, infection, HIV/AIDS, and other sexually transmitted diseases.[119] Those who experienced violent rapes suffered massive tears in the reproductive organs, which resulted in leaking of urine and feces. Without funds for surgery and repair, survivors have continued to not only suffer from pelvic infections, fetid odour, and infertility, but also shame from the leakage and odour affecting their daily lives. Survivors also contracted HIV and AIDs. For instance, out of 160 interviewees by Human Rights Watch,[120] 39 indicated that they had contracted HIV/AIDS from CRSV. Delays in seeking health care, particularly access to post-exposure prophylaxis (PEP), contributed to increased infections. For those who contracted HIV/AIDS, this was a double tragedy as they remained with invisible and visible scars of the conflict.

Survivors also suffered from social rejection and breakage of social relations. Kenya is a patriarchal society where sexual violation is abhorred. Among married survivors, some experienced spousal rejection, relocation to new areas, and/or divorce. Human Rights Watch[121] reported a case of a woman from the Rift Valley, who upon disclosure of being raped to her husband was verbally and physically abused, and eventually chased away from home. Such cases of rejection and abandonment by people whose support is most needed for the survivor to heal increase the severity of post-traumatic stress disorder. In communities where sexual violation is considered a taboo, disclosure leads to loss of social belonging and association. This leads to survivors isolating themselves, avoiding public places, or being silent about the ordeal. In some cases, where social stigma is heightened, some survivors relocate to places where they are unknown in order to lead peaceful lives. Stigma and rejection are less common in urban areas, compared to rural environs, due to weaker social norms and ties.

Several women and girls reported pregnancies resulting from the sexual violence experienced during the post-election period in 2007/2008. Most survivors didn't seek post-rape care due to fear, insecurity, lack of

---

[119] Makau (2018).
[120] HRW (2016).
[121] HRW (2016).

transport to hospital facilities, or ignorance. Accordingly, most pregnancies were either terminated or carried to term, each carrying significant health and social costs. As abortion is illegal in Kenya, women who opted to terminate the pregnancies utilized unsafe methods that led to additional health problems or even death, such as backstreet health practitioners or self-medication. For those who gave birth, they experienced the double effect of rejection by their families.[122]

Children born out of rape are a common phenomenon in conflicts.[123] Such children are often considered unwanted, as they are seen as children of the enemy, and therefore experience physical and psychological neglect and stigmatization from the mothers and community. It is common for mothers, especially young girls, to refuse to take care of the child, physically abuse them, and abandon them to the care of the survivors' parents. These mothers argue that the children remind them of the circumstances of their conception and thus cannot bear to even look at them. Below is an account from the mother of a survivor in such a situation:

> *My daughter is now 18 years. She was raped in Ainamoi. She did not want anything to do with the child. She left the child and went to Mombasa in 2009. She has never returned. When she calls home and I mention the child she disconnects the call. She called me recently crying badly. She asked, "Mum where will I take this child?" She hung up on me as I was trying to encourage her. I don't think her heart will ever like this baby. If anyone asks her about her baby she starts to cry. She says she is struggling in Mombasa, but she does not want to come home to this child. I am struggling to raise her child.*[124]

When such children are born to married women, both the child and the mother are often rejected by the spouse, mocked, and called derogatory names such as "bush babies" and "children of thugs."[125] These types of neglect and abuse have long-lasting effects on the children as they grow older, such as unequal opportunities in education, particularly if the mother or guardian is not economically stable. Just as in other armed

---

[122] HRW (2016), Makua (2018), TJRC (2014).

[123] Cohen, D. K., & Nordås, R. (2014). Sexual Violence in Armed Conflict: Introducing the SVAC Dataset, 1989–2009. Journal of Peace Research, 51(3).

[124] HRW (2016, p. 67).

[125] Wood, E. J. (2014). Conflict-Related Sexual Violence and the Policy Implications of Recent Research. International Review of the Red Cross, 96(894), 457–478.

conflicts, children born to married women in 2007/2008 post-election violence have also been stigmatized and rejected.[126] This can be associated with patriarchy, which leads to children with unknown fathers and lacking an inheritance and identity.

Sexual violence also impacted survivors' livelihoods and economic well-being. Most survivors were left impoverished after losing their assets, homes, businesses, and in some cases the family breadwinners; accordingly, they faced significant obstacles to future economic prospects. Coping with the act of sexual violence and related financial loss, physical injuries, and mental health problems prevent survivors from working long hours or doing heavy physical labour. This reduces their productivity and incomes, and hence their ability to support their families. Indeed, survivors struggle to feed their families, buy medication, and pay rent. For women who have been abandoned by their spouses and families, the situation is worse, sometimes resorting to commercial sex work in order to survive.

Various services were provided for survivors of CRSV in Kenya including counselling, medical, legal, and economic support. However, studies found that these services often were inadequate and riddled with challenges, such as limited prosecutions of perpetrators, economic support projects with short time horizons, and lack of financial compensation for victims.[127] Additionally, poor management of survivors resulted in insufficient counselling services, which lead to re-traumatization.[128]

While there were various initiatives to investigate sexual crimes committed in the 2007/2008, including a draft of measures to prevent, respond to, and hold perpetrators accountable, the implementation of these proposals has been unsatisfactory.[129] The result has been a continuation of cases of sexual violence in peacetime and neglect of the CRSV survivors.

These consequences of the 2007/2008 post-election violence, together with the ineffectiveness of the various services provided, had a great toll on survivors and the most commonly adopted strategies to cope and restore their lives.

[126] Makau (2018).
[127] UNOHCHR (2019), Makau (2018).
[128] HRW (2016), TJRC (2014).
[129] UNOHCHR (2019).

Coping Mechanism Employed by Survivors of CRSV in the 2007/2008 Post-Election Violence in Kenya

As survivors coped with the horrifying consequences of CRSV in the 2007/2008 post-election violence, Kenya had limited mental, medical, and legal services to offer. Moreover, few survivors accessed these services due to insecurity, lack of transport, ignorance, shame, and the poor handling of cases that were presented in health facilities.[130] Most survivors reported that they felt ashamed of the rape experience, and thus didn't disclose their experience to their spouses, families, communities, and health professionals.[131] As a result, these survivors turned to their internal capacities to cope with their experience with CRSV.

Some survivors used silence as a coping mechanism to ensure the people around them didn't know about their experience, and to avoid family and community stigmatization.[132] This experience is explained by one survivor of the Kenya post-election violence:

> *And then it is also embarrassing, you know issues of sexual violence. How would you go and tell the doctor that you were violated sexually? Because they are issues that are shameful. And sometimes you know the village is a small place. Maybe the doctor is your neighbour, the nurse maybe treats you then you hear him tell others outside that that one was raped. And you know the stigma that surrounds the issue of rape.*[133]

While silence reduces the shame and embarrassment to the survivor, and protects their dignity, it is not a healthy coping mechanism. Silence breeds a culture of self-blame and prevents the survivor from seeking health care in good time, which may exacerbate the consequences of CRSV.[134] This is illustrated in the following account:

> *My friend was raped and got HIV. She died. She did not tell her family and she did not go for treatment. We Kalenjins are very secretive. You cannot*

---

[130] Anastario, et al (2014), HRW (2016).

[131] Shackel, R., & Fiske, L. (2016). Making Justice Work for Women: Kenya Country Report; Makau (2018), HRW (2016).

[132] Makau (2018), Shackel and Fiske (2016), HRW (2016).

[133] Shackel and Fiske (2016, p. 70).

[134] Tankink, M. T. (2013). The Silence of South-Sudanese Women: Social Risks in Talking about Experiences of Sexual Violence. Cult Health Sex, 15(4), 391–403.

say anything [about being raped], because after that you are not seen as a human being.[135]

Rebecca Njuki et al.[136] concur that fear of stigmatization was a factor in the low utilization of health services for sexual violence victims in Kenya. The healing process after such traumatic experiences can only begin when one verbalizes what happened, accept it, make meaning of the experience, and move on positively.

Survivors of the post-election violence in Kenya also employed isolation as a coping mechanism. The trauma and stigma of rape make one develop a fear of the public and lose a sense of belonging and association with others. Additionally, survivors fear that they will be reminded of the traumatic experience through social interactions, as indicated by one survivor:

I don't socialize a lot because you may be talking to someone and they say something that reminds you of the rape. I would rather watch TV".[137]

As a result, survivors utilizing the isolation coping mechanism in Kenya kept away from public places, such as churches and markets, confining themselves to their houses. Isolation is a maladaptive practice that in most cases exacerbates the trauma and curtails recovery.[138] Positive social connections either in the family or community can thus help re-establish a person's sense of security, reducing shame while affirming the survivor's self-worth.

Reports on the 2007/2008 post-election violence also indicate that some survivors adopted self-harm as a coping mechanism. The use of self-harm in the aftermath of sexual violence is associated with feelings of anger, shame, disgust, and self-hate; and includes behaviour such as substance abuse, excessive eating, refusal to eat, or in worst case scenarios

---

[135] HRW (2016, p. 38).

[136] Njuki, R., et al. (2012, June 12). Exploring the Effectiveness of the Output-Based aid Voucher Program to Increase Uptake of Gender-Based Violence Recovery Services in Kenya: A Qualitative Evaluation. BMC Public Health, 12, 426.

[137] HRW (2016, p. 52).

[138] Spangaro, J., et al. (2013). What Evidence Exists for Initiatives to Reduce Risk and Incidence of Sexual Violence in Armed Conflict and Other Humanitarian Crises? A Systematic Review. PLoS ONE, 8(5), e62600.

suicidal tendencies. In Kenya, survivors turned to alcohol and drug abuse, while others contemplated, attempted, or committed suicide:

> *When I think of the things those people did, I can't think straight ... I want to die and leave this world.*[139]

Other survivors in Kenya engaged in reckless sexual behaviour such as prostitution as a coping mechanism. Survivors are motivated to adopt this strategy to gain acceptance from men, make them feel desirable and worthy, and make ends meet.[140] This coping strategy makes the survivor's situation more hopeless, with the possibility of future incidents of sexual abuse, and leads to rejection by society as one is considered immoral. Nevertheless, this is a common coping mechanisms among survivors who have no skills for gainful employment, and who have been rejected by their family and community.

CRSV survivors in Kenya also used social coping, especially through support from family or other external support. Studies show that when survivors get support from family and community they cope better with CRSV than when rejected and abandoned. Human Rights Watch[141] reported that spouses, families, and community rejected and shunned survivors after the 2007/2008 post-election violence. Some of these survivors joined counselling sessions that encouraged and supported them to form mutual support groups. Survivors indicated that the groups were very helpful in the process of accepting their experience, finding meaning, and moving forward in life.[142] As one survivor explained:

> *[A] counsellor from Kenyatta educated us and they also trained us and said that we should not be helped all the time, we should improve and that we should form groups. That is when we went and formed a group like that one so that someone can help herself. Not that we are being helped all the time but we also work hard to improve ourselves. So there is where we were we received care slowly by slowly as we were being counselled until I recovered. Those days I could not talk without crying the way I am talking now. So we*

---

[139] Shackel and Fiske (2016).
[140] Makau (2018).
[141] HRW (2016).
[142] Shackel and Fiske (2016), Makau (2018).

proceeded and formed a group, we have a group there in Kibera. We always go to encourage other.[143]

Social support through solidarity groups helps survivors gain confidence, share their experiences without fear of being stigmatized, and empower them economically through facilitation with start-up capital and training. Solidarity groups provide counselling to improve the management of social relations, which reduces stigma and helps survivors adopt better coping mechanisms.[144] Jeanne Ntete[145] submits that group counselling gives survivors of CRSV a sense of belonging and self-value, thus helping them overcome negative emotions associated with stigma and collective shame. Ultimately, this restores survivors' psychological health and enables them to move on with their lives.

CRSV survivors of the Kenya post-election violence also used relocation as a coping method, moving to new areas where they were anonymous.[146] Survivors used this method to avoid the shame of disclosure of their experience, disrespect by family and community, avoid threats by perpetrators who were known to them, and reduce the risk of similar incidents in the future. In some cases, they also avoided moving to their rural homes as they perceived that they would be more stigmatized in the rural areas where social norms are stronger. Hence, they remained in the city despite the hardships of urban life.

> *My family and my husband's family do not respect me. One time my daughter-in-law said I am useless, a broom that can take more than men. There are places I cannot go to. Here people don't know what happened to me. I cannot return where I used to live because I was so humiliated there. That is why I moved. They used to ask me, 'Are you really a woman, with no uterus?*[147]

---

[143] Shackel and Fiske (2016).

[144] Koegler, E., et al. (2019). Understanding How Solidarity Groups—A Community-Based Economic and Psychosocial Support Intervention—Can Affect Mental Health for Survivors of Conflict-Related Sexual Violence in Democratic Republic of the Congo. Violence against Women, 25(3), 359–374.

[145] Ntete, J. M. (2017). Effect of Group Therapy in Restoring Psychological Wellbeing of Sexually Violated Women of 1994 Tutsi Genocide in Rwanda (Doctoral Dissertation, Kenyatta University).

[146] Makau (2018), HRW (2016).

[147] HRW (2016, p. 52).

Those who relocated exhibited better psychological outcomes than those who remained in the same context where they experienced CRSV.[148] This resonates with the experiences of African refugees in the United States. Studies found that the new peaceful environment, coupled with new economic opportunities, helped sexual survivors grow out of post-traumatic stress faster than those who remained in the same circumstances.[149]

Conclusion

In conclusion, women survivors of CRSV in the 2007/2008 post-election violence have used various coping mechanisms on a continuum of adaptive to maladaptive practices. However, there is no concrete study documenting these strategies, with most focusing on the consequences of CRSV and the lack of legal accountability and reparations. There is therefore a need for a comprehensive study to inform academia and policymakers of the effectiveness of these coping strategies, and which characteristics lead some survivors to thrive more so than others. This will be useful in developing a new initiative that can enable those who are surviving to adopt adaptive coping mechanism that will enhance their functioning and capacities while learning from those who have been able to thrive.

Recommendations

1. From this study, it is apparent that CRSV occurred during the 2007/2008 post-election violence and continued after the 2017 elections. While there has been documentation of some of these cases none has been prosecuted successfully. There is a need for the government to take this matter seriously and ensure the perpetrators are brought to justice. This will deter future incidents and offer a sense of security to the CRSV survivors.

---

[148] HRW (2016).

[149] Leeman, Y., & van Koeven, E. (2019). New Immigrants. An Incentive for Intercultural Education? Education Inquiry, 10(3), 189–207.

2. One of the most cited effective coping mechanism that has been adopted by CRSV is social support through solidarity groups for counselling, as well as for economic purposes. These need to be coupled with legal and medical services. Actors in this field therefore need to integrate legal, counselling, and economic programmes for survivors to thrive, rather than the common standalone programmes.
3. It is also apparent that the only guided coping mechanisms are either spiritual or social. There is a need for organizations to work with survivors using problem and emotion-focused coping. Moreover, even where organizations provided space for social support this was short term in nature. This calls for the training of personnel but also the creation of spaces where such services can be provided for the long term.
4. There is also a need to work with cultural actors to promote survivor-centred approaches that censure stigmatization and shaming of CRSV victims and children born in these circumstances. Acceptance of CRSV survivors, and condemnation of perpetrators, would go a long way in ending this practice.

Limitations

The chapter sought to explore coping mechanisms used by CRSV survivors of the 2007/2008 post-election violence in Kenya through a literature review. However, there was very limited literature on the subject and hence this may not be representative of how survivors are coping. Thus, a more comprehensive study is needed based on primary data to exhaustively understand this subject.

References

Adedoyin, A. C., Bobbie, C., Griffin, M., Adedoyin, O. O., Ahmad, M., Nobles, C., & Neeland, K. (2016). Religious Coping Strategies among Traumatized African Refugees in the United States: A Systematic Review. Social Work and Christianity, 43(1), 95.

Adler, A. (1930). Individual Psychology. In C. Murchison (Ed.), Psychologies of 1930 (pp. 395–405). Clark University Press.

Albutt, K., Kelly, J., Kabanga, J., & Vanrooyen, M. (2017). Stigmatisation and Rejection of Survivors of Sexual Violence in Eastern Democratic Republic of the Congo. Disasters, 41(2), 211–227.

Amone-P'Olak, K., Otim, B. N., Opio, G., Ovuga, E., & Meiser-Stedman, R. (2015). War Experiences and Psychotic Symptoms among Former Child Soldiers in Northern Uganda: The Mediating Role of Post-war Hardships—The WAYS Study. South African Journal of Psychology, 45(2), 55–167.

Anastario, M. P., Adhiambo Onyango, M., Nyanyuki, J., Naimer, K., Muthoga, R., Sirkin, S., et al. (2014). Time Series Analysis of Sexual Assault Case Characteristics and the 2007–2008 Period of Post-Election Violence in Kenya. PLoS ONE, 9(8), e106443.

Anderson, K., Delić, A., Komproe, I., Avdibegović, E., Van Ee, E., & Glaesmer, H. (2019). Predictors of Posttraumatic Growth among Conflict-Related Sexual Violence Survivors from Bosnia and Herzegovina. Conflict and Health, 13(1), 23. Assessment of 2007–2008 election-related violence in Kenya. Conflict and Health, 8(2), 1–12.

Auchter, J. (2017). Forced Male Circumcision: Gender-Based Violence In Kenya. International Affairs, 93(6), 1339–1356.

Baaz, M. E., & Stern, M. (2009). Why Do Soldiers Rape? Masculinity, Violence, and Sexuality in the Armed Forces in the Congo (DRC). International Studies Quarterly, 53(2), 495–518.

Baker, J. P., & Berenbaum, H. (2007). Emotional Approach and Problem-Focused Coping: A Comparison of Potentially Adaptive Strategies. Cognition and Emotion, 21(1), 95–118.

Ben-Zur, H. (2020). Emotion-Focused Coping. In V. Zeigler-Hill & T. K. Shackelford (Eds.), Encyclopedia of Personality and Individual Differences. Cham: Springer. https://doi.org/10.1007/978-3-319-24612-3_512.

Bergoffen, D. (2013). Ungendering Justice: Constituting a Court, Securing a Conviction, Creating a Human Right. Transitional Justice Review, 1(2), 3.

Billings, A. G., & Moos, R. H. (1981, June). The Role of Coping Responses and Social Resources in Attenuating the Stress of Life Events. Journal of Behavioral Medicine, 4(2), 139–157.

Blackie, L. E. R., Jayawickreme, E., Hitchcott, N., & Joseph, S. (2017). Distinguishing Post-traumatic Growth from Psychological Adjustment among Rwandan Genocide Survivors. In D. Carr, J. Arthur, & K. Kristjánsson (Eds.), Varieties of Virtue Ethics (pp. 299–317). Palgrave Macmillan.

Boesten, J. 2014. Sexual Violence During War and Peace: Gender, Power, and Post-Conflict Justicein Peru. New York: Palgrave Macmillan.

Brown, S., & Sriram, C. L. (2012). The Big Fish Won't Fry Themselves: Criminal Accountability For Post-Election Violence In Kenya. African Affairs, 111(443), 244–260.

Brownmiller, S. (1975). Against Our Will: Men, Women, and Rape. New York: Simon and Schuster.
Buckley-Zistel, S. (2013). Redressing Sexual Violence in Transitional Justice and the Labelling of Women as "Victims". In T. Bonacker & C. Safferling (Eds.), Victims of International Crimes: An Interdisciplinary Discourse. The Hague, The Netherlands: T.M.C. Asser Press.
Cann, A., Calhoun, L. G., Tedeschi, R. G., Triplett, K. N., Vishnevsky, T., & Lindstrom, C. M. (2011). Assessing Posttraumatic Cognitive Processes: The Event Related Rumination Inventory. Anxiety, Stress, & Coping, 24(2), 137–156.
Carpenter, C. (2007). Gender, Ethnicity, and Children's Human Rights: Theorizing Babies Born of Wartime Rape and Sexual Exploitation. In Charli Carpenter (Ed.), Born of War: Protecting Children of Sexual Violence Survivors in Conflict Zones. Bloomfield: Kumarian Press.
Ceelen, I. (2016). Conflict-Related Sexual Violence and the Prevention of It. Royal Tropical Institute. Master Thesis. Available at https://bibalex.org/baifa/Attachment/Documents/pauwGznix7_20170424145031723.pdf
Cherewick, M., Doocy, S., Tol, W., Burnham, G., & Glass, N. (2016). Potentially Traumatic Events, Coping Strategies and Associations with Mental Health and Well-Being Measures among Conflict-Affected Youth in Eastern Democratic Republic of Congo. Global Health Research and Policy, 1(1), 8.
Cohen, D. K., Green, A. H., & Wood, E. J. (2013). Wartime Sexual Violence: Misconceptions, Implications, and Ways Forward. United States Institute of Peace. https://wcfia.harvard.edu/sites/projects.iq.harvard.edu/files/wcfia/files/dcohen_usip2013.pdf.
Cohen, D. K., & Nordås, R. (2014). Sexual Violence in Armed Conflict: Introducing the SVAC Dataset, 1989–2009. Journal of Peace Research, 51(3), 418–428. https://journals.sagepub.com/doi/10.1177/0022343314523028.
Costello, S. J. (2019). Applied Logotherapy: Viktor Frankl's Philosophical Psychology. Cambridge Scholars Publishing.
Courtois, C. A., & Ford, J. D. (2013). Treatment of Complex Trauma: A Sequenced, Relationship-Based Approach. Guilford Press.
Domingo, P., Holmes, R., Rocha Menocal, A., Jones, N., Bhuvanendra, D., & Wood, J. (2013). Assessment of the Evidence of Links between Gender Equality, Peacebuilding and Statebuilding: Literature Review. London: Overseas Development Institute.
Dijkman, N. E. J., Bijleveld, C., & Verwimp, P. (2014). Sexual Violence in Burundi: Victims, Perpetrators, and the Role of Conflict. HiCN Working Paper 172, Institute of Development Studies, University of Sussex, Brighton.
Elbert, T., Hinkel, H., Mädl, A., Hermenau, K., Hecker, T., & Schauer, M. (2013). Epidemiological Criminology's Response. "Response." Advances

in Applied Sociology, 2(01), 47–52. https://doi.org/10.4236/aasoci.2012. 21006.
Eriksson Baaz, M., & Stern, M. (2009, June 1). Why Do Soldiers Rape? Masculinity, Violence, and Sexuality in the Armed Forces in the Congo (DRC). International Studies Quarterly, 53(2), 495–518. https://doi.org/ 10.1111/j.1468-2478.2009.00543.x.
Folkman, S. (2008). The Case for Positive Emotions in the Stress Process. Anxiety, Stress & Coping, 21(1), 3–14.
Folkman, S. (Ed.). (2011). The Oxford Handbook of Stress, Health, and Coping. Oxford University Press.
Frankl, V. E. (1985). Man's Search for Meaning. Simon and Schuster.
Friedman, M. J., Resick, P. A., Bryant, R. A., & Brewin, C. R. (2011). Considering PTSD for DSM-5. Depression and Anxiety, 28(9), 750-769.
Gillihan, S. J., Williams, M. T., Malcoun, E., Yadin, E., & Foa, E. B. (2012, October 1). Common Pitfalls in Exposure and Response Prevention (EX/ RP) for OCD. Journal of Obsessive-Compulsive and Related Disorders, 1(4), 251–257.
Gladden, J. (2013). Coping Strategies of Sudanese Refugee Women in Kakuma Refugee Camp, Kenya. Refugee Survey Quarterly, 32(4), 66–89.
Gross J. J. (2015). Emotion Regulation: Current Status and Future Prospects. Psychological Inquiry, 26(1), 1–26.
Hagen, K., & Yohani, S. (2010). The Nature and Psychosocial Consequences of War Rape for Individuals and Communities. International Journal of Psychological Studies, 2(2), 14–25.
Hewitt Ramírez, N. O. H. E. L. I. A., Gantiva Díaz, C. A., Vera Maldonado, A. N. D. E. R. S. S. E. N., Cuervo Rodríguez, M. P., Liliam, N., Olaya, H., & Parada Baños, A. J. (2014). Psychological Effects on Children and Adolescents Exposed to Armed Conflict in a Rural Area of Colombia. Acta Colombiana De Psicología, 17(1), 79–89.
Human Rights Watch (New York, NY). (2016). "I Just Sit and Wait to Die" Reparations for Survivors of Kenya's 2007–2008 Post-Election Sexual Violence. Human Rights Watch.
Jayawickreme, E., & Blackie, L. E. R. (2014). Post-Traumatic Growth as Positive Personality Change: Evidence, Controversies and Future Directions. European Journal of Personality, 28(4), 312–331.
Kelly, J., Kabanga, J., Cragin, W., Alcayna-Stevens, L., Haider, S., & Vanrooyen, M. J. (2012). 'If Your Husband Doesn't Humiliate You, Other People Won't': Gendered Attitudes Towards Sexual Violence In Eastern Democratic Republic of Congo. Global Public Health, 7(3), 285–298.
Kinyanda, E., Musisi, S., Biryabarema, C., Ezati, I., Oboke, H., & Ojiambo-Ochieng, R. (2010, November 10). War Related Sexual Violence and It's Medical and Psychological Consequences as Seen in Kitgum, Northern

Uganda: A Cross-Sectional Study. BMC International Health and Human Rights, 10, 28.
KNCHR. (2018). Silhouettes of Brutality: An Account of Sexual Violence During and After the 2017 General Elections (2018). 5, ibid., p. 6.
KNCHR. (2008). On the Brink of the Precipice: A Human Rights Account of Kenya's Post-2007 Election Violence.
Koegler, E., Kennedy, C., Mrindi, J., Bachunguye, R., Winch, P., Ramazani, P., ... & Glass, N. (2019). Understanding How Solidarity Groups—A Community-Based Economic and Psychosocial Support Intervention—Can Affect Mental Health for Survivors of Conflict-Related Sexual Violence in Democratic Republic of the Congo. Violence Against Women, 25(3), 359–374.
Kohli, A., Perrin, N. A., Mpanano, R. M., Mullany, L. C., Murhula, C. M., Binkurhorhwa, A. K., Mirindi, A. B., Banywesize, J. H., Bufole, N. M., Ntwali, E. M., & Glass, N. (2014). Risk for Family Rejection and Associated Mental Health Outcomes among Conflict-Affected Adult Women Living in Rural Eastern Democratic Republic of the Congo. Health Care for Women International, 35(7–9), 789–807.
Koos, C. (2017). Sexual Violence in Armed Conflicts: Research Progress And Remaining Gaps. Third World Quarterly, 38(9), 1935–1951.
Koos, C. (2018). Decay or Resilience?: The Long-Term Social Consequences of Conflict-Related Sexual Violence in Sierra Leone. World Politics, 70(2), 194–238.
Kuria, M. W., Omondi, L., Olando, Y., Makenyengo, M., & Bukusi, D. (2013). Is Sexual Abuse a Part of War? A 4-Year Retrospective Study on Cases of Sexual Abuse at the Kenyatta National Hospital, Kenya. Journal of public health in Africa, 4(1), e5.
Lazarus, R. S., & Folkman, S. (1986). Cognitive Theories of Stress and the Issue of Circularity. In M. H. Appley, & R. Trumbull (Eds.), Dynamics of Stress. Physiological, Psychological, and Social Perspectives (pp. 63–80). New York: Plenum.
Leeman, Y., & van Koeven, E. (2019). New Immigrants. An Incentive for Intercultural Education? Education Inquiry, 10(3), 189–207.
Leiner, A. S., Kearns, M. C., Jackson, J. L., Astin, M. C., & Rothbaum, B. O. (2012). Avoidant Coping and Treatment Outcome in Rape-Related Posttraumatic Stress Disorder. Journal of Consulting and Clinical Psychology, 80(2), 317.
Mahoney, C. T., Lynch, S. M., & Benight, C. C. (2019). The Indirect Effect of Coping Self-Efficacy on the Relation Between Sexual Violence and PTSD Symptoms. Journal of Interpersonal Violence. https://doi.org/10.1177/0886260519881525.

Makau, E. M. (2018). Exploring the Intervention Efforts in Helping Women Survivors of Sexual Violence in the Aftermath of the 2007/2008 Post-election Violence in Kisumu County, Kenya (Doctoral dissertation).

Mannergren Selimovic, J. (2020). Gendered Silences in Post-Conflict Societies: A Typology. Peacebuilding, 8(1), 1–15.

Masinjila, M. (2013) in Thomas, K., Masinjila, M., & Bere, E. (2013). Political Transition and Sexual and Gender-Based Violence in South Africa, Kenya, and Zimbabwe: A Comparative Analysis. Gender & Development, 21(3), 519–532.

Moskowitz, J. T. (2011). Coping Interventions and the Regulation of Positive Affect. In S. Folkman (Ed.), The Oxford Handbook of Stress, Health, and Coping (pp. 407–427). Oxford University Press.

Moskowitz, J. T., Shmueli-Blumberg, D., Acree, M., & Folkman, S. (2012). Positive Affect in the Midst of Distress: Implications for Role Functioning. Journal of Community & Applied Social Psychology, 22(6), 502–518.

Mueller, S. (2012). The Political Economy of Kenya's Crisis. In D. Bekoe (Ed.), Voting in Fear. Washington, D.C.: U.S. Institute of Peace.

Njuki, R., Okal, J., Warren, C. E., Obare, F., Abuya, T., Kanya, L., Undie, C. C., Bellows, B., & Askew, I. (2012, June 12). Exploring the Effectiveness of the Output-Based aid Voucher Program to Increase Uptake of Gender-Based Violence Recovery Services in Kenya: A Qualitative Evaluation. BMC Public Health, 12, 426.

Nordås, R. (2011). Sexual Violence in African Countries. CSCW Policy Brief 01 | 2011. Center for the Study of Civil War (CSCW). Peace Research Institute (PRIO). https://www.usip.org/sites/default/files/missing-peace/Ragnhild-Nordas.pdf.

Nowrojee, B. (1996). Shattered Lives: Sexual Violence during the Rwandan Genocide and Its Aftermath. United States: Human Rights Watch.

Ntete, J. M. (2017). Effect of Group Therapy in Restoring Psychological Wellbeing of Sexually Violated Women of 1994 Tutsi Genocide In Rwanda (Doctoral Dissertation, Kenyatta University).

Nyaga, I. M. (2010). Prevalence of PTSD, Depression and Anxiety Among Female Survivors of Rape Following Post Election Violence 2007 December Nairobi-Kenya (Doctoral Dissertation, University of Nairobi, Kenya).

Palermo, T., & Peterman, A. (2011). Undercounting, Overcounting and the Longevity of Flawed Estimates: Statistics on Sexual Violence in Conflict. Bulletin of the World Health Organization, 89(12), 924–925. World Health Organization. https://doi.org/10.2471/BLT.11.089888.

Park, C. L., & Folkman, S. (1997). Meaning in the Context of Stress and Coping. Review of General Psychology, 1(2), 115–144.

Park, C. L., & Ai, A. L. (2006). Meaning Making and Growth: New Directions for Research on Survivors of Trauma. Journal of Loss and Trauma, 11(5), 389–407.
PeaceWomen: Women's International League of Peace and Freedom, United Nations Office, May 2018, https://www.peacewomen.org/node/102054#top.
Physicians for Human Rights (US), & United Nations Assistance Mission in Sierra Leone. (2002). War-Related Sexual Violence in Sierra Leone: A Population-Based Assessment: A Report. Physicians for Human Rights.
Rackley, E. (2014). Armed Violence against Women in Burundi—Issue 31—Humanitarian Exchange Magazine—Humanitarian Practice Network. Humanitarian Practice Network. Armed-Violence-Against-Women-in-burundi
Raleigh, C., & Dowd, C. (2013). Governance and Conflict in the Sahel's 'Ungoverned Space'. Stability: International Journal of Security and Development, 2(2), p. Art. 32
Rohwerder, B. (2015). Conflict Analysis of Kenya. Birmingham, UK: Gsdrc, University of Birmingham.
Ryanga, H. (2013). Women and Conflict in Mt. Elgon: Assessing Rape as a Weapon in Armed Conflict, 1991–2008 (Doctoral dissertation, University of Nairobi).
Selimovic, J. M. (2020). Gendered Silences in Post-Conflict Societies: A Typology. Peacebuilding 8(1), 1–15.
Seelinger, K. T. (2014). Domestic Accountability for Sexual Violence: The Potential of Specialized Units in Kenya, Liberia, Sierra Leone and Uganda. International Review of the Red Cross, 96(894), 539–564.
Shackel, R., & Fiske, L. (2016). Making Justice Work for Women: Kenya Country Report. Camperdown, Australia: University of Sydney
Spangaro, J., Adogu, C., Ranmuthugala, G., Powell Davies, G., Steinacker, L., & Zwi, A. (2013). What Evidence Exists for Initiatives to Reduce Risk and Incidence of Sexual Violence in Armed Conflict and Other Humanitarian Crises? A Systematic Review. PLoS ONE, 8(5), e62600. https://doi.org/10.1371/journal.pone.0062600.
Shin, H. J., Mwiti, G., Tomosada, M., & Eriksson, C. B. (2017). Associations between Trauma Exposure, Religious Coping, and Psychiatric Distress in a Community Sample in Nairobi, Kenya. Journal of Prevention & Intervention in the Community, 45(4), 250–260.
Simmelink, J., Lightfoot, E., Dube, A., Blevins, J., & Lum, T. (2013). Understanding the Health Beliefs and Practices of East African Refugees. American Journal of Health Behavior, 37(2), 155–161.
Somerville, K. (2011). Violence, Hate Speech and Inflammatory Broadcasting in Kenya: The Problems of Definition and Identification. Ecquid Novi: African Journalism Studies, 32(1), 82–101.

Tankink, M. T. (2013). The Silence of South-Sudanese Women: Social Risks in Talking about Experiences of Sexual Violence. Cult Health Sex, 15(4), 391–403.

Thomas, K. (2017). Women and Sexual Violence, Paths to Healing: Resistance, Rebellion, Resilience and Recovery (Doctoral Dissertation, Middlesex University).

Truth, Justice, and Reconciliation Commission. (2008). Commissions of Inquiry—CIPEV Report (Waki Report). IX. Government Documents and Regulations, 5.

Ubillos-Landa, S., Puente-Martínez, A., Arias-Rodríguez, G., Gracia-Leiva, M., & González-Castro, J. L. (2019). Coping Strategies Used By Female Victims of the Colombian Armed Conflict: The Women in the Colombian Conflict (Mucoco) Program. Sage Open, 9(4), 2158244019894072.

UN Security Council. (2000). Security Council Resolution 1325 (2000) [On Women and Peace and Security], 31 October 2000, S/Res/1325 (2000).

United Nations. (2018). Secretary General Report on the Protection of Civilians in Armed Conflict (S/2018/462)

UNOHCHR, UNWomen, Physicians for Human. (2019). Breaking Cycles of Violence Gaps in Prevention of and Response to Electoral Related Sexual Violence.

van Dijkhorst, H., & Vonhof, S. (2005). Gender and Humanitarian Aid: A Literature Review of Policy and Practice Wagenenin: Wagenien University 43 p.

Van Hook, M. P. (2016). Spirituality as a Potential Resource for Coping with Trauma. Social Work and Christianity, 43(1), 7.

Verelst, A., De Schryver, M., De Haene, L., Broekaert, E., & Derluyn, I. (2014). The Mediating Role of Stigmatization in the Mental Health of Adolescent Victims of Sexual Violence in Eastern Congo. Child Abuse & Neglect, 38(7), 1139–1146.

Violence in the Kivu Provinces of the Democratic Republic of Congo Insights from Former Combatants. Washington, DC: World Bank.

Walugembe. (2010). War Related Sexual Violence and It's Medical and Psychological Consequences as Seen in Kitgum, Northern Uganda: A Cross-Sectional Study. BMC International Health and Human Rights 10(1): 28.

White, R. W. (1974). Strategies of Adaptation: An Attempt at Systematic Description. In G. V. Coelho, D. A. Hamburg, & J. E. Adams (Eds.), Coping and Adaptation. New York: Basic Books.

WHO, World Health Organization. 2013. Global and Regional Estimates of Violence against Women: Prevalence and Health Effects of Intimate Partner Violence and Non-Partner Sexual Violence. Geneva: World Health Organization.

Woldetsadik, M. A. (2018). Long-Term Effects of Wartime Sexual Violence on Women and Families the Case of Northern Uganda. The Pardee RAND Graduate School.

Wood, E. J. (2014). Conflict-Related Sexual Violence and the Policy Implications of Recent Research. International Review of the Red Cross, 96(894), 457–478.

Wood, E. J. (2018). Rape as a Practice of War: Toward a Typology of Political Violence. Politics & Society, 46(4), 513–537.

World Bank. (2011). World Development Report 2012: Gender Equality and Development. Washington, DC: World Bank.

Zautra, A. J., Sheets, V. L., & Sandler, I. N. (1996). An Examination of the Construct Validity of Coping Dispositions for a Sample of Recently Divorced Mothers. Psychological Assessment, 8(3), 256–264.

CHAPTER 5

Transcending Inward Brokenness for Growth: A Determinant of Transformative Leadership

Nelly Jelagat Kibet

INTRODUCTION

In the aftermath of civil war and armed conflict lie "tangible" and "intangible" consequences[1] across societal strata, ranging from individuals and families to communities. The tangible costs of war have a significant impact on myriad sectors of society, including medical care, education, public infrastructure, and economic growth and development.[2] Beyond these physical disruptions is the invisible psychological impact of wars

---

[1] Bratti, M., Mendola M., & Miranda A. (2015). Hard to Forget: The Long-Lasting Impact of War on Mental Health. http://ftp.iza.org/dp9269.pdf. Accessed 30 Apr 2022.

[2] Moyer, J. D., Bohl, D., Hanna, T., Mapes, B. R., & Rafa M. (2019). Assessing the Impact of War on Development in Yemen. https://www.undp.org/content/dam/yemen/General/Docs/ImpactOfWarOnDevelopmentInYemen.pdf. Accessed 30 Apr 2020; Arab-hdr.org. (n.d). The Effects on Youth of War and Violent Conflict. http://www.arab-hdr.org/reports/2016/english/Ch6.pdf. Accessed 30 Apr 2022.

N. J. Kibet (✉)
Hekima Institute of Peace Studies and International Relations, Nairobi, Kenya
e-mail: nellykibeto@gmail.com

© The Author(s), under exclusive license to Springer Nature Switzerland AG 2023
J. Adero Ngala et al. (eds.), *Innovations in Peace and Security in Africa*, https://doi.org/10.1007/978-3-031-39043-2_5

on individual's mental health, which can be long-lasting and devastating. This impact is well documented among soldiers and/or combatants who are at risk of Post-traumatic Stress Disorder (PTSD) and depression[3] following exposure to traumas of war—confronting enemy lines, wounded civilians and combatants, death, and untold human suffering. In some instances, frontline combat officers survive to write first hand historical accounts in the aftermath of war or other armed conflict.

Various studies focus on the physical, social, and psychological impact of wars and conflicts on women and children.[4] However, there is limited coverage of political leaders who also experience psychological burdens in the aftermath of armed conflict. As they are at the helm of the country, occupying the highest echelons of society, it is critical to study cases of traumatized leaders governing a traumatized population. Such instances can be likened to the metaphoric biblical tale of the blind leading the blind,[5] or the psychological equivalent of transgenerational trauma, whereby a parent's trauma is passed on to their offspring if the seeds of family dysfunction are sown overtime. Indeed, transmission of trauma to future generations is a likely occurrence when the cycle of historical psychological burden is not treated; thus, "The trauma of one childhood can bleed into the next generation's childhood".[6] Similarly, a leader of a country, who in this case is a parent to his/her offspring (i.e., the citizens) existing in a family (i.e., the country), can pass his/her "collective emotional and psychological injury over the lifespan and across generations,"[7] leading to a dysfunctional country. Therefore, poor governance can be linked to the impact of trauma exposure on leadership.

---

[3] Gade, D. M., & Wenger, J. B. (2011). Combat Exposure and mental Health: The Long-Term Effects Among US Vietnam and Gulf war Veterans; Cesur, R., Sabia, J. J., & Tekin, E. (2013). The psychological Costs of War: Military Combat and mental Health.

[4] Snoubar, Y., & Duman, N. (2016). Impact of Wars and Conflicts on Women and Children in Middle East: Health, Psychological, Educational and Social Crisis.

[5] Matthew 15:14, The New King James Version.

[6] Schaeffer, M. C. (2012). Why Are You Crying?: The Impact of Parental Trauma on the Child. Retrieved from Sophia, the St. Catherine University Repository Website: https://sophia.stkate.edu/msw_papers/86. Accessed 12 May 2022.

[7] Muid, O. (2006). Then I Lost My Spirit: An Analytical Essay on transgenerational Theory and Its Application to Oppressed People of Color Nations, p. 36.

Studies on trauma and leadership broadly find that one's ability to lead is influenced by an individual's emotional, cognitive, and physical well-being.[8] As Nigerian Minister of Health, Olorunnimbe Momora observes "If you cannot lead yourself, how can you lead others?"[9] Any trauma experienced as a victim, witness or perpetrator changes aspects of a leaders' mental health and behaviour, whether positive or negative.[10] Indeed, a leader's past trauma impacts their inner theatre, and in turn influences their political action and leadership. In this manner, good or bad governance correlates with a leader's personal and/or collective memories of past events which shape problem perception and solving during decision-making. Additionally, leaders "make up their minds about new, complex, disturbing or otherwise exciting events about which they have only limited information at their disposal."[11]

In summary, when a leader is exposed to trauma, the degree to which and how he/she processes the experience in the aftermath of the exposure has the potential to influence the course of leadership taken.[12] As human beings, political leaders and policymakers carry around emotions that are "fundamental, unavoidable and inherent dimension of human life…"[13] shading their thoughts and perceptions. Hence the need for those in leadership positions to be aware of their emotional well-being.

A leader's emotional well-being can be significantly impacted by both psychological trauma and stressor events. Psychological trauma, and its

---

[8] Kramer, C., & Allen, S. (2018). Transformational Leadership Styles Pre- and Post-Trauma. https://journalofleadershiped.org/jole_articles/transformational-leadership-styles-pre-and-post-trauma/. Accessed 6 May 2022.

[9] Mamora (2012) as cited in Nicholas, S., Kehinde, O., Imhonopi, D., & Evbuoma, I. (2016). Good Governance and Leadership: Pathway to Sustainable National Development in Nigeria. https://www.researchgate.net/publication/295399476_Good_Governance_and_Leadership_Pathway_to_Sustainable_National_Development_in_Nigeria. Accessed 6 May 2022.

[10] Bennis, W. G., & Thomas, R. J. (2007). Leading for a Lifetime: How Defining Moments Shape the Leaders of Today and Tomorrow; Yip, J., & Wilson, M. S. (2010). Learning from Experience.

[11] Hart, P., & Walter, J. (2009). Political Psychology: Exploring the Human Factor in Political Life, p. 11.

[12] Kets de Vries, M. F. (2006). The Leadership Mystique: Leading Behavior in the Human Enterprise (2nd ed.). Harlow, England: Prentice Hall Financial Times.

[13] Hutchison, E. (2016). Affective Communities in World Politics: Collective Emotions after Trauma, p. xi.

emotional impact, can be caused by society-wide phenomena such as genocide, war, terrorism, epidemics, and mass disasters; as well as "private disasters" in the wake of deaths, injuries, threats to self or others, and abuse or violence in families or communities.[14] Stressor events are classified by their severity, frequency, predictability, duration, and the degree to which it disrupts normalcy. Events may be acute and temporary (e.g., 1994 Rwandan genocide), chronic and long-lasting (e.g., Iraq), repeated (e.g., South Sudan civil war), or isolated (e.g., world trade center bombing).[15] Regardless of the event's characteristics, trauma can be said to be in the eyes of the beholder,[16] hence the experience is traumatic if the individual perceives the negative event as a "watershed that divides a life into before and after" (e.g., witnessing the suffering of individuals or communities).[17] In the aftermath of the life-threatening event the emotional toll shapes the nature of individual experience, rendering them helpless to prevent or stop the resulting mental harm.

Individuals and particularly leaders can have a range of responses in the aftermath of a crisis. Some individuals succumb to the trauma or never fully recover, while others may portray a more positive trajectory. For example, despite enduring stress and trauma there may be positive outcomes that a person can experience such as "greater appreciation for life [and] sense of mastery."[18] Other survivors emerge as leaders of prosocial change, inspired by their experiences to lead others to wholeness and prevent tragedies similar to theirs from re-occurring.[19]

Indeed, there are trauma survivors who have risen from life-threatening tragedies such as imprisonment, genocide, and civil wars, and transformed their adversity for the common good. For instance, Nelson Mandela was imprisoned on Robben Island and elsewhere for 27 years (1962–1990), continuously subjected to stressors that had "differential

---

[14] Reyes et al. (2012). The Encyclopedia of Psychological Trauma.

[15] Berger, R. (2015). Stress, Trauma, and Posttraumatic Growth, p. 18.

[16] Berger, R. (2015). Stress, Trauma, and Posttraumatic Growth, p. 8.

[17] Calhoun, L., & Tedeschi, R. (2014). The Foundations of Posttraumatic Growth: In an Expanded Framework, p. 9.

[18] Vasterling, J. J., et al. (2011). Posttraumatic Stress Reactions Over Time: The Battlefield, Homecoming, and Long-Term Course, p. 35.

[19] Frazier, P., et al. (2012). The Relations Between Trauma Exposure and Prosocial Behavior.

effects on organismic functioning."[20] In a bid to portray their power and control, Mandela's adversaries inflicted degradation through harsh treatment, depriving him of liberty and dislocating his previous social existence. All this cruelty amounted to stressors inflicted by adversity and trauma on a continuum. Despite his experiences and sufferings while in prison, Nelson Mandela transformed himself and his relationships with others and their actions. His experience of forced social displacement has been described to stir "strong feelings of fear, sorrow and anger."[21] Mandela was propelled by his traumatic personal experiences to advocate for an end to apartheid in South Africa. His legacy portrays an aspect of prosocial leadership that is "positive, effective influence, with constructive goals that serve the common good."[22] Mandela was able to address feelings of hatred and revenge towards his perpetrators by embracing intrapersonal forgiveness.[23]

As illustrated in Mandela's singular experience, prosocial behaviour and attitudes have been associated with self-forgiveness,[24] which facilitates intrapersonal restoration and promotes positive mental health. This is in line with the fact that reconciliation with oneself comprises addressing one's traumatic history.[25] Ideally, reconciliation applies to everyone ranging from those who suffered the pain, those who caused the suffering, and the community at large. It takes both top–down approaches (e.g., truth commissions, national reparation programmes, public reconciliation forums, legal reforms, official apologies, national tribunals) and bottom–up approaches (e.g., community-level initiatives, interpersonal

[20] Wilson, J. P. (2004). PTSD and Complex PTSD: Symptoms, Syndromes, and Diagnoses, p. 8.

[21] Demertzis, N. (2013). *Emotions in Politics*: The Affect Dimension in Political Tension, p. 62.

[22] Lorenzi, P. (2004). Managing for the Common Good: Prosocial Leadership, p. 238.

[23] Kalayjian, A., & Paloutzian, R. (2009). Forgiveness and Reconciliation, p. 7.

[24] Hall, J. H., & Fincham, F. D. (2005). Self-Forgiveness: The Stepchild of Forgiveness Research; Hall, J. H., & Fincham, F. D. (2008). The Temporal Course of Self-Forgiveness; María Prieto-Ursúa, M., & Echegoyen, I. (2015). Self-Forgiveness, Self-Acceptance or Intrapersonal Restoration? Open Issues in the Psychology of Forgiveness. https://www.researchgate.net/publication/283082022_Self-forgiveness_self-acceptance_or_intrapersonal_restoration_Open_issues_in_the_Psychology_of_Forgiveness. Accessed 13 May 2022.

[25] Werle, G. (2006). Justice in Transition – Prosecution and Amnesty in Germany and South Africa, p. 137.

reconciliation initiatives). Although the process may begin either with leaders or at the grassroots level, effective reconciliation proceeds in both dimensions simultaneously.[26] Indeed, both approaches are complementary since the top–down approach (i.e., structural) achieves political reconstruction while the bottom-up approach (i.e., cultural and grass-root level) ensures that interpersonal reconciliation is achieved.[27] Lastly, the ability of leaders to foster peaceful coexistence after conflict and support post-conflict reconstruction lies in intrapersonal reconciliation—assisting them to address past trauma as was the case for Nelson Mandela.

In essence, adverse life events can propel leadership development, enable lasting impact and impel individuals.[28] In his quest to transform the apartheid violence, Mandela initiated the South Africa's Truth and Reconciliation Commission (TRC) which acknowledged suffering and ameliorated trauma to avert resurgent violence. Truth commissions have a direct link to reconciling and healing individuals and upholding political legitimacy in post-conflict societies.[29] Truth telling constituted in truth commissions facilitates "the social process of reconciliation and peacebuilding"[30] as it provides psychological and emotional benefits to victims (trauma healing).

Mandela's choice of the reconciliatory path for South Africa illustrates that leaders in post-conflict societies have a central role in reconstructing and rebuilding a country and setting a path for its future. Drawing from Posttraumatic Growth Theory (PTG) and the trauma model of violence this chapter cross-examines two African leaders—Paul Kagame and Salva Kiir to analyse why some individuals thrive after post-tragedy (such as civil war and genocide) while others stagnate or succumb to the trauma. Could leaders who have experienced positive growth in the aftermath of

---

[26] Bar-Tal, D., et al. (2004). The Nature of Reconciliation as an Outcome and as a Process, pp. 11–38.

[27] As discussed by Bloomfield, D., Barnes, T., & Huyse, L. (2003). Reconciliation After Violent Conflict. A Handbook.

[28] Turner, J., & Mavin, S. (2008). What Can We Learn from Senior Leader Narratives? The Strutting and Fretting of Becoming a Leader, p. 380.

[29] https://www.tandfonline.com/doi/pdf/10.1080/14754830902717726. Accessed 10 May 2022.

[30] WHO 2002 cited in Pupavac 2004a: 386 World Health Organization. (2002) Report on the second WHO consultation on health as a bridge for peace (July 8–9, Geneva).

psychological brokenness be in a better position to advocate for reconciliation and post-conflict reconstruction of states? Despite holding echelons of power as heads of state, these leaders remain persons with distinct intrinsic selves that influence their ideologies, decision-making, motivation, and performance. These political leaders (namely the two presidents assessed in this chapter) have exceptional influences whether good or ill on political systems.

PAUL KAGAME OF RWANDA

The arc of Paul Kagame's life reflects a metamorphosis from an exiled child refugee, guerrilla warrior and rebel politician, to the President of Rwanda. The degree to which Kagame transformed personal adversity and trauma exposure to the prosperity of a country sheds light on the impact of posttraumatic growth on leadership and governance.

Born into a Tutsi family in 1959, Paul Kagame experienced a challenging upbringing where at three years old his village in Ntambwe commune was attacked by Hutu gangs. At such a tender age, young Kagame witnessed beatings, arson, looting, deaths, and sufferings in villages, while his family experienced forced displacement to safeguard their physical integrity.[31] After fleeing home, Kagame settled among thousands of other Rwandan Tutsis in a refugee camp in Uganda where he spent his childhood.[32]

In the early 1970s, Kagame witnessed family separation as a refugee in Nshungerezi camp in Toro District in Uganda, and as an exiled student encountered social and financial hardships. Together with other refugees, Kagame was often reminded of their "outsider status"[33] by their hosts in western Uganda. In addition to feelings of alienation from being accorded second-class status while in exile, Kagame and his peers encountered dangerous periods of uncertainty in the 1980s. When he revisited his

---

[31] Waugh, C. (2004). Paul Kagame and Rwanda: Power, Genocide and the Rwandan Patriotic Front.

[32] Bartrop, P. (2012). A Biographical Encyclopedia of Contemporary Genocide Portraits of Evil and Good. p. 150.

[33] Waugh, C. (2004). Paul Kagame and Rwanda: Power, Genocide and the Rwandan Patriotic Front.

birthplace—Ntambwe village—in later years, Kagame found "an almost empty hill and just one or two older survivors of the massacres...".[34]

In the late 1970s Kagame joined the political and military opposition in Uganda, supporting Yoweri Museveni in his quest to fight against Idi Amin, who had overthrown Milton Obote through a coup. Upon formation of the Front for National Salvation (FRONASA), Kagame and his classmate Fred Rwigyema joined Museveni in Tanzania in 1978 to help overthrow Amin. Later in the 1980s, he joined the National Resistance Army to support Obote's (second) removal from power.[35] Overall, Kagame trained in military fighting and intelligence gathering in Uganda, Cuba, and the United States.[36]

In April 1994 with the onset of the genocide, the Rwandan Patriotic Front (RPF) renewed and expanded their civil war with the Rwanda government; and in July 1994 the RPF seized power, bringing the genocide to an end. In the aftermath of genocide and years of personal adversity and exposure to trauma, Kagame utilized his presidency to build Rwandan national unity.[37] Referred to as an "indomitably resilient dynamo" and "driving force of Rwanda"[38] Kagame is seen as the architect of Rwanda's development. He is also acclaimed for prioritizing post-genocide justice, reconciliation, peacebuilding, economic development, women empowerment, and good governance.[39] By any measure, Rwanda is considerably better off than before Kagame's leadership.

Rwanda was a devastated country after years of war and genocide, which exacted an enormous toll on civilian populations, with nearly one million deaths, two million refugees, and a million internally displaced; as well as an annihilated physical infrastructure, marked by dysfunctional

---

[34] Waugh, C. (2004). Paul Kagame and Rwanda: Power, Genocide and the Rwandan Patriotic Front, p. 8.

[35] Waugh, C. (2004). Paul Kagame and Rwanda: Power, Genocide and the Rwandan Patriotic Front.

[36] Pruitt, W. R. (2018). Why Kagame Should Not Seek Another Term. https://www.umes.edu/uploadedFiles/_WEBSITES/AJCJS/Content/VOL%2011%20PRUITT%20FINAL.pdf. Accessed 14 May 2022.

[37] Bartrop, P. (2012). A Biographical Encyclopedia of Contemporary Genocide Portraits of Evil and Good, p. 151.

[38] Soudan, F. (2015). *Kagame*: The President of Rwanda Speaks.

[39] Bartrop, P. (2012). A Biographical Encyclopedia of Contemporary Genocide Portraits of Evil and Good.

health care, education, and justice systems.[40] To contend with this reality, President Kagame instituted reforms that resulted in numerous socio-economic gains. In less than two decades since 1994 Rwanda's economy has soared across key metrics, such as an average of 7.5% growth over the decade to 2018.[41] The country registered economic growth by 10.9%, the most since 2008,[42] and poverty declined from 59 to 39% between 2001 and 2014. While it is likely that this upward trend will slow due to the COVID-19 global pandemic,[43] other economic indicators in Rwanda show the promise of Kagame's economic reform drive. For example, Rwanda ranked 38 out of 190 on ease of doing business according to the World Bank's (2020). Doing Business report, and the second easiest place to do business in Africa.[44] This makes Rwanda the only low-income country and one of only two African countries (along with Mauritius) to rank in the top 50.[45]

Rwanda has also performed well in closing gaps in representation, expanding public services infrastructure, and respect for the rule of law. According to the global gender gap index 2021 rankings, Rwanda is ranked seventh place in bridging the gender gap in the world and the first in Africa,[46] in addition to other advances in promoting women's empowerment.[47] Rwanda is a leading country in the world with the highest women's representation in parliament, with 64% of the seats garnered by

---

[40] Reyntjens, F. (2004). Rwanda, Ten Years On: From Genocide to Dictatorship.

[41] National institute of statistics of Rwanda. (2020). GDP National Accounts, 2019. http://www.statistics.gov.rw/publication/gdp-national-accounts-2019. Accessed 28 May 2020.

[42] Rwanda GDP Annual Growth Rate. https://tradingeconomics.com/rwanda/gdp-growth-annual. Accessed 13 May 2022.

[43] The World Bank. (2020). The World Bank In Rwanda: Overview. https://www.worldbank.org/en/country/rwanda/overview. Accessed 12 May 2020.

[44] World Bank Group. (2020). Doing Business 2020: Comparing Business Regulation in 190 Economies.

[45] World Bank Group. (2020). Doing Business 2020: Comparing Business Regulation in 190 Economies, p. 4.

[46] World Economic Forum. (2021). Global Results. https://www3.weforum.org/docs/WEF_GGGR_2021.pdf. Accessed 13 May 2022.

[47] Congressional Research Service. (2019).Rwanda: In Brief. https://fas.org/sgp/crs/row/R44402.pdf. Accessed 15 May 2020.

women during elections in September 2018.[48] Alongside this, Rwanda provides a national health service for basic primary care[49] that has contributed to Rwanda's life expectancy rising from 45 to 65 years. Additionally, Kagame's government has introduced a national health service, reduced child mortality by two-thirds, increased life expectancy from dash to dash, and advocated investments in primary school enrolment. Finally, Rwanda ranks as the safest and cleanest country[50] in Africa with orderly and law-abiding citizens.[51] All these successes demonstrate why Rwanda is one of the world's fastest growing developing countries.

From the foregoing, it can be seen that Paul Kagame bounced back from trauma and devastating experiences and used his adversity as a springboard to further personal growth as well as that of his country. Stephen Joseph explains that people who grow following adversity "may remain emotionally affected, but their sense of self, views on life, priorities, goals for the future and their behaviours have been reconfigured in positive ways in light of their experiences."[52]

The aspect of growth and positive outcomes in the aftermath of adversity has received attention in the literature.[53] Posttraumatic growth (PTG) comprises "the experience of positive change that occurs as a result of the struggle with highly challenging life crises."[54] It is the tendency for some

---

[48] The World Bank. (2020). The World Bank In Rwanda: Overview. https://www.worldbank.org/en/country/rwanda/overview. Accessed 12 May 2022.

[49] University of Rwanda, Management Sciences for Health, and the Rockefeller Foundation (2016). Technical Brief: The Development of Community-Based Health Insurance in Rwanda: Experiences and Lessons. https://www.msh.org/sites/default/files/the_development_of_cbhi_in_rwanda_experiences_and_lessons_-_technical_brief.pdf. Accessed 29 Apr 2022.

[50] Grant 2010.

[51] Montague, J. (2014). Thirty-One Nil – On the Road with Football's Outsiders: A World Cup Odyssey.

[52] Stephen Joseph, S. (2011). What Doesn't Kill Us: The New Psychology of Posttraumatic Growth, pp. 71–72.

[53] Calhoun, L. G., & Tedeschi, R. G. (2006). The Foundations of Posttraumatic Growth: An Expanded Framework; Joseph, S., & Linley, P. A. (2008). Psychological Assessment of Growth Following Adversity: A Review; Weiss, T., & Berger, R. (Eds.) (2010). Posttraumatic Growth and Culturally Competent Practice: Lessons Learned from Around the World.

[54] Tedeschi, R. G., & Calhoun, L. G. (2004). Posttraumatic Growth: Conceptual Foundations and Empirical Evidence, p. 1.

individuals to build a new way of life following a traumatic event. Individuals who experience PTG display a variety of growth areas, including changed priorities, improved relationships, increased appreciation for life, and increased personal strength, spiritual development, and openness to new possibilities. PTG manifests itself in three aspects: self-perception (e.g., a greater sense of autonomy and self-reliance); interpersonal relationships (e.g., enhanced feelings of compassion or intimacy); and life philosophy (e.g., a new sense of meaning, a greater appreciation for life or an increased spiritual awareness).[55]

An important aspect in the domain of perception-of-self lies in how an individual perceives themselves in the aftermath of trauma whether as a victim of trauma or survivor of trauma. The survivor label enables the individual to have a greater sense of self with "special status and strength."[56] This self-perception impacts how an individual responds to life transitions; and in the case of Paul Kagame he views his survival as a chance to contribute to his personal life and that of his country. In his words, President Kagame disclosed that "… I'm not merely living my life; I'm also contributing to their lives."[57] This implies that a leader's experiences of trauma shapes how he or she perceives and responds to life.

In the aftermath of a traumatic event, survivors experience increased awareness of their "vulnerability, mortality and the preciousness and fragility of life."[58] With this sense of vulnerability, such individuals are more appreciative of life, spend time on vital life priorities, and invest in interpersonal relationships. By recognizing his vulnerabilities, President Kagame is keen on promoting national unity; and with his experience of genocide and its devastating effects he seeks to be assertive in appreciating human life, often advocating for no more genocide in Rwanda.

Trauma affects fundamental aspects of life, hence surviving it sets in motion the sense that "one has been spared, and that this gift of a second

---

[55] Calhoun, L. G., & Tedeschi, R. G. (2006). The Foundations of Posttraumatic Growth: An Expanded Framework.

[56] Tedeschi, R. G., Park, C. L., & Calhoun, L. G. (1998). Posttraumatic Growth: Conceptual Issues, p. 10.

[57] Soudan, F. (2015). *Kagame*: The President of Rwanda Speaks.

[58] Tedeschi, R. G., Park, C. L., & Calhoun, L. G. (1998). Posttraumatic Growth: Conceptual Issues, p. 11.

chance should be treated with care."[59] Recognizing his life as a second chance, Kagame is keenly focused on his legacy—what contribution he can make—and to make his life meaningful for the sake of self and countrymen. Survivors of a traumatic event possess an increased self-efficacy with a sense that "if I survived this, I can handle anything."[60] This self-reliance and stronger self-image explains the self-belief that President Kagame has when addressing issues in his homeland.

As discussed above, trauma has the potential to have a highly positive impact. PTG can create "psychological preparedness" allowing trauma survivors to confront subsequent events with less anxiety.[61] Despite some instances in which Kagame has been described as an "authoritarian"—"ruthless and repressive" leader that suppresses human rights and disregards public opinion,[62] he is generally lauded for his visionary leadership.[63] This portrays PTG in action as President Kagame deters to seek refuge in victimhood but prosperity.

Salva Kiir of South Sudan

Salva Kiir, President of the Government of South Sudan (GOSS) and one of South Sudan's liberation fighter, has struggled to unite and ensure that citizens lead dignified lives. For instance, 8.9 million out of the 12.4 million population are in need of humanitarian assistance,[64] and the country ranks 185 out of 189 countries in the Human Development

---

[59] Tedeschi, R. G., Park, C. L., & Calhoun, L. G. (1998). Posttraumatic Growth: Conceptual Issues, p. 12.

[60] Aldwin, C. M., Levenson, M. R., & Spiro, A. (1994). Vulnerability and Resilience to Combat Exposure: Can Stress Have Lifelong Effects?

[61] Janoff-Bulman, R. (1992). Shattered Assumptions: Towards a New Psychology of Trauma.

[62] Agaba, A. K. The Case for Kagame's third term in Rwanda, Washington Post, August 3, 2017; Kinzer, S. Rwanda and the Dangers of Democracy, Boston Globe, July 22, 2017.

[63] Bartrop, P. (2012). A Biographical Encyclopedia of Contemporary Genocide Portraits of Evil and Good.

[64] USAID. South Sudan–Complex Emergencies. https://www.usaid.gov/sites/default/files/documents/2022-03-25_USG_South_Sudan_Complex_Emergency_Fact_Sheet_3.pdf. Accessed 14 May 2022.

Index.[65] Unlike Kagame who was able to transform personal adversity and trauma exposure to the prosperity of Rwanda, Salva Kiir is yet to realize the aspects of posttraumatic growth for personal and collective gains.

Salva Kiir is one of the founders of the Sudan People's Liberation Movement/Army (SPLM/A). An ethnic Dinka from Bahr al-Ghazal, Kiir was born in September 1951. Prior to joining the SPLM in 1983, Kiir served as an intelligence officer in the Sudanese army and fought in the first civil war in Sudan (1955–1972). In a quest for independence from Khartoum, South Sudan was involved in a struggle that stretched more than five decades[66] to resist Arabo-Islamic power among other grievances related to Southern political, economic, and cultural autonomy. This conflict has been described as the longest and bloodiest in Africa amidst a legacy of neglect, exclusion, and marginalization of the South.[67] In January 2005, under the leadership of John Garang in the South and Omar al-Bashir in the North, the SPLM/A and Khartoum signed the Comprehensive Peace Agreement (CPA) ending the second twenty-year civil war (1983–2005). The conflict was characterized by widespread

---

[65] OCHA. Humanitarian Response Plan South Sudan; Humanitarian Programme Cycle 2022. https://reliefweb.int/sites/reliefweb.int/files/resources/hrp_ssd_2022_3 0mar_2022.pdf. Accessed 14 May 2022.

[66] This First Civil War between the Arab/Muslim North and the African/Christian South, which took place from 1955 to 1972, was led by a group of insurgents known as the Anya-Nya. Anya-Nya means "snake venom" in Madi Language, spoken in parts of Uganda and South Sudan. The AnyaNya were a group of separatists led by Joseph Lagu, and formed the military wing of the Southern Sudan Resistance Movement (SSRM). They fought the First Sudanese Civil War, or AnyaNya Rebellion, from 1963 until 1972, when Lagu and the Sudanese president, Jaafar Muhammad an-Numeiry, signed the Addis Ababa Agreement (Boddy-Evans, n.d.). The war ended in 1972 with the Addis Ababa Agreement, which granted Southern Sudan semi-autonomy through a regional government with a representative assembly and created constitutional provisions for religious and cultural protection. The Addis Ababa Agreement, however, did not last due to the inability of Southern Sudanese to unite politically in its defence, and the failure of the Khartoum regime of Jaafar Mohammad an-Numeiry, to meet its provisions (LeRiche and Arnold 2012). The Second Civil War began in 1983, led by the Sudan People's Liberation Army (SPLA) with John Garang de Mabior as the leader.

[67] See Kumsa, A. (2017), Amir (2013) and Malwal (2015). https://www.researchgate.net/publication/321142466_South_Sudan_struggle_for_independence_and_it's_implications_for_Africa. Accessed 04 May 2022.

violence[68] and suffering inflicted on the people, leaving its survivors with deep wounds that can last a lifetime when not addressed.

After Garang's death in 2005, Kiir became the head of the SPLM/A and president of the autonomous southern regional government.[69] Following a pro-secession referendum provided for in the CPA South Sudan finally got its independence in 2011, after years of bloodshed along ethnic and religious fault lines. Over time Kiir's government sought to maintain unity and strive for reconciliation, but with mixed results. This outcome is attributed to political rivalries, armed rebellions, and external interference.[70] Acknowledging the challenge in state building, President Kiir noted that "We have over sixty tribes in South Sudan; it is not easy with such diversity. We must accept ourselves as one nation and use different tribes to build that one nation which we can be proud of."[71] In the period between 2005 and independence in 2011 South Sudan enjoyed relative peace; however, despite the vision of unity, prosperity, and stability South Sudan slid back to crisis in 2013, three years after gaining its independence.

In December 2013 violence erupted in Juba and quickly spread throughout the Greater Upper Nile region (i.e., Jonglei, Unity and Upper Nile states). The slide back into armed conflict followed growing political tensions between President Kiir, his deputy Dr Riek Machar and their loyalists, ultimately mushrooming into brutal nationalized violence.[72] The intensity and the speed of the spread of the violence has been attributed to

---

[68] Roberts, B., Damundu, E. Y., Lomoro O., & Sondorp E. (2009). Post-conflict Mental Health Needs: A Cross-Sectional Survey of Trauma, Depression and Associated Factors in Juba, Southern Sudan.

[69] Dagne, T. (2011). The Republic of South Sudan: Opportunities and Challenges for Africa's Newest Country, p. 12; Natsios, A. S. (2012). Sudan, South Sudan, and Darfur: What Everyone Needs to Know. New York, NY: Oxford University Press.

[70] Dagne, T. (2011). The Republic of South Sudan: Opportunities and Challenges for Africa's Newest Country, https://fas.org/sgp/crs/row/R41900.pdf. Accessed 10 May 2022.

[71] Herbst, J., Mills, G., & McNamee, T. (2012). On the Fault Line: Managing Tensions and Divisions Within Societies.

[72] UN Mission in South Sudan (UNMISS). (2014). Conflict in South Sudan: A Human Rights Report. https://reliefweb.int/sites/reliefweb.int/files/resources/UNMISS%20Conflict%20in%20South%20Sudan%20-%20A%20Human%20Rights%20Report.pdf. Accessed 28 May 2020; Amnesty International. (2014). Nowhere Safe: Civilians Under Attack in South Sudan. https://www.amnesty.org/download/Documents/8000/afr650032014en.pdf. Accessed 8 May 2022.

various factors, including lack of independence of the military from politics, oil wealth, power struggles over control of the state, and unresolved grievances linked to decades of violence and trauma from past wars.[73]

As a veteran of both Sudanese civil wars, fighting with the Anyanya and then the SPLM/A, Salva Kiir experienced war trauma while in combat, in addition to surviving other near-death experiences. For instance, in 1994, he survived a plane crash in Kapenguria, Kenya. Travelling from Wilson Airport, Nairobi to Nimule, and the chartered plane in which he was a passenger fell from over 25,000 feet, killing all passengers including the pilot, except Kiir and his bodyguard. He later survived a joint Egyptian-Sudanese assassination plot on his life. These encounters are traumatic events since they are "out of the ordinary and are directly experienced as threats to survival and preservation."[74] In some cases when trauma is not addressed it can potentially fuel cycles of violence, since the presence of trauma hinders reconciliation and perceived solutions to a crisis.[75]

Even though not all forms of trauma are predictive of future violent behaviour the trauma model of violence indicates that trauma is a contributor to the cycle of violence. In support of the trauma model of violence, Pomeroy indicates that "persons who have been traumatized, by whatever circumstances, are more likely to choose violence as an option to resolve future conflicts and stress."[76] As an antithesis to posttraumatic growth, the trauma theory illustrates that unlike Kagame who to a greater extent "grew" and transformed his traumatic painful experience into prosperity, Salva Kiir might have "stagnated" in his experiences given the situation in South Sudan. This offers an explanation of the on–off nature of peace negotiations and the limited progress towards achieving a mediated solution in South Sudan. The ambivalence in agreeing to the terms of peace settlements could be a result of unaddressed traumatic

---

[73] UNDP. 2015. Search for a New Beginning: Perceptions of Truth, Justice, Reconciliation and Healing in South Sudan, p. vi. https://www.undp.org/content/dam/southsudan/library/Rule%20of%20Law/Perception%20Survey%20Report%20Transitional%20Justice%20Reconciliation%20and%20Healing%20-.pdf. Accessed 05 May 2022.

[74] Janoff-Bulman, R. (1992). Shattered Assumptions: Towards a New Psychology of Trauma, p. 53.

[75] Ng, L. C., et al. (2017). Posttraumatic Stress Disorder, Trauma, and Reconciliation in South Sudan.

[76] Pomeroy, W. (1995). A Working Model for Trauma: The Relationship Between Trauma and Violence, p. 89.

experiences. Consequently, encounters with human suffering, crisis and adversity usually produce "distress, disrupts one's understanding of the world, makes salient one's vulnerabilities and lack of power and control, and may make more salient one's mortality."[77]

Exposure to war-related violence and the resultant psychological impacts have been linked to influencing attitudes on reconciliation, justice and sustainable peace in post-conflict societies. This is because those who have gone through violent traumatic events are more likely to favour violence over nonviolence.[78] Previous studies show that traumatic exposure during armed conflict affects how individuals perceive post-conflict societal rebuilding mechanisms such as amnesties, criminal trials and truth commissions.[79] Hence, efforts to promote societal reconstruction and peacebuilding call for assisting the traumatized populace to address their trauma. This should include political leaders given that their suffered psychological trauma impacts the transformation of society. Indeed, political leaders and their emotional well-being greatly impact the trajectory of transitions from fragility through state building and development processes in post-conflict contexts.

Recommendations

The following are pointers that leaders in or out of crises, or struggling with past trauma, can explore to be effective in their leadership and governance. Trauma has profound effects on emotional intelligence (EI), which relates to how an individual's cognitive capacities are informed by emotions and the extent to which emotions are managed by one's cognition.[80] Hence, life-threatening occurrences impact one's self-awareness and conflict management capacity, shut down senses, and narrow one's "window of tolerance."[81] Leaders that strengthen their emotional intelligence can process trauma and eventually be effective and conscious.

---

[77] Calhoun, L., et al. (2006). Handbook of Posttraumatic Growth: Research and Practice, p. 7.

[78] Vinck, P., et al. (2007). Exposure to War Crimes and Implications for Peace Building in Northern Uganda.

[79] Weine, S. M., et al. (1995). Psychiatric Consequences of "ethnic cleansing": Clinical Assessments and Trauma Testimonies of Newly Resettled Bosnian Refugees.

[80] George, J. M. (2000). Emotions and Leadership: The Role of Emotional Intelligence.

[81] Siegel, D. J. (2010). Mindsight: The New Science of Personal Transformation.

Leaders with high EI create positive climates and garner better results.[82] Therefore, leaders need to foster dialogue to reconnect with self and community since "there can be no peace without inner healing and no inner healing without reforming relations with the self and the other."[83]

Brubaker discusses the importance of self-awareness among leaders, akin to a dentist needing to brush their own teeth or a counsellor tending to their own wounds lest "patients and clients suffer."[84] Similar to the patients and clients in a medical care system, citizens in a political system should have leaders who are self-aware and as a result equipped to deal with others during times of crisis, destabilization, or polarization. Alternatively, if leaders remain emotionally distant in their responses to atrocities committed, witnessed, or experienced, they can exacerbate and recreate internal trauma.[85] To ensure successful conflict prevention and post-war recovery, leaders should find ways to address their deep-seated traumatic set of circumstances since self-awareness makes a difference in preventing cycles of violence.

A cross-examination of wars in Africa and Eastern Europe indicates that "…trauma has come to be understood not only as a consequence of war but a possible factor in its perpetuation."[86] Accordingly, treatment and other assistance for individuals who have encountered traumatic experiences are crucial to breaking chronic cycles of violence. The mental health of citizens and its leaders should be prioritized in post-conflict contexts to avert a return to violence and prevent traumatized victims from becoming future perpetrators. Nonetheless, most stakeholders focus on the psychological health of citizens in post-violence societies yet there is a need to also look into the intrapersonal state and well-being of political leaders (as individuals).

---

[82] Schmelzer, G. (2018). Journey Through Trauma: A Trail Guide to the 5-Phase Cycle of Healing Repeated Trauma; Goleman, D. (2000). Leadership That Gets Results.

[83] Institute for Justice and Reconciliation and the War Trauma Foundation. (2015). Healing Communities – Transforming Society: Exploring the Interconnectedness Betweenpsychosocial Needs, Practice and Peacebuilding, p. 15.

[84] Brubaker, D., Brubaker, E., Yoder, C., & Haase, T. (2019). When the Center Does Not Hold: Leading in an Age of Polarization, p. 91.

[85] Audergon, A. (2005). The War Hotel: Psychological Dynamics in Violent Conflict, p. 181.

[86] Moon, C. (2009). Healing Past Violence: Traumatic Assumptions and Therapeutic Interventions in War and Reconciliation, p. 75.

International and regional experts and other actors working in the aftermath of violent conflict largely focus on peacebuilding; humanitarian assistance, and economic rehabilitation, with a comparatively limited focus on transforming leadership. The failure to prioritize leaders' psychological health in post-conflict reconstruction raises the likelihood of a temporary peace settlement that is not sustainable.[87] Hence, organizations supporting societal reconstruction and transformation should channel funds towards appropriate support and intervention for political leaders. The chronic cycle of violence can be interrupted by treating traumatized political leaders. If left untreated, leaders run the risk of becoming future perpetrators given that unhealed trauma is transferred trauma. In this manner, the process of reconciliation and peacebuilding can be facilitated by responsive trauma healing centred on leaders.

A practicable policy mechanism that could be implemented during post-conflict reconstruction is the training and appointment of psychological advisers to political leaders. In the same way that politicians are surrounded by focal persons providing counsel on political and economic matters, a leader should have chaplains or psychotherapists that they can consult to process psychological needs. Spiritual advisers should offer insight based on morality, hold the leader accountable to the ideals pursued during campaigns, while remaining apolitical and objective. As human beings presidents and politicians in general require experts with relevant and appropriate skills to carry out regular psychological assessments along with related treatment and assistance. Apart from having subject matter experts, those running for elective posts should receive training on psychotherapy and coaching as a baseline qualification for office. This will go a long way in assisting traumatized leaders in transcending their brokenness and preventing them from bleeding their wounds on others.

---

[87] Mayanja, E. (2013). Strengthening Ethical Political Leadership for Sustainable Peace and Social Justice in Africa: Uganda as a Case Study. Accord. https://www.accord.org.za/ajcr-issues/strengthening-ethical-political-leadership-for-sustainable-peace-and-social-justice-in-africa/. Accessed 28 Apr 2022.

Even with the availability of mental health strategies and policies, some political leaders might not seek out such support due to the stigma associated with mental health conditions.[88] The situation is worsened by the fact that the majority of political leaders are men who are less likely than women to seek professional support and far less likely to disclose a mental health problem to friends and family.[89] There is therefore a need to push for a cultural shift away from the stigmas attached to mental health since the status quo is detrimental to individuals, namely leaders, and society at large. To that end, mental health literacy in proactive coping methods can alleviate societal stereotypes and prejudicial attitudes, and in turn dismantle existing barriers to leaders seeking professional psychological support.

Conclusion

Communities affected by the brunt of war and violence suffer from losses that range from economic hardship, political division, destruction of infrastructure, and social fragmentation. Armed conflict affects the social, economic, political, and psychological well-being of the populace. With human suffering as the common denominator, leaders are as vulnerable as anyone else to the effects of trauma regardless of the timing of the traumatic event. However, an encounter with great suffering and loss can lead to significant positive changes if an individual does not succumb to its wrath. Ultimately, leaders should strive to address their struggles with past trauma since overcoming them has the possibility of improving leadership and governance.

References

Agaba, A. K. (2017). The Case for Kagame's Third Term in Rwanda. The Washington Post. Retrieved from https://www.washingtonpost.com/news/global-opinions/wp/2017/08/03/the-case-for-kagames-third-term-in-rwanda/. Accessed 13 May 2022.

---

[88] Clement, S., Schauman, O., Graham, T., Maggioni, F., Evans-Lacko, S., Bezborodovs, N., Morgan, C., Rüsch, N., Brown, J. S., & Thornicroft, G. (2015). What Is the Impact of Mental Health-Related Stigma on Help-Seeking?

[89] Doward, J. (2016). Men Much Less Likely to Seek Mental Health Help Than Women. The Guardian. Retrieved from https://www.theguardian.com/society/2016/nov/05/men-less-likely-to-get-help--mental-health Accessed 8 May 2022.

Aldwin, C. M., Levenson, M. R., & Spiro, A. (1994). Vulnerability and Resilience to Combat Exposure: Can Stress Have Lifelong Effects? Psychology and Aging, 9(1), 34–44. https://doi.org/10.1037/0882-7974.9.1.34

Amnesty International. (2014). Nowhere Safe: Civilians Under Attack in South Sudan. London: Amnesty International Ltd.

Arab-hdr.org. (n.d). The Effects on Youth of War and Violent Conflict. http://www.arab-hdr.org/reports/2016/english/Ch6.pdf. Accessed 28 Apr 2022.

Audergon, A. (2005). The War Hotel: Psychological Dynamics in Violent Conflict. London: Whurr Publishers/John Wiley.

Bar-Tal, D., & Bennink, G. H. (2004). The Nature of Reconciliation as an Outcome and as a Process. In Y. Bar-Siman-Tov (Ed.), From conflict Resolution to Reconciliation (pp. 11–38). New York, NY: Oxford University Press.

Bartrop, P. (2012). A Biographical Encyclopedia of Contemporary Genocide Portraits of Evil and Good. Santa Barbara, California: ABC-CLIO.

Bennis, W. G., & Thomas, R. J. (2007). Leading for a Lifetime: How Defining Moments Shape the Leaders of Today and Tomorrow. Boston, MA: Harvard Business School Press.

Berger, R. (2015). Stress, Trauma, and Posttraumatic Growth. New York, NY: Routledge.

Bloomfield, D., Barnes, T., & Huyse, L. (2003). Reconciliation After Violent Conflict. A Handbook. Stockholm: International Institute for Democracy and Electoral Assistance.

Bratti, M., Mendola M., & Miranda A. (2015). Hard to Forget: The Long-Lasting Impact of War on Mental Health. SSRN Electronic Journal. https://doi.org/10.2139/ssrn.2759365.

Brubaker, D., Brubaker, E., Yoder, C., & Haase, T. (2019). When the Center Does Not Hold: Leading in an Age of Polarization. Minneapolis: Augsburg Fortress. doi:https://doi.org/10.2307/j.ctvcb5bsg.

Calhoun, L. G., & Tedeschi, R. G. (2006). The Foundations of Posttraumatic Growth: An Expanded Framework. In L. G. Calhoun & R. G. Tedeschi (Eds.), Handbook of Posttraumatic Growth: Research & Practice (pp. 3–23). Lawrence Erlbaum Associates Publishers.

Calhoun, L., & Tedeschi, R. (2014). The Foundations of Posttraumatic Growth: An Expanded Framework. In L. Calhoun, & R. Tedeschi (Eds.), Handbook of Posttraumatic Growth (pp. 3–23). Taylor and Francis.

Calhoun, L., & Tedeschi. R. (Eds.). (2006). Handbook of Posttraumatic Growth: Research and Practice. New York, NY: Psychology Press.

Cesur, R., Sabia, J. J., &Tekin, E. (2013). The Psychological Costs of War: Military Combat and Mental Health. Journal of Health Economics, 32(1), 51–65.

Clancy, M. A., & Hamber, B. (2009). Trauma, Peacebuilding, and Development: An Overview of Key Positions and Critical Questions. Unknown Host Publication International Conflict Research Institute.
Clement, S., Schauman, O., Graham, T., Maggioni, F., Evans-Lacko, S., Bezborodovs, N., Morgan, C., Rüsch, N., Brown, J. S., & Thornicroft, G. (2015). What Is the Impact of Mental Health-Related Stigma on Help-Seeking? A Systematic Review of Quantitative and Qualitative Studies. Psychological Medicine, 45(1), 11–27. https://doi.org/10.1017/S0033291714000129.
Congressional Research Service. (2019). Rwanda: In Brief. https://fas.org/sgp/crs/row/R44402.pdf. Accessed 15 May 2022.
Dagne, T. (2011). The Republic of South Sudan: Opportunities and Challenges for Africa's Newest Country. https://fas.org/sgp/crs/row/R41900.pdf. Accessed 20 May 2020.
Demertzis, N. (2013). Emotions in Politics. Basingstoke: Palgrave Macmillan.
Doward, J. (2016). Men Much Less Likely to Seek Mental Health Help Than Women. The Guardian. Retrieved from https://www.theguardian.com/society/2016/nov/05/men-less-likely-to-get-help--mental-health. Accessed 28 May 2020.
Frazier, P., Greer, C., Gabrielsen, S., Tennen, H., Tomich, P., & Park, C. (2012). The Relations Between Trauma Exposure and Prosocial Behavior. Psychological Trauma: Theory, Research, Practice, and Policy, 5(3), 286–294.
Gade, D., & Wenger, J. (2011). Combat Exposure and Mental Health: The Long-Term Effects Among US Vietnam and Gulf war Veterans. Health Economics, 20(4), 401–416. https://doi.org/10.1002/hec.1594.
George, J. M. (2000). Emotions and Leadership: The Role of Emotional Intelligence. Human Relations, 53(8), 1027–1055. https://doi.org/10.1177/0018726700538001.
Goleman, D. (2000). Leadership That Gets Results. Harvard Business Review, 78(2), 78.
Hall, J. H., & Fincham, F. D. (2005). Self-Forgiveness: The Stepchild of Forgiveness Research. Journal of Social and Clinical Psychology, 24(5), 621–637.
Hall, J. H., & Fincham, F. D. (2008). The Temporal Course of Self-Forgiveness. Journal of Social and Clinical Psychology, 27(2), 174–202.
Hart, P., & Walter, J. (2009). Political Psychology: Exploring the Human Factor in Political Life. In D. Marsh & G. Stoker (Eds.), Theory and Methods in Political Science (3rd ed.). Basingstoke: Palgrave.
Herbst, J., Mills, G., & McNamee, T. (2012). On the Fault Line: Managing Tensions and Divisions Within Societies. London, The Brenthurst Foundation.

Hutchison, E. (2016). Affective Communities in World Politics: Collective Emotions after Trauma (Cambridge Studies in International Relations). Cambridge: Cambridge University Press.
Institute for Justice and Reconciliation and the War Trauma Foundation. (2015). Healing communities – Transforming Society: Exploring the Interconnectedness Between Psychosocial Needs, Practice and Peacebuilding. http://www.ijr.org.za/home/wp-content/uploads/2016/11/IJR-Healing-communities-conference-WEB.pdf. Accessed 28 Apr 2020.
Janoff-Bulman, R. (1992). Shattered Assumptions: Towards a New Psychology of Trauma. New York, NY: Free Press.
Joseph, S., & Linley, P. A. (2008). Psychological Assessment of Growth Following Adversity: A Review. In S. Joseph & P. A. Linley (Eds.), Trauma, Recovery, and Growth: Positive Psychological Perspectives on Posttraumatic Stress (pp. 21–36). John Wiley & Sons Inc.
Kalayjian, A., & Paloutzian, R. (2009). Forgiveness and Reconciliation. New York: Springer-Verlag.
Kets de Vries, M. F. (2006). The Leadership Mystique: Leading Behavior in the Human Enterprise (2nd ed.). Harlow, England: Prentice Hall Financial Times.
Kinzer, S. (2017). Rwanda and the Dangers of Democracy. Boston Globe. http://stephenkinzer.com/2017/07/rwanda-and-the-dangers-of-democracy/. Accessed 28 Apr 2022.
Kramer, C., & Allen, S. (2018). Transformational Leadership Styles Pre- and Post-Trauma. Journal of Leadership Education, 7(3), 81–97. https://doi.org/10.12806/V17/I3/R5.
Kumsa, A. (2017). South Sudan Struggle for Independence, and It's Implications for Africa. RUDN Journal of Sociology, 17(4), 513–523.
Lorenzi, P. (2004). Managing for the Common Good: Prosocial Leadership. Organizational Dynamics, 33(3), 282–291.
María Prieto-Ursúa, M., & Echegoyen, I. (2015). Self-Forgiveness, Self-Acceptance or Intrapersonal Restoration? Open Issues in the Psychology of Forgiveness. https://www.researchgate.net/publication/283082022_Selffo rgiveness_self-acceptance_or_intrapersonal_restoration_Open_issues_in_the_ Psychology_of_Forgiveness. Accessed 13 May 2022.
Mayanja, E. (2013). Strengthening Ethical Political Leadership for Sustainable Peace and Social Justice in Africa: Uganda as a Case Study. Accord. https://www.accord.org.za/ajcr-issues/strengthening-ethical-political-leadership-for-sustainable-peace-and-social-justice-in-africa/. Accessed 28 Apr 2020.
Mayardit, S., Wel, P., & Yel, S. (2016). President Salva Kiir Mayardit: The Joshua of South Sudan - President Kiir's Speeches Before Independence. South Carolina: CreateSpace Independent Publishing Platform.

Montague, J. (2014). Thirty-One Nil - On the Road with Football's Outsiders: A World Cup Odyssey. London: Bloomsbury publishing.
Moon, C. (2009). Healing Past Violence: Traumatic Assumptions and Therapeutic Interventions in War and Reconciliation. Journal of Human Rights, 8(1), 71–91.
Moyer, J. D., Bohl, D., Hanna, T., Mapes, B. R., & Rafa M. (2019). Assessing the Impact of War on Development in Yemen. UNDP: Yemen.
Muid, O. (2006). Then I Lost My Spirit: An Analytical Essay on Transgenerational Theory and Its Application to Oppressed People of Color Nations. Ann Arbor, MI: UMI dissertation Services/ProQuest.
National Institute of Statistics of Rwanda. (2020). GDP National Accounts, 2019. http://www.statistics.gov.rw/publication/gdp-national-accounts-2019. Accessed 28 May 2020.
Natsios, A. S. (2012). Sudan, South Sudan, and Darfur: What Everyone Needs to Know. New York, NY: Oxford University Press.
Ng, L. C., López, B., Pritchard, M., & Deng, D. (2017). Posttraumatic Stress Disorder, Trauma, and Reconciliation in South Sudan. Social Psychiatry and Psychiatric Epidemiology, 52(6), 705–714. https://doi.org/10.1007/s00127-017-1376-y.
Nicholas, S., Kehinde, O., Imhonopi, D., & Evbuoma, I. (2016). Good Governance and Leadership: Pathway to Sustainable National Development in Nigeria. Journal of Public Administration and Governance, 6(1), 35–49.
Pomeroy, W. (1995). A working Model for Trauma: The Relationship Between Trauma and Violence. Pre- and Peri-Natal Psychology Journal, 10(2), 89–91.
Pruitt, W. R. (2018). Why Kagame Should Not Seek Another Term. African Journal of Criminology and Justice Studies, 11(1), 55–70.
Reyes, G., Ford, J., & Elhai, J. (2013). The Encyclopedia of Psychological Trauma. Wiley.
Reyntjens, F. (2004). Rwanda, Ten Years on: From Genocide to Dictatorship. African Affairs, 103, 177–210.
Roberts B., Damundu, E. Y., Lomoro O., & Sondorp E. (2009). Post-conflict Mental Health Needs: A Cross-Sectional Survey of Trauma, Depression and Associated Factors in Juba, Southern Sudan. BMC Psychiatry, 9(7). https://doi.org/10.1186/1471-244X-9-7.
Rothì, D., & Leavey, G. (2006). Mental Health Help-Seeking and Young People: A Review. Pastoral Care in Education, 24(3), 4–13. https://doi.org/10.1111/j.1468-0122.2006.00373.x.
Schaeffer, M. C. (2012). Why Are You Crying? The Impact of Parental Trauma on the Child. Retrieved from Sophia, the St. Catherine University repository website: https://sophia.stkate.edu/msw_papers/86. Accessed 12 May 2022.
Schmelzer, G. (2018). Journey Through Trauma: A Trail Guide to the 5-Phase Cycle of Healing Repeated Trauma. NY: Avery Pub Group.

Siegel, D. J. (2010). Mindsight: The New Science of Personal Transformation. New York, NY: Bantam Books.

Snoubar, Y., & Duman, N. (2016). Impact of Wars and Conflicts on Women and Children in Middle East: Health, Psychological, Educational and Social Crisis. European Journal of Social Sciences Education And Research, 6(2), 211–215. https://doi.org/10.26417/ejser.v6i2.

Soudan, F. (2015). Kagame: The President of Rwanda Speaks. New York, NY: Enigma Books.

Stephen Joseph, S. (2011). What Doesn't Kill Us: The New Psychology of Posttraumatic Growth. London: Hachette Digital.

Tedeschi, R. G., & Calhoun, L. G. (2004). Posttraumatic Growth: Conceptual Foundations and Empirical Evidence. Psychological Inquiry, 15, 1–18. https://doi.org/10.1207/s15327965pli1501_01.

Tedeschi, R. G., Park, C. L., & Calhoun, L. G. (1998). Posttraumatic Growth: Conceptual Issues. In R. G. Tedeschi, C. L. Park, & L. G. Calhoun (Eds.), The LEA Series in Personality and Clinical Psychology. Posttraumatic Growth: Positive Changes in the Aftermath of Crisis (pp. 2–22). Lawrence Erlbaum Associates Publishers.

The Holy Bible, New International Version. (1984). Matthew 15:14. Grand Rapids: Zondervan Publishing House.

The World Bank. (2020). The World Bank In Rwanda: Overview. https://www.worldbank.org/en/country/rwanda/overview. Accessed 12 May 2022.

Truman Library Institute. (2020). Historic Speeches: Truman's Farewell Address. Retrieved 29 June 2020, from https://www.trumanlibraryinstitute.org/farewell-address/.

Turner, J., & Mavin, S. (2008). What Can We Learn from Senior Leader Narratives? The Strutting and Fretting of Becoming a Leader. Journal of Leadership and Organization Development Journal,

UN Mission in South Sudan (UNMISS) (2014). Conflict in South Sudan: A Human Rights Report. https://reliefweb.int/sites/reliefweb.int/files/resources/UNMISS%20Conflict%20in%20South%20Sudan%20-%20A%20Human%20Rights%20Report.pdf. Accessed 28 May 2020.

UNDP. 2015. Search for a New Beginning: Perceptions of Truth, Justice, Reconciliation and Healing in South Sudan. https://www.undp.org/content/dam/southsudan/library/Rule%20of%20Law/Perception%20Survey%20Report%20Transitional%20Justice%20Reconciliation%20and%20Healing%20-.pdf. Accessed 05 May 2022.

University of Rwanda, Management Sciences for Health, and the Rockefeller Foundation. (2016). Technical Brief: The Development of Community-Based Health Insurance in Rwanda: Experiences and Lessons. https://www.msh.org/sites/default/files/the_development_of_cbhi_in_rwanda_experiences_and_lessons_-_technical_brief.pdf. Accessed 29 June 2020.

Vasterling, J. J., Daly, E. S., & Friedman, M. J. (2011). Posttraumatic Stress Reactions Over Time: The Battlefield, Homecoming, and Long-Term Course. In J. I. Ruzek, P. P. Schnurr, J. J. Vasterling, M. J. Friedman, J. I. Ruzek, P. P. Schnurr, ... M. J. Friedman (Eds.), Caring for Veterans with Deployment-Related Stress Disorders (pp. 35–55). Washington, DC: American Psychological Association.

Vinck, P., Pham, P. N., Stover, E., & Weinstein, H. M. (2007). Exposure to War Crimes and Implications for Peace Building in Northern Uganda. Journal of the American Medical Association, 298(5), 543–554. https://doi.org/10.1001/jama.298.5.543.

Waugh, C. (2004). Paul Kagame and Rwanda: Power, Genocide and the Rwandan Patriotic Front. Jefferson, N.C.: McFarland & Company, Inc., Publishers.

Weine, S. M., Becker, D. F., McGlashan, T. H., Laub, D., Lazrove, S., Vojvoda, D., & Hyman, L. (1995). Psychiatric Consequences of "Ethnic Cleansing": Clinical Assessments and Trauma Testimonies of Newly Resettled Bosnian Refugees. The American journal of psychiatry, 152(4), 536–542. https://doi.org/10.1176/ajp.152.4.536.

Weiss, T., & Berger, R. (Eds.) (2010). Posttraumatic Growth and Culturally Competent Practice: Lessons Learned from Around the World. Hoboken, NJ: John Wiley & Sons.

Werle, G. (2006). Justice in Transition – Prosecution and Amnesty in Germany and South Africa. Berlin: BWV, Berliner Wissenschafts-Verlag.

Wilson, J. P. (2004). PTSD and Complex PTSD: Symptoms, Syndromes, and Diagnoses. In J. P. Wilson & T. M. Keane (Eds.), Assessing Psychological Trauma and PTSD (2nd ed., pp. 7–44). New York, NY: The Guilford Press.

World Bank Group. (2020). Doing Business 2020: Comparing Business Regulation in 190 Economies. Washington, DC: International Bank for Reconstruction and Development.

World Economic Forum. (2020). Global Results. http://reports.weforum.org/global-gender-gap-report-2020/the-global-gender-gap-index-2020/results-and-analysis/. Accessed 28 May 2020.

Yip, J., & Wilson, M. S. (2010). Learning from Experience. In E. VanVelsor, C. D. McCauley, & M. N. Ruderman (Eds.), Handbook of Leadership Development (3rd ed., pp. 63–95). San Francisco, CA: Jossey-Bass.

CHAPTER 6

A Systematic Review on the Effects of PTSD Associated Alcohol Abuse on Social Economic Status Among Youth Living in Kiambu County, Kenya

Joseph Theuri

INTRODUCTION

Problem Statement

There is a plethora of literature on Post-Traumatic Stress Disorder (PTSD)-related alcohol abuse and its negative effect on the socio-economic well-being of the youth. Most extant literature focuses on various parts of the world but not Kenya. Although studies have been undertaken in Kenya, most studies do not relate PTSD and alcohol abuse and by extension, socio-economic status. Thus, there is a knowledge lacuna regarding the effect of PTSD-related alcohol abuse on the socio-economic status of youth in Kenya. Accordingly, more studies are needed to bridge this gap, and produce findings that can inform government and psychosocial support professionals on how to best mitigate the negative

J. Theuri (✉)
Tangaza University College, Nairobi, Kenya

© The Author(s), under exclusive license to Springer Nature Switzerland AG 2023
J. Adero Ngala et al. (eds.), *Innovations in Peace and Security in Africa*, https://doi.org/10.1007/978-3-031-39043-2_6

influences of alcohol abuse on the socio-economic status of youth with PTSD. Indeed, it is critical that this social phenomenon is addressed as the youth are a vital contributing sector of the economic development of the country.

Methods

This study adopts a systematic review approach with data being collected from existing literature articles. The study used qualitative meta-synthesis. The findings obtained confirmed that there was a significant effect of alcohol-related PTSD on the socio-economic status among the youth living in Kiambu County, Kenya. Alcohol abuse PTSD has social and economic effects that include relationships breakdown and loss of income among other related effects. This paper reviews various effects of alcohol use and PTSD further stresses the importance of treating alcoholism through initiating rehabilitation programs which should be individualized according to the specific situation of the affected person(s).

Theoretical Foundation

This study is based on The Social-Ecological Model (SEM). The Social-Ecological Model (SEM) as expounded by Stokols (1996) is a theory-based framework that considers the multifaceted and interactive effects of personal and environmental factors that determine behaviours. It can be argued that five nested, hierarchical levels of the SEM namely: individual, interpersonal, community, organizational, and policy/enabling environment predict behaviour. Within the scope of this study, it can be claimed that individual factors related to traumatic experiences and PTSD could affect alcohol abuse behaviours of the youth. As such, and as conceptualized by this current study, the presence of traumatic experiences at community and family levels could contribute to the likelihood of the youth to abuse alcohol and drugs, factors that can affect their socio-economic status.

The issue of alcohol abuse in Kenya is deeply rooted and has continued to affect the well-being of the youthful population. This study could benefit psychosocial support professionals to come up with tangible ways of helping youth with PTSD. The government could also learn how to put in place policy measures aimed at helping persons who suffer from PTSD to control their propensity to take to alcohol abuse which could predispose them to alcohol abuse. Other researchers and scholars could also benefit from this study through increased literature on the study subject. Non-state actors could also garner valuable information that could guide their programming processes.

Background

Research shows Post Traumatic Stress Disorder (PTSD) is often linked with alcohol abuse. Khoury et al. (2010) posit that exposure to traumatic experiences has positive linkages with substance use disorders (SUDs). This is more severe among the young. In their study, Khoury et al. found out that in a highly traumatized population, there were high levels of lifetime dependence on various substances. In such populations, the most abused substances were marijuana (44.8%), alcohol (39%), cocaine (34.1%), and heroin/opiates (6.2%). This abuse has significant socio-economic consequences such as endemic poverty.

In South Korea, Emery et al. (2016) PTSD-related and non-PTSD-related alcohol abuse pushed families to put in place mechanisms aimed at controlling physical intimate partner violence (IPV). The study shows that random effects regression and zero-inflated Poisson Regression models show that family members' interventions checked the negative effects of such alcohol abuse such as wastage of family resources. In a study focused on a sample of 171 African-American women, Watson-Singleton et al. (2019) show that alcohol abuse is catalysed by IPV as well as PTSD and that this was mediated by and other psychosocial factors mediate this link.

Magidson et al. (2016) argue that PTSD experiences led to increases in alcohol and other drug abuse among adolescents (16–18 years) in Johannesburg, South Africa. Indeed exposure to violence, other traumatic experiences, and sexual activity were related to alcoholism in females and males. This went on to affect the future of teenagers as well as their well-being.

Adere et al. (2017) in South Africa posit that some of the catalysts of psychoactive substance use among students of Woldia University in Ethiopia were traumatic experiences in the lives of teenagers as well as challenges related to their background such as poverty. The study shows that continuous abuse of such substances had lasting effects on the socio-economic well-being of the children studied.

In Liberia, Petruzzi et al. (2018) posits that exposure to substance abuse has risks such as emotional instability, academic failure, and community poverty. Although the study was not directly linked to PTSD, it shows that alcohol abuse, irrespective of its causes, was closely linked to success in poverty at individual and community levels.

In Lebanon a study by Yassin et al. (2018) undertaken using the social ecology framework shows that alcohols use is a result of various social relations and lax policies. It was also attributable to personal challenges such as exposure to PTSD among other challenges. Maniglio (2016) shows that peer victimization and other challenges in the lives of teenagers PTSD and family background contributed to alcohol use and misuse.

Smith et al. (2017) show that PTSD and depression play a major role as links between deployment stressors to work, and family outcomes as well as alcohol abuse. Ruglass et al. (2016) show that there is a positive association of cumulative trauma, PTSD, and substance use disorder (SUD) and arrest probability among the socio-economically disadvantaged African-American and Latino mothers. This went on to further affect their social economic status.

A study by Karsberg and Elklit (2015) in "Victimization and PTSD in A rural Kenyan youth sample" shows that exposure of Potentially Traumatic Events (PTEs) and Post Traumatic Distress Disorder (PTSD) prevalence among adolescents leads to alcohol abuse; which may have lasting effects in their future such financial instability.

As shown in the preceding discourse there is a positive link between PTSD-related alcohol abuse and socio-economic challenges and impoverishment. This current study sets out to carry out a systematic review of the effects of PTSD associated alcohol abuse on social economic status among youth in Kenya.

Literature Review

Post-traumatic stress disorder (PTSD) is a psychopathological outcome of being exposed to a stressful experience that puts one's psychological and/or bodily well-being at jeopardy. Several psychoactive substances, including cannabis, alcohol, cocaine, MDMA, and synthetic cannabinoid, have been related to PTSD. According to Adere et al. (2017), psychoactive substance usage is very common among students. Substance misuse can lead to mental instability, scholastic failure, and poverty in the community (Petruzzi et al., 2018).

Cannabis usage has been related to PTSD, especially in people who have experienced trauma in the past (Metrik et al. 2022). Cannabis users have been reported to have a PTSD-like impact in several studies, with heightened alertness and negative mood (Adere et al., 2017). Continued cannabis usage has been linked to addiction, which has been demonstrated to have a negative influence on academic performance (Suerken et al. 2016).

Alcohol abuse is considered a severe public health issue that stems from a variety of social relationships, permissive policies, and PTSD, among other factors. Alcohol abuse is a global public health issue that has resulted in a slew of social, psychological, and physiological issues. It's a big part of a lot of different kinds of violence, and it's tied to a lot of mental illnesses like despair and anxiety. Many car accidents and other mishaps are caused by alcohol. Alcoholism, or the excessive consumption of alcohol, is a serious health issue that can lead to death. This condition is caused by a complicated combination of circumstances. PTSD has been connected to alcohol misuse, regardless of the etiology. Karsberg and Elklit (2015) found that homeless individuals with PTSD were more likely to be substance abusers, and substance abusers with PTSD were less likely to have legitimate jobs and more likely to be homeless.

Brown et al. (2016) discovered that women with post-traumatic stress disorder (PTSD) exhibited higher neuroticism scores than healthy women, which was linked to higher alcohol use in the PTSD group. PTSD is a disorder that is brought on by a traumatic incident and manifests as flashbacks and nightmares. The researchers reasoned that because patients with PTSD are more likely to experience physiological and emotional symptoms following a stressful event, they may have a stronger urge for alcohol to help them cope.

Breet et al. (2016) carried out a study titled "Posttraumatic Stress Disorder and Depression in Men and Women Who Perpetrate Intimate Partner Violence". This study aimed at examining the prevalence of intimate partner violence (IPV) perpetrated by men and women and the association between symptoms of depression or post-traumatic stress disorder (PTSD) and IPV perpetration between men and women. Data were collected through self-report questionnaires administered to a sample size of 210 people from three peri-urban areas in South Africa. The findings show that gender differences were not a contributing factor to physical assault and psychological aggression.

Adolescents with a history of trauma, depression, or post-traumatic stress disorder (PTSD) are more likely to be exposed to communal violence. This could have a significant impact on their mental health, possibly leading to comorbidity. Nöthling et al. (2016) conducted research to determine the role of demographic characteristics, trauma, community violence, and different types of abuse and neglect in the prediction of PTSD levels in people with and without the disorder. A sample of 215 adolescents with emotional and behavioural issues was chosen from the Western Cape region of South Africa for the study. The findings demonstrate that teenagers with a history of trauma, depression, or PTSD had a greater level of emotional distress after clinical examinations and regression analysis.

PTSD and depression, according to Smith et al. (2017), play a significant role in the linkages between deployment stresses and job and family outcomes. The researchers discovered a high correlation between a person's chance of acquiring PTSD and their level of depression when they returned from deployment in this study. The research is the first to establish a bidirectional association between deployment pressures and mental health difficulties. Although depression and PTSD symptoms frequently coexist, the researchers discovered that increased levels of depression were linked to deployment-related stressors, such as witnessing violence or being exposed to traumatic events, and had a stronger relationship with PTSD than the other way around in the study.

According to Ruglass et al. (2016), PTSD and substance use disorders (SUD) are risk factors for individuals experiencing trauma and, as a result, increasing their vulnerability to criminal conduct. Their findings suggest that those with PTSD and SUD have a higher chance of being arrested than people who only have PTSD. Furthermore, the study suggested that those who have both PTSD and SUD had a higher chance of getting arrested than people who only have SUD.

In adolescents who have been exposed to substance misuse, PTSD symptoms can emerge in a variety of ways. Students, for example, may experience anxiety, irritation, hostility, and hyperarousal, all of which are signs of PTSD (Brown et al. 2014). These symptoms might make it difficult to function on a daily basis, which can lead to academic failure. Furthermore, individuals with PTSD symptoms may have a more difficult time recovering from academic stress and may require more time to finish assignments and tests.

Examining the link between depression, substance addiction, and general stress and four symptom clusters in the Dysphoria factor model is a crucial step toward understanding the complicated relationship between PTSD and other illnesses. Schwartz et al. (2019) looked at the links between depression, substance misuse, and general stress and four symptom clusters in the Dysphoria factor model, two of which were also linked to PTSD. Cognitive avoidance, hyper arousal, emotional numbness, and poor attention were the four symptom clusters identified. In order to help students reach their academic goals, it is critical to identify and treat pupils who are suffering from PTSD. Determining a student's level of social anxiety is one technique to identify those who are suffering from PTSD (Adere et al. 2017).

Analysis

Various studies were reviewed. These were drawn from over relevant 30 studies. Most of these were excluded and 5 of them analysed since they met the inclusion criteria. PTSD-related alcohol abuse was recorded by Kinyua et al. (2019) in "Socio-economic Factors Influencing Alcohol and Substance Abuse among College Students in Murang'a County, Kenya". A sample of 417 students from 5 colleges was selected using descriptive cross-sectional research design, stratified sampling, and systematic random sampling. Quantitative and qualitative methods were used where data was collected using structured questionnaires and analysed using SPSS version 23 and chi-square test. The findings show that there is a need to increase awareness of alcohol abuse resulting from PTSD and its effects such as diminishing socio-economic impacts.

Chege et al. (2017) in "An Investigation of the Factors Contributing to Drug and Substance Abuse among the Youth in Kenya: A Survey of Select Rehabilitation Centres in Mombasa County" sampled 89 students. Data was collected using questionnaires and analysed using SPSS Version 21 and descriptive and inferential statistics. Students suffering from PTSD were more prone to abuse drugs compared to those not doing so. High levels of substance abuse challenge the performance of students and could have long-lasting implications on the socio-economic status of the students.

Jenkins et al. studied "PTSD in Kenya and Its Associated Risk Factors: A Cross-Sectional Household Survey." The findings show that 48% have experience of severe trauma and a 10.6% prevalence of PTSD which indicates a prevalence of PTSD in rural Kenya. The risk factors included being female, single, self-employed, previous life experiences, and having a common mental disorder (CMD). Those who took to alcohol as a coping mechanism ended up more impoverished than those who did not do so. This emanates from the fact that alcohol abuse reduced their abilities to work or access other socio-economic opportunities.

Mbwayo et al. (2020) carried out a study titled "Trauma among Kenyan School Children in Urban and Rural Settings: PTSD Prevalence and Correlates". This study focused on estimating the prevalence and correlates of PTSD during the post-election violence period among Kenyan school children. The UCLA PTSD index was used in data collection and analysis in a sample of 2482 school children aged 11–17 years both in urban and rural Kenya. The findings show that a majority of these children had experienced or witnessed a form of violence during this period translating to high levels of PTSD. They went on to be more prone to poverty and missed opportunities due to the propensity to abuse alcohol and other hard drugs.

Kiambi (2018) carried out a study titled "Factors Influencing Drugs and Substance Abuse among Public Secondary School Students in Kiambu County, Kenya." This study used the descriptive survey study design to achieve its objective. A sample of 140 respondents drawn from form three students and teachers using simple random sampling and purposive sampling techniques was used during this study. Data was collected by the use of questionnaires, analysed using SPSS software version 21.0, and presented in the form of frequencies and percentages. The findings show that there is a high prevalence of the use of drugs and substance abuse among the student population, especially in the male students, and this behaviour was influenced by PTSD and peer pressure among others. Alcohol abuse had immense negative socio-economic ramifications on the abusers especially after school due to the likelihood to score poor grades; affecting their transition to higher levels of learning.

Conclusion

The issue of alcohol abuse in Kenya is deeply rooted and has continued to affect the well-being of the youthful population. This analysis of the literature shows that PTSD related to alcohol abuse, though not well studied in Kenya, impacts youth in significant ways including their learning processes (e.g. transition to colleges and other institutions of higher learning), as well as employment prospects and susceptibility to impoverishment. This study can benefit psychosocial support professionals to come up with tangible ways of helping youth with PTSD. Other researchers and scholars could also benefit from this study through additional research that can deepen scholarship and policy prescriptions for this important subject. Non-governmental organizations could garner valuable information that could guide their programming processes. The government could also learn how to implement policy measures aimed at helping persons who suffer from PTSD to control their propensity to take alcohol, which could predispose them to its abuse. Additionally, the government should put in place funding strategies for the rehabilitation of youth suffering from PTSD. Government empowerment programs in Kenya should factor in mechanisms for ensuring that youth with PTSD-related alcohol abuse can access funding to enhance their socio-economic status.

References

Adere, A., Yimer, N. B., Kumsa, H., & Liben M. L. (2017). Determinants of Psychoactive Substances Use Among Woldia University Students in North-Eastern Ethiopia. BMC Res Notes, 10, 441. https://doi.org/10.1186/s13 104-017-2763-x.

Arbona, C., & Schwartz, J. P. (2016). Posttraumatic Stress Disorder Symptom Clusters, Depression, Alcohol Abuse, and General Stress among Hispanic Male Fire-fighters. Hispanic Journal of Behavioural Sciences, 38(4), 507–522.

Breet, E., Seedat, S., & Kagee, A. (2016). Posttraumatic Stress Disorder and Depression in Men and Women Who Perpetrate Intimate Partner Violence. Journal of Interpersonal Violence, 34(10), 2181–2198.

Brown, N., Wojtalik, J. A., & Turkel, M. et al. (2016). Neuroticism and It's Associated Brain Activation in Women with PTSD. Journal of Interpersonal Violence, 35(1–2), 341–363.

Brown, W. J., Bruce, S. E., & Buchholz, K. R. et al. (2014). Affective Dispositions and PTSD Symptom Clusters in Female Interpersonal Trauma Survivors. Journal of Interpersonal Violence, 31(3), 407–424.

Chege, R., Mungai, P., & Oresi, S. (2017). An Investigation of the Factors Contributing To Drug and Substance Abuse among the Youth in Kenya: A Survey of Select Rehabilitation Centres in Mombasa County. International Journal of Public Health, 1, 1.

Daw, J., Margolis, R., & Wright, L. (2017). Emerging Adulthood, Emergent Health Lifestyles: Sociodemographic Determinants of Trajectories of Smoking, Binge Drinking, Obesity, and Sedentary Behaviour. Journal of

Health and Social Behaviour, 58(2), 181–197. Retrieved March 14, 2020, from www.jstor.org/stable/44504733.

Emery, C. R., Wu, S., Yang, H., et al. (2016, May 8). Informal Control by Family and Risk Markers for Alcohol Abuse/Dependence in Seoul. Journal of Interpersonal Violence, 34(5), 1000–1020.

Ferrajão, P. C., & Oliveira, R. A. (2015). Portuguese War Veterans: Moral Injury and Factors Related to Recovery From PTSD. Qualitative Health Research, 26(2), 204–214.

Hollingsworth, D. W., Gauthier J. M., McGuire A. P. et al. (2018). Intolerance of Uncertainty Mediates Symptoms of PTSD and Depression in African American Veterans with Comorbid PTSD and Substance Use Disorders. Journal of Black Psychology, 44(7), 667–688.

Jenkins, R., Othieno, C., & Omollo, R. et al. (2015). Probable Post Traumatic Stress Disorder in Kenya and Its Associated Risk Factors: A Cross-Sectional Household Survey. International Journal of Environmental Research and Public Health, 12, 13494–13509. ISSN 1660-4601. www.mdpi.com/jou rnal/ijerph, https://doi.org/10.3390/ijerph121013494.

Kaminer, D., Eagle, G. & Crawford-Browne, S. (2016). Continuous Traumatic Stress as a Mental and Physical Health Challenge: Case Studies from South Africa. Journal of Health Psychology, 23(8), 1038–1049.

Karsberg, S., & Elklit, A. (2015). Victimization and PTSD in A Rural Kenyan Youth Sample. Clinical Practice and Epidemiology in Mental Health, 8(1), 91–101.

Khoury, L., Tang, Y. L., Bradley, B., Cubells, J. F., & Ressler, K. J. (2010). Substance Use, Childhood Traumatic Experience, and Posttraumatic Stress Disorder in an Urban Civilian Population. Depression and Anxiety, 27(12), 1077–1086.

Kiambi, M. J. (2018). Factors Influencing Drugs and Substance Abuse among Public Secondary School Students in Kiambu County, Kenya. International Journal of Psychology, 3(1), 1–23.

Kinyua, D. G., Nyamai, J. J., Nyaberi, J. M., & Wanyoike P. K. (2019). Socio-economic Factors Influencing Alcohol and Substance Abuse among College Students in Murang'a County, Kenya. International Journals of Academics & Research, IJARKE Science & Technology Journal, 1(4), 8–18.

Magidson, J. F., Dietrich, J., Otwombe, K. N. et al. (2016). Psychosocial Correlates of Alcohol and Other Substance Use Among Low-Income Adolescents in Peri-Urban Johannesburg, South Africa: A Focus on Gender Differences. Journal of Health Psychology, 22(11), 1415–1425.

Maniglio, R. (2016). Bullying and Other Forms of Peer Victimization in Adolescence and Alcohol Use. Trauma, Violence, & Abuse, 18(4), 457–473.

Mbwayo, A. W., Mathai, M., Harder, V. S. et al. (2020). Trauma among Kenyan School Children in Urban and Rural Settings: PTSD Prevalence and Correlates. Journal of Child & Adolescent Trauma, 13, 63–73. https://doi.org/10.1007/s40653-019-00256-2.
Metrik, J., Stevens, A. K., Gunn, R. L., Borsari, B., & Jackson, K. M. (2022). Cannabis use and posttraumatic stress disorder: prospective evidence from a longitudinal study of veterans. Psychological medicine, 52(3), 446–456. https://doi.org/10.1017/S003329172000197X.
Mwangi, C. (2018). Media Influence on Public Policy in Kenya: The Case of Illicit Brew Consumption. SAGE Open, 8(2), 88–109.
Mwangi, J. W. (2019). Nature and Causes of Conflicts Existing Between and Among Women and Men Living in Informal Settlement Areas. A Case of Kiandutu Informal Settlement in Kiambu County, Kenya. International Journal of Academic Research in Business, Arts and Science, 1(4), 1–14.
Nöthling, J., Suliman, S., Martin L., et al. (2016). Differences in Abuse, Neglect, and Exposure to Community Violence in Adolescents With and Without PTSD and Depression. Journal of Interpersonal Violence, 34(21–22), 4357–4383.
Petruzzi, L. J., Pullen, S. J., Lange, B. C. L. et al. (2018). Contributing Risk Factors for Substance Use among Youth in Post-Conflict Liberia. Qualitative Health Research, 28(12), 1827–1838.
Pollard, M. W., & McKinney, C. (2016). Parental Physical Force and Alcohol Use in Emerging Adults: Mediation by Psychological Problems. Journal of Interpersonal Violence, 34(10), 2087–2109.
Riber, K. (2017). Trauma Complexity and Child Abuse: A Qualitative Study of Attachment Narratives in Adult Refugees with PTSD. Transcultural Psychiatry, 54(5–6), 840–869.
Ruglass, L. M., Espinosa, A., Sykes, M. et al. (2016). Direct and Indirect Effects of Cumulative Trauma, PTSD, and Substance Use Disorder on Probability of Arrest Among Lower-Income African American and Latina Women. Race and Justice, 8(2), 126–153.
Russell, C. A., Hamby, A. M., Grube, J. W., & Russell, D. W. (2019). When Do Public Health Epilogues Correct the Influence of Alcohol Story Lines on Youth? The Interplay of Narrative Transportation and Persuasion Knowledge. Journal of Public Policy & Marketing, 38(3), 316–331.
Schwartz, B., Kaminer, D., & Hardy A., et al. (2019). Gender Differences in the Violence Exposure Types That Predict PTSD and Depression in Adolescents. Journal of Interpersonal Violence, 37. https://doi.org/10.1016/j.chiabu.2012.12.011.
Smith, B. N., Taverna, A. B., & Fox, A. B., et al. (2017). The Role of PTSD, Depression, and Alcohol Misuse Symptom Severity in Linking Deployment

Stressor Exposure and Post-Military Work and Family Outcomes in Male and Female Veterans. Clinical Psychological Science, 5(4), 664–682.

Stokols, D. (1996). Translating Social Ecological Theory into Guidelines for Community Health Promotion. American journal of health promotion, 10 (4), 282–298.

Suerken, C. K., Reboussin, B. A., Egan, K. L., Sutfin, E. L., Wagoner, K. G., Spangler, J., & Wolfson, M. (2016). Marijuana use trajectories and academic outcomes among college students. Drug and alcohol dependence, 162, 137–145. https://doi.org/10.1016/j.drugalcdep.2016.02.041.

Watson-Singleton, N. N., Florez, I. A., Clunnie, A. M., et al. (2019). Psychosocial Mediators between Intimate Partner Violence and Alcohol Abuse in Low-Income African American Women. Violence against Women. Advance online publication. https://doi.org/10.1177/1077801219850331.

Yassin, N., Afifi, R., & Singh, N., et al. (2018). "There Is Zero Regulation on the Selling of Alcohol": The Voice of the Youth on the Context and Determinants of Alcohol Drinking in Lebanon. Qualitative Health Research, 28(5), 733–744.

CHAPTER 7

The Nexus Between Peacekeeping and Counterterrorism: A Case of African Union Mission in Somalia

Michelle A. Digolo Nyandong

INTRODUCTION

Peacekeeping has become more sophisticated since the end of the Cold War, occupying a significant role as a mechanism for conflict management for institutions such as the United Nations (UN) and the African Union (AU). Peace operations in Africa cover a broad spectrum of activities aimed at promoting peace and stability in deadly armed conflicts. Reeling from the failures in Somalia and Rwanda, peacekeeping in Africa shifted from traditional peacekeeping models to multidimensional operations. Traditional models of peacekeeping are characterized by strict neutrality,[1] monitoring and observer missions, and the creation of buffer

[1] Kenkel, Kai Michael. (2013). Five Generations of Peace Operations: From the "Thin Blue Line" to "Painting a Country Blue". Brasiliera Politica Internacionale 56(1), 122–143.

M. A. D. Nyandong (✉)
Life & Peace Institute, Nairobi, Kenya
e-mail: michellenyandong@gmail.com

© The Author(s), under exclusive license to Springer Nature Switzerland AG 2023
J. Adero Ngala et al. (eds.), *Innovations in Peace and Security in Africa*,
https://doi.org/10.1007/978-3-031-39043-2_7

zones[2] between belligerents. Multi-dimensional operations on the other hand involve myriad peacebuilding tasks and indirect actions in the transition from war to peace, such as participating in the organization of elections and ferrying ballot boxes. As violent conflict has shifted from interstate war to largely sub-state violence, these peacebuilding activities are intended to aid in rebuilding the economic, social, political, and legal institutions of a nation in transition. However, such a broad portfolio arguably deviates from the limitations within traditional conceptions of peacekeeping. For example, twenty-two years ago the Brahimi Report (2000)[3] recommended that UN peacekeepers should not be deployed in peace operations where there is no peace to keep; and, in "An Agenda for Peace (1992)" former UN Secretary General Boutros Boutros-Ghali stated that peacekeeping is "a technique that expands the possibilities for both the prevention of conflict and the making of peace."[4] Indeed, peacekeeping should not be put in the same box as conflict resolution, peacemaking, and diplomacy, as it is not designed to address the root causes of conflicts. Without a course-correction this expanded approach to peacekeeping will plague future operations in a Sisyphean cycle of repeated mistakes. We will unpack this component in this chapter.

The terrorist attack on the Twin Towers on September 11, 2001, was a tipping point in international security, as it was an encroachment of extremely dangerous non-state actors on US soil. It was a defining moment in the conceptualization of security, and the means of ensuring and maintaining it. African states also felt the effects of the terror attack, due to increased conflict and insecurity instigated by terrorist activities within their borders. According to the Global Terrorism Index, terrorism attacks rapidly increased over the last two decades.[5] This directly affected the nature, mandates and tasks assigned to components in Peace Keeping

---

[2] Adebajo, Adekeye. (2011). UN Peacekeeping in Africa: From the Suez Crisis to the Sudan Conflicts (p. 10). Lynne Rienner Publishers.

[3] United Nations. (2000). Report of the Panel on United Nations Peace Operations, A/55/305–S/2000/809. https://www.un.org/ruleoflaw/files/brahimi%20report%20peacekeeping.pdf.

[4] O'Neill, John Terence, & Rees, Nick. (2005). United Nations Peacekeeping in the Post-Cold War Era (p. 5). Routledge.

[5] Institute for Economics & Peace. Global Terrorism Index 2019: Measuring the Impact of Terrorism (pp. 1–12). Sydney. http://visionofhumanity.org/app/uploads/2019/11/GTI-2019web.pdf.

Operations (PKO) especially in relation to the principle of impartiality.[6] The ambivalent relationship on the African continent between PKOs and terrorism is critical. PKOs are now compelled to respond in weak states, where rebel groups are fragmented and jihadist groups and insurgencies flourish. Instead of dealing with states, peacekeepers deal with armed groups pushing to achieve their unholy goals. In contrast to Brahimi, the rise of terrorism has meant that peacekeepers are mandated to fight terrorism in counterterrorism theatres, posing great challenges to their own personal safety, thus begging the question—should peacekeepers fight terrorism?

In 2015, the United Nations High Level Independent Panel on Peace Operations (HIPPO) recommended that due to doctrinal reasons the UN could not go beyond peacekeeping and suggested that the United Nations Security Council (UNSC) should consult the AU and other bodies regarding peace enforcement mandates.[7] This is pegged on the fact that UN peacekeeping operations do not have the appropriate unity of command. In order to have a successful mission, UN staff officers need to have synergy of efforts as well as the requisite military hardware (air support, artillery, troops, etc.) to conduct offensive combat operations when necessary.[8] Although in theory this argument is quite plausible, the AU lacks the array of multidimensional capabilities or financial power which would permit it to take on or sustain peacekeeping operations. Owing to these comparative advantages and inadequacies, a complimentary model has emerged. This involves the UN looking to the AU to take on the role as the first responder to steady eruptions of violent conflicts on the continent. Once relative stability has been reinstated, the responsibility is shifted to the UN.[9] This model has been used in Central African Republic and Mali. The point was later buttressed by UN Secretary

---

[6] Tardy, Thierry. (2007). The UN and the Use of Force: A Marriage Against Nature. Security Dialogue, 38(1), 4–8, 49–70.

[7] United Nations. (2015). Report of the High-Level Independent Panel on Peace Operations. https://peaceoperationsreview.org/wp-content/uploads/2015/08/HIPPO_Report_1_June_2015.pdf.

[8] United Nations. (2008). United Nations Peacekeeping Operations Principles and Guidelines. https://peacekeeping.un.org/sites/default/files/capstone_eng_0.pdf.

[9] Cedric de Coning. (2017). Peace enforcement in Africa: Doctrinal distinctions between the African Union and United Nations. Contemporary Security Policy, 38(1), 145–160.

General António Guterres when he stated on 20 November 2018 that UN peacekeeping has its constraints in conducting operations with peace enforcement and counterterrorism mandates, and is therefore looking for symbiotic partnerships with the AU and other sub-regional organizations to fill the gap.[10] Using the principle of subsidiarity, the AU has stronger political legitimacy as it is closer to the African governance systems, which means that it has closer links to Africans in comparison to the UN.[11] This symbiotic association between the UN and AU has dovetailed some of the institutional challenges while simultaneously strengthening PKO on the continent.

This shifting of lenses through which peacekeeping is viewed can be seen in the evolution of the AMISOM mandates over the years. With the adoption of UNSCR 1744 (2007),[12] and UNSCR 1772 six months later,[13] AMISOM was deployed under Chapter VII as a peacekeeping mission in an active warzone. UNSCR 1772 only authorized AMISOM to conduct "all necessary measures" to protect the locations under its supervision such as the Transitional Institutions of the Somali government.[14] The mission was not to fight against al-Shabaab actively and offensively, as the United States and Ethiopian troops did before them. Rather, they were to support "dialogue and reconciliation" by providing protection to all parties involved.[15] In 2012, UNSCR 2036 under Chapter VII of the United Nations Charter authorized AMISOM to increase its presence in the four sectors outlined in its strategic concept "to reduce the

---

[10] UN Web TV, The United Nations Live & On Demand. (2018). Remarks of António Guterres to the 8407th Meeting of the United Nations Security Council Open Debate on Strengthening Peacekeeping Operations in Africa. http://webtv.un.org/watch/ant%C3%B3nio-guterresun-secretary-general-on-strengthening-peacekeepingoperations-in-africa-security-council-8407thmeeting/5969510237001/.

[11] Ndiaye, Michelle. (2016). The Relationship between the AU and the RECs/RMs in Relation to Peace and Security in Africa: Subsidiarity and Inevitable Common Destiny in the Future of African Peace Operations From the Janjaweed to Boko Haram (p. 52). Cédric de Coning, Linnéa Gelot and John Karlsrud (Eds.), Uppsala, Nordiska Afrikainstutet. http://nai.divaportal.org/smash/get/diva2:913028/FULLTEXT02.pdf.

[12] http://unscr.com/en/resolutions/1744 UNSCR 1744.

[13] http://unscr.com/en/resolutions/1772 UNSCR 1722.

[14] https://www.un.org/ga/search/view_doc.asp?symbol=S/RES/1744(2007) S/RES/1744 (2007). UNSCR.

[15] Cellamare, Giovanni, & Ingravallo, Ivan. (2018). Peace Maintenance in Africa: Open Legal Issues (p. 89). Springer.

threat posed by Al-Shabaab and other armed opposition groups in order to establish conditions for effective and legitimate governance across Somalia."[16]

Notably, the merger between PKOs and counterterrorism is not unique to Somalia. In Mali, for example, this convergence is complex and constantly developing. The mandates of several PKOs in Africa also have been modified by the UNSC for peacekeepers to fight against violent non-state actors. However, if peace must be enforced, is it a peace that will last? While the Brahimi Report (2000) cautioned the UN of intervening in several conflicts, especially when there is no peace to keep, this principle has de facto set aside by providing PKOs with robust mandates. This is evident in Mali, the Democratic Republic of Congo— United Nations Force Intervention Brigade, Central African Republic, and Somalia where peace enforcement and the usage of offensive military capabilities is part of the mandate rather than an exception. Moreover, these UN stabilization missions have all been modified at great human, economic and political costs. Somalia has had to contend with well-financed and unfaltering Islamist-stirred insurgencies, which have taken advantage of centre-periphery political pressures, perpetual humanitarian crises, weak governance, internationally linked organized criminal networks, banditry, and lawlessness. In both Mali and Somalia, AU-led peace support operations have been a central pillar in the political and security stabilization efforts, albeit with deficiencies and challenges that characterized AMISOM's early struggle to secure Mogadishu. However, the distinctiveness of AMISOM lies in the fact that it is the first AU-led mission to be deployed in a terrorist sponsored armed conflict. Additionally, AMISOM had the greatest number of personnel among peacekeeping missions, boasting a strength of 22,126 military and police officers.[17]

This era of peacekeeping involves robust mandates, engaging in asymmetric warfare; and peacekeepers are being deployed to regions where there was no peace to keep in the first place. This implies "the biggest challenge for future peace operations, probably, will be the war on

---

[16] Security Council, SC/10550. (2012). Security Council Requests African Union to Increase Troop Level of Somalia Mission to 17,700, Establish Expanded Presence in Keeping with Strategic Concept. https://www.un.org/press/en/2012/sc10550.doc.htm.

[17] African Union, AMISOM (2014). https://amisom-au.org/2014/03/amisom-and-somali-national-army-drive-al-shabaab-out-of-six-towns/. AMISOM and Somali National Army Drive Al-Shabaab Out of Six Towns.

terrorism."[18] But where there is no peace to keep what do we do? Merge two doctrines with a wide range of activities to attain decisive victory—a favourable achievement in military parlance that determines the result of a war and hence shapes the post-war landscape.[19]

Changing the modus operandi of UN peacekeeping missions, particularly as regards counterterrorism operations, is complicated by questions of legitimacy, capability (human resource, finances, lack of strong counterterrorism frameworks to guide peacekeeping operations), and ethics. This chapter discusses these issues in three parts. Firstly, it provides an analysis of AMISOM, how it came to be and its mandate. Secondly, it discusses the push and pull between peacekeeping principles such as impartiality and non-use of force and counterterrorism. Can peacekeeping as it were, lose its meaning once more focus is placed on the militarization of peace in places where there is no peace to keep in comparison to focusing on political processes which are supposed to be more sustainable? Thirdly, it captures the role of the AU in peacekeeping and the need to develop new rules of engagement for counterterrorism operations. The chapter concludes with a reflection on the convergence of peacekeeping and counterterrorism in AMISOM and argues that the binaries of peacekeeping and counterterrorism, which are often seen to be at cross purposes, are no longer polar opposites but jointed by the constantly evolving threats to the international security system. This shift is espoused by the United Nations Global Counter-Terrorism Strategy a one-of-a-kind tool for bolstering counterterrorism efforts at the national, regional, and worldwide levels. In this chapter counterinsurgency and counterterrorism will be used interchangeably as the AU and, by extension the UN, has not made a distinction in its operations regarding the two principles in multidimensional PKOs as they respond to new transnational non-state complexities.

---

[18] Leurdijk, Dick. (2004). NATO's Shifting Priorities: From Peace Support Operations to Counter-Terrorism. In Tardy, Thierry (Ed.), Peace Operations after 11 September 2001 (pp. 66, 75). London, Frank Cass.

[19] Gray, C. S. (2002). Defining and Achieving Decisive Victory (pp. 10–11). U.S. Army War College.

The Inception of AMISOM

Harakat al-Shabaab al-Mujahedeen, frequently referred to as al-Shabaab, is an offshoot of the Union of Islamic Courts (UIC), which had origins in the now defunct Al-Itihaad Al-Islamiyah (AIAI). The UIC controlled Mogadishu from 2006 and expanded its reach to the southeast of Somalia, with the purpose of creating a Greater Somali state through the unification of all Somalis in Kenya, Ethiopia, and Djibouti and the establishment of Sharia law[20] (This was an agenda previously held by al-Itihaad al-Islamiyah). On 24 December 2006, Ethiopian armed forces, supported logistically by the George Bush administration in the United States, arrived in Somalia to support the Transitional Federation Government (TFG) in efforts to dislodge the UIC.[21] Ethiopia's geopolitical interest was fearing an Islamist regime on its doorstep which would jeopardize its sovereignty[22] as well as regional and international interests as al-Itihaad al-Islamiyah was seeking to unify Ethiopia's eastern Ogaden area with Somalia. The United States' political interest in Somalia's stabilization was threefold: first, preventing the spread of instability across Somalia's boundaries, particularly UIC suspected ties to Al Qaeda and other US-designated terrorist organizations; secondly, since the 1991 famine, which lasted more than two decades, Washington had attempted to address humanitarian concerns arising from drought and cyclical food shortages. Third, as the world's leading maritime security guarantor, the United States had pursued a strategic interest in defending the large international shipping lanes that run off Somalia's coast and across the Gulf of Aden.[23] In addition to its own interests, Ethiopia could be seen as fighting a proxy war for the United States, which had been wary of Islamic militants acquiring a foothold in the Horn of Africa, one of the busiest maritime passageways to the Middle East, since the terrorist

---

[20] Lapidus, Ira M. (2014). A History of Islamic Societies Front Cover (p. 789). Cambridge University Press.

[21] Ellis, Stephen, & van Kessel, Ineke. (2009). Movers and Shakers: Social Movements in Africa (p. 103). BRILL.

[22] Guardian News and Media. (2009, January 26). Ethiopia Ends Somalia Occupation. The Guardian. Retrieved April 17, 2022, from https://www.theguardian.com/world/2009/jan/26/ethiopia-ends-somalia-occupation.

[23] Samatar, A. I. (2007). Ethiopian Invasion of Somalia, US Warlordism & AU Shame. Review of African Political Economy, 34(111), 155–165. http://www.jstor.org/stable/20406369.

attacks of September 11, 2001. In 2004, the thousands-strong Ethiopian troops helped relocate the TFG to Somalia from Kenya where it had been initially constituted and governed for two years.[24] The TFG was not home grown or organically Somali, but rather considered a government in exile in Kenya firstly then in Baidoa.[25] On the back of a Christian nation, Ethiopian troops brought down the UIC and lodged the TFG—a decisive event. The Islamic courts were rapidly eradicated by collaborative military efforts and split into several factions—among them a group called al-Shabaab.[26] Al-Shabaab became a nationalist movement fighting the invasion of Somalia by a Christian nation and ostensibly to save it from the influences of foreigners.[27]

Shabaab which means youth in Arabic[28] intrigued the Somali youth to join the national resistance movement to expel the Ethiopian invaders, as they were viewed by locals. Al-Shabaab's identity had thus mutated from a small extremist faction into a powerful military force in national resistance. Al-Shabaab was able to appeal to a wide group of Somalis' with its agenda of Somali occupation and integration of all Somali people under one flag, an ideal previously held by UIC and AIAI.[29] In 2012, al-Shabaab became more charged and transformed into a global jihadist group pledging allegiance to al-Qaeda thus showcasing efforts to garner more support from the well-established and resourced jihadist movement.[30] Al-Shabaab was well funded and had boasted thousands of

---

[24] Bruton, B. E., Action, C. for P., & Relations, C. on F. (2010). Somalia: A New Approach (p. 7). Council on Foreign Relations.

[25] Ibid.

[26] Ibid., 104.

[27] Wise, Rob. (2011). Al-Shabaab. AQAM Futures Project: Case Studies Series. http://www.operationspaix.net/DATA/DOCUMENT/4039~v~Al_Shabaab.pdf.

[28] Ibid.

[29] Ndegwa, Loise W. (2018). An Analysis of the Counterterrorism (CT) and Counterinsurgency (COIN) Operations Employed by African Union Mission in Somalia (AMISOM) to Counter the Threat of Al-Shabaab in Somalia (2007–2016) (pp. 25–28). Cape Town, South Africa: University of Cape Town.

[30] Maszka, John. (2017). Al-Shabaab and Boko Haram: Guerrilla Insurgency or Strategic Terrorism? World Scientific.

fighters locally and in sleeper cells in neighbouring countries, as would be witnessed in later years by attacks in Kenya and Uganda.[31]

The state of affairs in Somalia worsened as al-Shabaab took over Mogadishu. The UN issued a directive to the AU to become more engaged in the peace and stability of the country. The AU Peace and Security Council then formed the African Union Mission in Somalia (AMISOM) in January 2007. AMISOM was deployed as a stop gap measure to prevent the exploitation of a security vacuum, following the withdrawal of Ethiopian forces[32] and the unsuccessful effort by Inter-governmental Authority on Development (IGAD) to deploy the Inter-Governmental Authority on Development Peace Support Mission to Somalia (IGASOM).[33] It became a UN-mandated PKO under UNSCR 1744 (2007) with a preliminary six-month mission and hand over to the UN[34]; however, this timeline became implausible. Following the departure of Ethiopian troops from Somalia in 2009, AMISOM's theatre of operation increased with less military power. AMISOM became the only lawful force in Somalia to fight against al-Shabaab to create an enabling environment for the Transitional Federal Government to function.[35] Geographically, the PKO set forth protecting only some districts of Mogadishu but subsequently expanded to cover the entire south-central Somalia. During this period al-Shabaab continued to launch an anti-Transitional Federal Government (TFG) military campaign. The acts of terror conducted by al-Shabaab fighters intended to show that it had the capability of harming and defeating the government and its nascent security architecture. Additionally, AMISOM's battles were linked to the

---

[31] Ellis, Stephen, & van Kessel, Ineke. (2009). Movers and Shakers: Social Movements in Africa (p. 103). BRILL.

[32] Dersso, Solomon Ayele. (2010). Somalia Dilemmas: Changing Security Dynamics, Limited Policy Options. ISS Paper no. 218, Addis Ababa: Institute for Security Studies. https://issafrica.org/research/papers/somalia-dilemmas-changing-security-dynamics-but-limited-policy-choices.

[33] African Union. (n.d). AMISOM Background. http://amisom-au.org/amisom-background/.

[34] United Nations Security Council. (2007). SC/8960 Security Council Authorizes Six-Month African Union Mission in Somalia, Unanimously Adopting Resolution 1744 (2007). https://www.un.org/press/en/2007/sc8960.doc.htm.

[35] United Nations. (2019). Yearbook of the United Nations 2014 (p. 375). United Nations; Orakhelashvili Alexander. (2001). Collective Security (p. 305). Oxford United Press: Oxford.

power al-Shabaab exhibited. The insurgency had dominated in-country economic resources. This afforded them power over vast territories. Moreover, the backing from some influential clans made al-Shabaab harder to neutralize. The TFG did not present the same power base to AMISOM, as the locals did not consider the transitional government to be legitimate.[36]

In retaliation to AMISOM, al-Shabaab carried out several bombings in Kenya and one in Uganda. The 2010 attack in Uganda left 76 people dead. These attacks were to deter allied countries from training the Somali National Security Agents and sending additional troops.[37] Immediately after the attack of AMISOM's largest troop contributor, Uganda, the mission took on a peace enforcement mandate and carried out offensive operations against al-Shabaab. Four years after its formation, AMISOM captured Mogadishu in 2011. In 2012, the TFG was dissolved, and elections were held in the country. A Federal Government was established, while the threat of al-Shabaab continued to loom. During this period AMISOM's approach was threefold: execution of key al-Shabaab leaders; liberation of cities/villages; and, growing its troops' strength.[38] Although this approach assisted AMISOM and the TFG to achieve control over more regions in Somalia, it did not exterminate al-Shabaab completely. The terrorist group repeated its attacks in different locations, changing tactics regularly and broadening its capability in rural and remote areas where AMISOM's resources could not reach. The strategy al-Shabaab used to control territories outside Mogadishu was not purely fighting but negotiation with various clan leaders. The support they received from the clans gave them an edge over AMISOM and the Federal Government of Somalia as it indicated less support for the AU mission.[39] The support from the clan elders camouflaged al-Shabaab with free movement

---

[36] Bruton, Bronwyn E., & Williams, Paul D. (2014). Report on Counterinsurgency in Somalia: Lessons Learned from the African Union Mission in Somalia (p. 16). JSOU Report 14–5. https://www.socom.mil/JSOU/JSOUPublications/JSOU14-5_BrutonWilliams_AMISOM_FINAL.pdf.

[37] Philpott, Don. (2019). Is America Safe?: Terrorism, Homeland Security, and Emergency Preparedness (p. 132). Rowman & Littlefield.

[38] United Nations Security Council. (2009). United Nations Security Council. Retrieved from https://www.un.org/securitycouncil/content/secretary-generals-reports-submitted-security-council-2009.

[39] Maruf, Harun, & Joseph, Dan. (2018). Inside Al-Shabaab: The Secret History of Al-Qaeda's Most Powerful Ally (p. 142). Indiana University Press.

in different territories. As Mateja (2015) posits, insurgent groups against which the UN peacekeeping mandates target have very little legitimacy from the lens of the outside world. However, in the eyes of the local population, they have many supporters as is the case with al-Shabaab and its sympathizers.[40]

Analysis of AMISOM Mandates

From its genesis, AMISOM's mandate was cognizant of the disintegration of government institutions accountable for delivery of security and other public services and for upholding law and order. This has been a constant in UNSCR's mandate from 2007 to 2019. Its first mandate was to safeguard the transitional federal institutions, important infrastructure, installations, and equipment in line with the mission's capability.[41] The initial mandate authorized eight thousand troops although fewer troops were deployed. In defence of this mandate and self-defence, use of force was authorized. It was viewed as a mission with a defensive approach aside from the recovery of a small number of towns from the rebel group al-Shabaab, particularly around Mogadishu and its surrounding area. This was pegged on the fact that AMISOM's initial capability did not match peace enforcement tasks necessary for the intense military battle it experienced. However, over the years AMISOM has transformed into a counterterror operation. Its metamorphosis was dictated by the type of threat al-Shabaab posed as well as the reality that the mission was only significant to the extent to which it could guarantee the exit of the transitional federal institutions in Mogadishu. This has been realized and currently Somalia has a Federal Government. Containing al-Shabaab then became a key driver and indicator in the success of the AU mission. Some discontent has also been raised by Somali's regarding the participation of AMISOM in counterterrorism operations and the amplification of military strategies compared to more diplomatically centred approaches. Inadvertently it raises suspicions about the AU's impartiality in Somalia

---

[40] Mateja, Peter (2015). Between Doctrine and Practice: The UN Peacekeeping Dilemma. Global Governance: A Review of Multilateralism and International Organizations, 21(3), 351–70.

[41] Wondemagegnehu, Dawit Yohannes, & Kebede, Daniel Gebreegziabher. (2017). AMISOM: Charting a New Course for African Union Peace Missions. African Security Review, 26(2), 199–219.

and has the potential to affect any psychological operations AMISOM will engage in to win the trust and respect of the population, particularly in peacebuilding as AMISOM transitioned to the African Union Transition Mission (ATMIS) on 1 April 2022, in which all responsibilities transferred to the Somali Security Forces.[42]

In an effort to protect and foster strategies to rebuild Somalia, UNSCR 1772 (2007) mandated the mission. Firstly, to hand support to the Transnational Federal Institutions (TFIs) in their endeavours to stabilize the state in the country and promote dialogue and reconciliation. Secondly, to open channels for the provision of humanitarian assistance to internally displaced persons. Thirdly, to establish conducive conditions for prolonged stabilization, reconstruction, and development actioned through the training of Somali security forces (as authorized in the National Security and Stabilization Plan). Finally, to ensure the safeguarding of all mission resources (human and equipment) to guarantee security and freedom of movement.[43] The principal objective of the mission was to use "all necessary measures" to support the TFG.

The protection offered by AMISOM was critical due to the existence of different armed factions in the Somali society that aggressively disputed these initiatives and contested the legitimacy of a nascent type of central state authority. The most daunting challenge to AMISOM came from al-Shabaab, which at the time controlled the important sections of south-central Somalia. In its initial deployment in Mogadishu, AMISOM was very constrained with 1600 Ugandan troops deployed, covering a wide area of operation including air and seaports. This number can be compared with the military strength of 38,000 troops with armoured brigades from the United States and other Western countries in the previous UN peacekeeping mission in Somalia between 1993 and 1995.[44] The Ugandan troops found themselves enmeshed in a deadly battle between different anti-TFG forces- particularly al-Shabaab. This

---

[42] ATMIS. (n.d.). The African Union Transition Mission in Somalia. Retrieved from https://atmis-au.org/.

[43] African Union (2007). Communique of the 69th Meeting of the Peace and Security Council, PSC/PR/Comm(LXIX) (p. 2) https://www.peaceau.org/uploads/communiqueeng-69th.pdf.

[44] Wondemagegnehu, Dawit Yohannes, & Kebede, Daniel Gebreegziabher. (2017). AMISOM: Charting a New Course for African Union Peace Missions. African Security Review, 26(2), 199–219.

compelled the military to focus on its core military tasks, protecting the TFG and ensuring its own troop's safety. Tasks such as patrolling and civilian engagement were constrained decreasing the mission's access to intelligence. Notably, the AMISOM mandate did not stipulate what circumstances would be a sign of mission success, although a transition to a UN peacekeeping force after six months was recommended. In May 2008, the African Union Commission released AMISOM's Strategic Directive[45] specifying nine conditions for the mission's success. These criteria comprised a number of sections: "involvement of the TFG in the inter-Somali dialogues; assimilation of militias within national security forces; relocation of the TFIs to Mogadishu; establishment of the TFIs in all regions; mission handover to a UN advance contingent; stabilisation of the current hostile environment in the country; commencement and completion of disarmament of armed groups; completion of planning for support to an election process; and the return of all Internally Displaced Persons (IDPs) and refugees."[46] It became evident that this was a herculean task to be completed in six months. Troops from Burundi later joined the Ugandan army to secure part of Mogadishu in 2009 increasing confidence and robustness in the mission. Both contingents fought without air support and paid heavy costs in relation to direct confrontation in the streets and sniper shots. Nevertheless, resolute in their task the troops managed to establish authority in Mogadishu.

In UNSCR 2036 (2012) the UNSC was more explicit in permitting AMISOM to diminish the threats caused by al-Shabaab and other anti-TFG armed groups in order to create conditions requisite for effective and legitimate governance across Somalia. In spite of the political objectives, AMISOM's position was restricted by the scope and direction of the UNSC. It was primarily viewed as a military contribution, designed to create an enabling security setting, part of a broader political strategy that is still developing. The resolution also authorized the aerial capacity of twelve military helicopters, three utility and nine attack, to conduct offensive operations. These would have been extremely useful in swiftly striking al-Shabaab thereby decimating some of its valued combat capabilities.

---

[45] Williams, Paul. (2019). Fighting for Peace in Somalia: A History and Analysis of the African Union Mission (AMISOM), 2007–2017 (p. 63). Oxford University Press.

[46] Wondemagegnehu, Dawit Yohannes, & Kebede, Daniel Gebreegziabher. (2017). AMISOM: Charting a New Course for African Union Peace Missions. African Security Review, 26(2), 199–219.

It would have also assisted in delivering air cover for military contingents, escorting convoys, providing immediate response teams through evacuation rescue missions, and airlift capacity.[47]

As a general principle in military doctrine, any force which seeks to intervene should primarily be proportionate in number to the biggest enemy force they are likely to face. "With comparable numbers, as well as superior skills, mobility, and repower, intervening forces would then be well placed to dominate the ensuing battles.[48]" A Hobbesian sentiment with deep realism roots. In similar fashion, a robust force is a requisite element of successful peacekeeping, a view stressed in the Brahimi Report—"no amount of good intentions can substitute for the fundamental ability to project credible force."[49] However, without a single military attack helicopter AMISOM's capacity was limited to achieve this mandate especially in view of al-Shabaab's shift to asymmetric operations. Additionally, notwithstanding the setting up of AMISOM's Strategic Concept, the defence forces deployed were inadequate to ensure the stabilization of its operational environment. For example, it is uncertain how 2,500 Ugandan and Burundian military troops could secure the Baidoa sector. The same was also expected of the Djiboutian soldiers in the Belet Weyne sector. The mandate of the PKO was wide in comparison to the human and financial assets required or available. AMISOM troops continued to face threats to their safety and security which was unevenly distributed based on the capacities of each troop contributing country to protect itself from the asymmetrical threats. Military operating bases which were remote faced deadly attacks as forces were spread too thin. Additionally, many countries were unwilling to contribute troops or police officers due to its dark past which pushed the United States to pull out its troops (as dramatized in the film "Black Hawk Down"). The issue of troop strength and capacity will be discussed further in a later section.

---

[47] Lotze, Walter, & Williams, Paul D. (2016). The Surge to Stabilize: Lessons for the UN from the AU's Experience in Somalia (p. 12). IPI Publications.

[48] O'Hanlon, Michael. (2003). Expanding Global Military Capacity for Humanitarian Intervention (p. 46). Washington DC.: Brookings Institution Press.

[49] United Nations General Assembly and Security Council (UNGASC). (2000). Report of the Panel on United Nations Peace Operations A/55/305-S/2000/809. http://www.un.org/documents/ga/docs/55/a55305.pdf.

At the strategic level, AMISOM's mandate since its inception involved providing protection to high-level personalities affiliated with the political reconciliation process in Somalia; and to contain and neutralize al-Shabaab and other armed anti-government actors. Nonetheless, at the operational level, it meant that AMISOM was expected to protect civilians in its operational environment in accordance with International Humanitarian Law. Another source of contention occurred at the operational level in relation to AMISOM's Rules of Engagement (ROE). AMISOM's earliest ROE ordered its troops to take preventative measures to ensure that there is no collateral damage. Accordingly, it authorized its troops to use force in cases of self-defence and the protection of civilians and humanitarian workers facing grave physical violence in keeping with its mandate. It was uncertain however what level of force was allowable in the protection of civilians.[50] Moreover, fighting a faceless al-Shabaab meant that it was difficult to differentiate a civilian from a combatant. Occasionally, al-Shabaab would use civilians as human shields leading to civilian deaths.

AMISOM then had to bear the brunt of unintended harm to civilians in its iron-handed responses because of the asymmetrical nature of the conflict and failure to protect the population from al-Shabaab snipers. This obscured and complicated AMISOM's ability to observe International Laws of Armed Conflict and protect civilians from threat. Additionally, the mandate did not provide guidance to address this tension and lack of clarity.[51] There was a glaring gap between the Protection of Civilians (POC) mandate, and the ROEs issued which negatively affected local perceptions of AMISOM operations, undermining its effectiveness. Al-Shabaab took advantage of this and launched a campaign against the mission while actively targeting AMISOM troops, local security agents, and civilians.[52] AMISOM troops were portrayed as a party to the conflict and a ruthless occupying force in Mogadishu. Reports by Civilians In Armed Conflict indicated that locals began to question the

---

[50] Williams, Paul. (2018). Fighting for Peace in Somalia: A History and Analysis of the African Union Mission (AMISOM), 2007–2017 (p. 261).

[51] Williams, Paul D. (2018). Fighting Peace in Somalia: A History and Analysis of the African Union Mission in Somalia 2007–2017. Oxford University Press.

[52] United Nations High Commissioner of Refugees & Centre for Civilians in Conflict (CIVIC). (2011). Civilian Harm in Somalia: Creating an Appropriate Response (pp. 1–67). https://issuu.com/civiliansinconflict/docs/civic_somalia_2011/67.

difference between AMISOM and al-Shabaab because both killed civilians. As a result, some youth joined al-Shabaab driven by the desire to seek revenge because of AMISOM's offensive tactics.[53]

While POC is crucial in active combat operations on moral, legal, and strategic grounds, it turned out to be even more significant as operations turn to broader stabilization tasks. For example, although al-Shabaab was dislodged from Mogadishu in 2011 it was not until 2013 that AMISOM formally embraced a mission wide POC approach.[54] As AMISOM's theatre of operation expanded to the south-central part of Somalia, it was critical for the mission to minimize civilian harm as it could force more locals to aid the opponents thereby undermining the mission's effectiveness. POC was therefore key for that plan of operation because the Somali population was the centre of gravity needed to defend against al-Shabaab, who were ready to use violence to compel civilian conformity to their agendas. In such settings, effecting compliance with Laws of Armed Conflict is not sufficient to succeed. More pre-emptive measures need to be employed to protect civilians from harm such as assigning "no-fire zones" and exerting a high level of restraint in places where civilians are many and exiting.

COUNTERTERRORISM AND PEACEKEEPING

As discussed in the previous section, counterterrorism has been pushed from the margins to the foreground and therefore the UN will ultimately carry on deploying peacekeepers in complex environments, ceding counterterrorism operations to its partners like the AU.[55] Such an agenda is greatly supported in the Action for Peacekeeping Initiative (A4P) which underscores the need for partnerships. However, the notion of UN peacekeepers operating and participating in counterterrorism operations is not without its complications. The respective ethics, logic, and purposes of counterterrorism and peacekeeping are often seen to be in contradiction.

---

[53] Hassan, Muhsin. (2012) Understanding Drivers of Violent Extremism: The Case of Al-Shabab and Somali Youth. CTC Sentinel, 5(8), 18–20.

[54] Bouchet-Saulnier, Françoise. (2013). The Practical Guide to Humanitarian Law (p. 11). Rowman & Littlefield Publishers.

[55] Charbonneau, Bruno. (2018, June 28). Counterterrorism and Challenges to Peacekeeping Impartiality. The Global Observatory. https://theglobalobservatory.org/2018/06/counterterrorism-peacekeeping-impartiality/.

Peacekeeping is premised on the idea of supporting a political process, impartiality and having no enemies to eliminate; while counterterrorism operates according to a military logic justified by the goal of creating space for politics and the obligation to pursue, capture, or neutralize the enemy. In this section, I submit that although peacekeeping and counterterrorism denote two different ethical frameworks, there are some tactical and doctrinal similarities. Hence, the conception of a division of labour between peacekeeping and counterterrorism is unwarranted, as in praxis no such delineation exists. Unpacking the principles of peacekeeping is critical to understand the divergence from traditional peacekeeping and the merger of counterterrorism roles in fighting continuously aggressive non-state actors threatening global peace and security.

Principles of Peacekeeping

The United Nations traditional peacekeeping doctrine is set apart by three concepts, specifically: consent from host nation, impartiality,[56] and the minimum use of force except in instances of self-defence, whereas in contemporary Peace Keeping Operations (PKOs) the use of force is permitted in self-defence and defence of the mandate. According to the UN peacekeeping principles, peacekeeping is consensual; therefore, the protagonists or the principal actors in a conflict must acknowledge that there is a problem in the state and approve to the assistance of the UN. This could be through the implementation of a peace agreement or ceasefire. Although these three principles continue to be applicable, their meaning and interpretations have morphed over the years due to changes in the global security structure. Since the end of the Cold War, majority of the PKOs on the continent have been progressively deployed in theatres where the enforcement of a ceasefire or peace agreement is critical, primarily where the protection of civilians is of urgent concern. In such circumstances, the UN greatly depends on the approval of the host nation. According to the United Nations Peacekeeping Operations Principles and Guidelines commonly referred to as the Capstone Doctrine (2008), when consent is lacking PKOs peacekeeping operation runs the risk of becoming a party to the conflict; and being pushed towards

---

[56] Willmot, Haidi, Mamiya, Ralph, Weller, Marc, & Sheeran, Scott (Eds.). (2016). Protection of Civilians (p. 126). Oxford University Press.

enforcement action, a move inherent to its role of keeping the peace.[57] Consent is not only championed for principled reasons but practical ones as well, namely to make the job and tasks of peacekeepers more feasible. While consent is usually acquired through a peace agreement among the main parties to the conflict, in many contemporary conflicts such comprehensive agreements are not in place rendering consent questionable. In the case of AMISOM, peacekeepers were deployed to support the state's government and assist it defeat al-Shabaab which is one of the parties to the conflict. Notably, al-Shabaab commands ample political and military power that the then TFG and the current federal government have been incapable of defeating them on their own. Therefore, this insurgent group is a main party to the conflict. Yet, the missions mandate called for expansion of state authority from the TFG to the Federal Government of Somalia.

The second principle is impartiality which was considered the lifeline of traditional peacekeeping operations—UN peacekeeping strives not to take any sides in the conflict and is expected to treat all parties to the conflict equally. Nevertheless, impartiality in UN peacekeeping should not be mistaken for neutrality. Although UN PKOs are impartial in their relations with the parties to the conflict, they are not neutral in the way the mandate is executed, implying that peacekeepers ought to be assertive in conducting their operations. This distinction is witnessed in missions with a protection of civilians' mandate, which in most cases is implicit. In such mandates, peacekeepers will not be neutral when civilians are faced with situations which place them in imminent danger. Moreover, impartiality is essential to ensuring a PKOs legitimacy as well as the security and safety of peacekeeping personnel. Sometimes, the actors in conflict may view PKOs as a party to the conflict and thereby target it.

In the case of AMISOM, impartiality was challenged on several fronts. While the deployment of troops was UN-mandated, the full support of the local population was weak. The involvement of neighbouring countries in Somalia was not welcomed, particularly in view of a record of meddling in Somali internal affairs. Moreover, a portion of the population likened the Troop Contributing Countries (TCCs) to the English and French in view of the fact that they invaded an Islamic nation and by

---

[57] United Nations. United Nations Department of Peacekeeping Operations Department of Field Support Capstone Doctrine (p. 32). https://peacekeeping.un.org/sites/def ault/files/capstone_eng_0.pdf.

extension launched a full-scale war on Islam targeting Muslims.[58] Indeed, many youths and other recruits joined al-Shabaab in part due to increased civilian casualties, corruption,[59] and reports of sexual exploitation and abuse of women.[60] As al-Shabaab launched attacks on AMISOM operating bases, it was evident that PKOs and their aggressive counterterror operations were not viewed with impartiality but rather as hostile targets, raising questions about troop safety and security.

The third principle of traditional PKOs is the limited use of force with the exception of self-defence. This denotes that UN peacekeepers are authorized to use minimum force to protect themselves and the individuals stipulated in the mandate.[61] However, in the Brahimi Report (2000) the concept of self-defence is unpacked further and expanded at the doctrinal level from merely self-defence to the defence of the authorized mission. It formed part of the doctrinal advancement of the authorization of legitimate force by peacekeepers, extending from an individual's self-defence and the freedom of movement and protection of positions, to the defence of the mandate and the protection of third parties such as civilians.[62] As in AMISOM this threshold between the nature and level of force permitted was difficult to balance in praxis of asymmetrical warfare. The use of force oscillates like a pendulum from military combat operations to armed police operations. Such a murky territory for peacekeepers because they have been deployed in a dangerous setting with a robust mandate to employ counterterrorism tasks. According to Nagl (2005) the concept of "minimum force" should only be considered when fighting an insurgency, as failure to comply

---

[58] United States Congress House Committee on Foreign Affairs. (2014, October 3). Al-Shabaab: How Great a Threat? Hearing before the Committee on Foreign Affairs, House of Representatives, One Hundred Thirteenth Congress, First Session (p. 12). U.S. Government Printing Office. https://www.govinfo.gov/content/pkg/CHRG-113hhrg85 104/pdf/CHRG-113hhrg85104.pdf.

[59] Menkhaus, Ken. (2012, September 24). The Somali Spring. Foreign Policy. www.for eignpolicy.com/articles/2012/09/24/the_somali_spring?page=0,1.

[60] Davies, Sara E., & True, Jacqui. (2019). The Oxford Handbook of Women, Peace, and Security (p. 383). Oxford University Press.

[61] United Nations. (2008). United Nations, Department of Peacekeeping Operations Principles and Guidelines (Capstone Doctrine) (p. 26). New York: UN 2008.

[62] Tsagourias, Nicholas. (2006), Consent, Neutrality/Impartiality and the Use of Force in Peacekeeping Operations: Their Constitutional Dimension. Journal of Conflict & Security Law, 11(3), 465–482.

leads to diminished support for the government.[63] Former al-Shabaab fighters referred to the fact that AMISOM's bombing of towns led to the increased hatred of the mission.[64] In other civilian-related examples, AMISOM sprayed bullets on civilians who were mistaken for al-Shabaab fighters. A public transport bus was accidentally fired upon by AMISOM troops ensnared by a sequence of roadside bombs and machine gun fire.[65] A similar incident occurred when an AMISOM soldier of Kenyan origin allegedly shot six civilians after the assault on Kismayo. He had mistaken them for al-Shabaab militia who had launched an attack on his unit that day.[66] Consequently, the use of force in such violent settings puts greater demands on PKOs due to the mandate of implicit protection of civilians.[67]

Notably, the three principles of peacekeeping mentioned above are only used as planning guidelines rather than principles which characterize AU peace support operations.[68] This is because AU's interventions are guided by the African Standby Forces Policy Framework (2003) which outlines six scenarios within which interventions are permissible.[69] These range from small observer missions to multidimensional interventions to stop mass crimes against humanity. According to the AU the purpose of the mission and the circumstance within which the intervention is

---

[63] Nagl, John A. (2005). Learning to Eat Soup with a Knife: Counterinsurgency Lessons from Malaya and Vietnam (p. 30). In Paperback ed. Chicago: University of Chicago Press.

[64] Hassan, Muhsin. (2012, August 23). "Understanding Drivers of Violent Extremism: The Case of al-Shabab and Somali Youth." Combating Terrorism Center at West Point. http://www.ctc.usma.edu/posts/understanding-drivers-of-violent-extremism-the-case-of-al-shabab-andsomali-youth.

[65] United Nations High Commissioner of Refugees & Center for Civilians in Conflict (CIVIC). (2011). Civilian Harm in Somalia: Creating an Appropriate Response (p. 20). https://issuu.com/civiliansinconflict/docs/civic_somalia_2011/67.

[66] Gabriel Gatehouse. (2012, September 24). Kenyan AMISOM Soldier Kills Six Somali Civilians. Nairobi: BBC News. https://www.bbc.com/news/world-africa-19698348.

[67] Kaldor, Mary. (1999). New and Old Wars: Organized Violence in a Global Era (p. 125). Stanford University Press.

[68] De Coning, Cedric, Gelot, Linnéa, & Karlsrud, John. (2013). The Future of African Peace Operations: From the Janjaweed to Boko Haram (p. 44). Zed Books Ltd.

[69] African Union. (2003). Policy Framework for the Establishment of the African Standby Force and the Military Staff Committee Exp/ASF-MSC/2 (I), See paragraph 1.6. https://www.peaceau.org/uploads/asf-policy-framework-en.pdf.

conducted guides the extent to which consent, impartiality and other critical factors influence the mission. Similarly, the level to which force may be applied is governed by assessments concerning the level of force that may be required to achieve the mandate and risk factor in a given context.

Counterterrorism

There is no universally agreed upon definition of the term terrorism. However, in this chapter, the definition provided by Koffi Anan Annan will be used. He describes terrorism as an act "intended to cause death or serious bodily harm to civilians or non-combatants with the purpose of intimidating a population or compelling a government or an international organisation to do or abstain from doing any act."[70] Counterterrorism therefore is an effort(s) taken by governments to cease terrorist activity. The United Nations developed the UN Global Counter-Terrorism Strategy (2006) to address rising trends in terrorism. The strategy adopted by the General Assembly has four pillars: addressing conditions favourable for the spread of terrorism; preventing and fighting against terrorism; building countries' capability to fight against terrorism and to improve the role of the United Nations system in that respect; and ensuring respect for human rights and the rule of law while conducting counterterrorism operations.[71] It is reviewed every two years and gives a roadmap for UN and member states at all levels, global, regional, and national, to address counterterrorism. Though all UN member states signed the strategy it does not have the same legal or authoritative status as an international treaty. This is linked to the lack of a clear definition of terrorism and what it entails, which has two key consequences: prevents the development of laws that would lead to uniform execution across the international system; and relegates the strategy as a list of highly regarded principles that ought to guide counterterrorism. That said, the ambiguity in definition and implementation of the strategy has the effect of preventing a "one-size-fits-all" approach to countering terrorism as

---

[70] Botha, Anneli. (2008). Challenges in Understanding Terrorism in Africa: A Human Security Perspective. African Security Review, 17(2), 28–41.

[71] Security Council Counter Terrorism Committee. (2010). United Nations Global Counter-Terrorism Strategy. https://www.un.org/sc/ctc/resources/general-assembly/un-global-counter-terrorism-strategy/.

every terrorism-related conflict has its distinctive characteristics.[72] The four tenets provided by the UN Global Counter-Terrorism Strategy (UN GCTS) are suitable for states with functioning institutions because the principal obligation for preventing and countering terrorism lies with national Governments.[73] The strategy therefore cannot be implementable in war-torn areas. In the case of Somalia, which is a recovering failed state, the institutions are not strong enough to address terrorism posed by al-Shabaab unilaterally. Hence the deployment of AMISOM to assist in conflict management. As indicated in an earlier section, counterinsurgency and counterterrorism will be used interchangeably. Counterinsurgency (COIN) encompasses the harmonized response of a national government and its external supporters to incorporate political, socio-economic, legal, police, and military methods to thwart and in the long run defeat an insurgency. Counterterrorism comprises defensive measures to diminish the capability of a terrorist/insurgent group to perpetrate violence against the population therefore falls within the COIN framework.[74]

The Inevitable Merger of Peacekeeping and Counterterrorism

Peacekeeping and counterterrorism operations are often perceived to be at cross purposes, however there are some similarities given the nature of contemporary warfare. Both doctrines are employed in order to prevent an unstable security situation from worsening. In peacekeeping impartiality coupled with limited use of force except in defence of the mandate or self-defence is approved and often recognized as a distinguishing factor. In counterterrorism/counterinsurgency operations, considerable force is permitted to counteract the acts of violence from insurgents whose goal is territorial control and toppling democratic authorities.[75] Additionally,

---

[72] Wilkinson, Paul. (2006). Terrorism Versus Democracy: The Liberal State Response (p. 203). New York: Routledge.

[73] United Nations General Assembly A/72/840*. (2018). Activities of the United Nations System in Implementing the United Nations Global Counter-Terrorism Strategy (p. 6/87). https://undocs.org/pdf?symbol=en/A/72/840.

[74] Geraint, Hughes. (2011, May). Letort Paper the Military's Role in Counterterrorism: Examples and Implications for Liberal Democracies (pp. 21–22). https://publications.arm ywarcollege.edu/pubs/2140.pdf.

[75] Miles, Kitts R. (2019). The Strategic Use of Force in Counterinsurgency: Find, Fix, Fight (p. 37). Rowman & Littlefield; (2006). Headquarters, Department of the Army. Counterinsurgency Operations (pp. vi–vii). Field Manual—Interim.

peacekeeping operations are continuously deployed under Chapter VII of the UN Charter, while counterterrorism operations are heavily kinetic with restraint on the protection of civilians. This distinction in the African Union operations are merged in peace support operations doctrine which comprises a broad spectrum of operations not characterized by the UN peacekeeping principles impartiality, consent and use of force but instead function and intent.[76] Additionally, in comparing the two doctrines, the following similarities were drawn: emphasis on civilian protection; attention to kinetic and non-kinetic approaches to establishing peace such as training local security agents and developing strong institutions. The divergences between the principles of Counterterrorism (CT) and Peacekeeping (PK) lie in the mandates issued by the UNSC, political grounding of the operation and strategies employed.

Counterterrorism Approaches

Brigitte Nacos (2016) distinguishes hard and soft counterterrorism strategies employed in terrorism mitigation. Hard strategies can be described as command power that can be applied to provoke others to alter their positions and identified by military offensives, drone strikes, and different kinds of special operations.[77] Soft strategies on the other hand can be described as actions aimed at co-opting or embracing people rather than forcing them to take a particular stand. It comprises humanitarian/economic aid, community policing, and diplomacy with primary concentration on the long-term goals of terrorism mitigation.[78] AMISOM has encompassed both strategies simultaneously, due to its mandate to stabilize the situation on the ground to establish conditions conducive for humanitarian activities as well as get rid of the threat posed by al-Shabaab. The hard approach was primarily enforced by the military component while the soft approach by the police and civilian components. AMISOM's Police Component was tasked to safeguard the rule of law in Mogadishu and provide capacity building of the Somali Police Force (e.g.

---

[76] Norheim-Martinsen, Per M., & Nyhamar, Tore. (2015). International Military Operations in the 21st Century: Global Trends and the Future of Intervention (p. 125). Routledge.

[77] Nacos, Brigitte L. (2016). Terrorism and Counterterrorism (p. 257). New York: Routledge.

[78] Ibid.

mentoring and training) with the goal of changing it into a trustworthy body that could provide security to the Somali population.[79] The African Union Police (AUPOL) was therefore greatly involved in reforming, restructuring, and rebuilding Somalis police force as over 4000 Police officers benefited from different trainings since the mission's inception.[80]

The Civilian Component which comprises five departments; "Mission Support, Political Processes, Stabilisation and Early Recovery, Protection, Human Rights and Gender and Security Sector Reform" was tasked with facilitating the building of legitimate and effective political institutions in the country.[81] The component has been dedicated to promoting the launch of civil reconciliation programs in order to seek political inclusiveness and representation by fostering loyalty to the Somali state instead of clan leaders or warlords. These hard and soft approaches to counterterrorism are synonymous to tasks employed by peacekeepers. Peacekeeping is reliant on both kinetic and non-kinetic approaches to win the trust and respect of the local population realizing that hard offensive counterterrorism-oriented approaches should be balanced with soft counterterrorism approaches.

On the other hand, the AMISOM is engaged in classic war models of countering terrorism which is distinguished by the usage of a great level of force intended to subdue the enemy. In the traditional sense, victory is defined by the ability to overpower the enemy.[82] Consequently, counterterrorism interventions are continuously pursued until the terrorist threat is non-existent.[83] This can be seen in the United States' involvement in eliminating terrorists in Somalia alongside AMISOM.

---

[79] African Union Police Component. https://amisom-au.org/wp-content/cache/page_enhanced/amisom-au.org/mission-profile/amisom-police/_index.html_gzip.

[80] AMISOM Police. https://amisom-au.org/mission-profile/amisom-police/.

[81] AMISOM Civilian Component. http://amisom-au.org/mission-profile/amisom-civilian-component/.

[82] Crelinsten, Ronald. (2014). Perspectives on Counterterrorism: From Stovepipes to a Comprehensive Approach. http://www.terrorismanalysts.com/pt/index.php/pot/article/view/321/html.

[83] Ibid.

AMISOM Operations in Perspective

The more the lines are blurred the more mergers between peacekeeping and counterterrorism are expected because of the type of operations taken to neutralize the opponent. The goal being to realize a decisive local superiority, that will overpower the adversary, break the balance, and permit a step forward to victory. In order to show the merger of the concepts of PK and CT, I will use Clausewitz's Principles of War to illustrate the merger. These principles are objective, surprise, manoeuvre, economy of force, offensive, simplicity, unity of command, and security.[84] These principles are not expansive however the nature of al-Shabaab is a great example of the ageless nature of the principles. As peacekeepers are continuously deployed in counterterrorism theatres, these principles of war show the importance of launching an offensive. Al-Shabaab's success in Somalia can be credited to adherence to these principles, even though the organization might not be aware of them, can lead to success of their operations. Similarly, denying al-Shabaab the power to follow and adhere to these principles results in their defeat.

The approach employed by AMISOM at the strategic and operational level indicates a fusion of peacekeeping, counterterrorism/counterinsurgency. At the top level, strategic, AMISOM is an authorized PKO in tune with Article 13 of the Protocol Relating to the Establishment of the Peace and Security Council (2002).[85] However, at the operational level, the plan of attack deployed to weaken the capabilities of al-Shabaab resembles counterinsurgency. In the United States for example, the military doctrine FM 3–24[86] is counterinsurgency framework which follows three principles, "Clear, Hold, Build."[87] The principles in concert constitute reclaiming control from insurgent groups through capturing and neutralizing to force withdrawal; sustaining

---

[84] Gray, Colin S. (2013). War, Peace and International Relations: An Introduction to Strategic History (p. 23). Routledge.

[85] African Union. (2002). Protocol Relating to the Establishment of the Peace and Security Council of the African Union. https://au.int/en/treaties/protocol-relating-est ablishment-peace-and-security-council-african-union.

[86] Paul, Christopher, Clarke, Colin P., & Grill, Beth. (2010). Victory Has a Thousand Fathers: Sources of Success in Counterinsurgency (p. xv). Rand Corporation.

[87] John A. United States Army, United States Marine Corps. (2008). The U.S. Army/Marine Corps Counterinsurgency Field Manual (pp. 174–175). University of Chicago Press.

control of recaptured territories and promoting the presence of the host nation at local levels by assisting governments to develop strong national institutions.[88] These counterinsurgency tactics have been widely used in Somalia to defeat al-Shabaab. This narrative gains more traction with the UNSCR 2093 (2013) with the increased responsibility given to the Somali government through trainings and mentoring by AMISOM and its partners.[89] If AMISOM was a purely counterterrorism mission it would focus exclusively on destroying al-Shabaab operatives, extending little or no support to the Somali government. In both settings the centre of gravity (where efforts need to be focused) is the local population and the personnel deployed to assist the host government in this effort. Aside from offensive attacks which in most settings will be necessary, building strong institutions and developing political support for state authorities is critical to achieve buy-in from the locals. The fusion of military and non-military tasks is championed to build a positive peace process.

Though the United States has not formally declared war in Somalia, it intensified its interventions in the country. It labelled Somalia an active area of hostilities and blacklisted al-Shabaab in 2008 following threats issued against the United States by al-Shabaab even though the terrorist organization had pledged allegiance to Al Qaeda in 2012.[90] This explains the increased counterterrorism operations such as airstrikes and lethal operations in Somalia which have killed thousands of al-Shabaab militants. The United States has occasionally provided AMISOM with advanced intelligence, surveillance, and reconnaissance.[91] In March 2016, US Special Forces worked with Somali National Army and AMISOM to conduct multiple airstrikes and raids, including a notable operation

---

[88] Ibid.

[89] United Nations Security Council Resolution. (2013). Resolution 2093. http://unscr.com/en/resolutions/2093.

[90] Harnisch, Chris. (2010). The Terror Threat from Somalia: The Internationalization of Al Shabaab. Critical Threats, Project of the American Enterprise Institute. https://www.criticalthreats.org/analysis/the-terror-threat-from-somalia-the-internationalization-of-al-shabaab.

[91] Olayiwola Abegunrin, Sabella Abidde. (2018). African Intellectuals and the State of the Continent: Essays in Honor of Professor Sulayman S. Nyang Cambridge Scholars Publishing (p. 175).

involving the neutralization of 159 al-Shabaab recruits during a graduation ceremony.[92] The Trump administration in March 2017 approved the military to conduct precision strikes targeting al-Shabaab loosening the rules of engagement to permit more aggressive targeting of the jihadist militants. Previously the US military was authorized to conduct airstrikes only in defence of its advisors on the ground. The administration considered the fight against al-Shabaab crucial to protecting America's Eastern African allies Ethiopia and Kenya which suffered greatly due to terror attacks. The United States and its allies the United Kingdom, European Union, and United Nations agreed on a long-term strategy to replace AMISOM with a Somali National Army (SNA), the Danaab (which means lighting in Somali).

The Danaab troops are a commando unit of the Somali National Army. They were first trained by Bancroft Global Development, a private security company and further trained by Turkey and the United Arab Emirates, and equipped and mentored by the United States. The 3000 Somali special forces have been conducting offensive operations to dislodge al-Shabaab alongside the United States and AMISOM.[93] The Danaab are held in high regard by the Somali and are widely viewed as clan neutral and effective in counterterrorism.[94] This battalion's strong special forces units have eliminated al-Shabaab terrorists alongside their mentors. In January 2020, the special forces unit's 13th battalion killed 12 al-Shabaab militants who had been terrorizing locals in Lower Juba[95] while the 16th battalion eliminated 20 fighters in an offensive battle in Lower Shebelle,[96] an area prone to attacks like the ones in Leggo and Janaale.

[92] Ibid. (p. 177).

[93] Defence Post. (2020, January 3). AFRICOM responds to Al-Shabaab Ambush on Somalia Troops with Airstrike, Staff Writer. https://thedefensepost.com/2020/01/03/somalia-africom-airstrike-shabaab-ambush/.

[94] Military Times. (2019, September 30). US Launches Airstrikes on Al-Shabab in Response to Attack on US Commando Outpost in Somalia. https://www.militarytimes.com/news/your-military/2019/09/30/extremists-launch-2-attacks-on-military-targets-in-somalia/ShawnSnow.

[95] Garowe Online. (2020). US Trained Forces Operations Kills Al-Shabaab Militants in Somalia, 20/01/20, Staff Correspondent. https://www.garoweonline.com/en/news/somalia/us-trained-forces-operation-kills-al-shabaab-militants-in-somalia.

[96] Garowe Online. (2018). US Trained Somalia Danaab Forces Kill Dozens of Al-Shabaab Militants, Staff Correspondent https://www.garoweonline.com/en/news/somalia/us-trained-somalias-danab-forces-kill-dozens-of-al-shabaab-militants.

The United States have used manned and unmanned aerial vehicles to spy on al-Shabaab locations and launch airstrikes which has hampered the organization's ability to communicate. Al-Shabaab defectors have noted that the strikes have planted extensive distrust among its members and limited its leaders' mobility.[97] The United States has continued to launch airstrikes against al-Shabaab because it has changed its tactics and begun targeting high security zones in the country.[98] According to US Africa Command, they intend to build two Danaab companies a year to secure territories captured by al-Shabaab[99] across the six sectors.[100] Moreover, supporting the elite Danaab unit and Gashan (shield in Somali), the SNA rapid reaction force with tactical advice as they carry out offensive operations is critical for the US African Command as the United States has special operation capabilities, particularly in regions where al-Shabaab has left behind sleeper cells.[101]

The United States has also on numerous occasions assisted in coordinating AMISOM efforts by operations with AMISOM chiefs of defence. The Combined Joint Task Force–Horn of Africa (CJTF–HOA) travelled between AMISOM capitals to support planned joint operations such as Juba Corridor, Indian Ocean which led to the liberation of the coastal

[97] Goldbaum, Christina. (2018). A Trumpian War on Terror that Just Keeps Getting Bigger "Drone Strikes May Have a Purpose, But They Are No Substitute for a Political Strategy. https://www.theatlantic.com/international/archive/2018/09/drone-somalia-al-shabaab-al-qaeda-terrorist-africa-trump/569680/.

[98] Goldenberg. (2020, January 21). US Airstrike Kills Three Al Shabaab Terrorists in Bangeeni, Lower Jubba In Support of Danaab Forces. https://intelligencebriefs.com/us-airstrike-kills-three-al-shabaab-terrorists-in-bangeeni-lower-jubba-in-support-of-danaab-forces/.

[99] Military Times. (2019, September 30). US Launches Airstrikes on Al-Shabab in Response to Attack on US Commando Outpost in Somalia Shawn Snow. https://www.militarytimes.com/news/your-military/2019/09/30/extremists-launch-2-attacks-on-military-targets-in-somalia/.

[100] Rempfer, Kyle. (2019). Lightning Brigade: Training Advanced Infantry—Not Airstrikes—Is Africom's Primary Effort In Somalia. Military Times. https://www.militarytimes.com/news/your-military/2019/03/27/lightning-brigade-training-advanced-infantry-not-airstrikes-is-africoms-primary-effort-in-somalia/.

[101] Jonsson, Michael, & Torbjörnsson, Daniel. (n.d.). Resurgent, Reinvented or Simply Resilient? The Growing Threat of al-Shabaab in Somalia. Studies in African Security. https://www.foi.se/download/18.7fd35d7f166c56ebe0bb3bd/1544269060470/Resurgent-Reinvented-or-Simply-Resilient_FOI-Memo-5913.pdf.

towns and Eagle which led to the liberation of ten cities.[102] The CJTF-HOA also incorporated liaison officers from AMISOM and other nations into its headquarters in Djibouti which provided military, political, and intelligence assistance.[103]

Principles of War

Getting to a location the fastest with heavy military hardware encapsulates the principle of mass, one of the nine principles of war[104] The two most important elements in mass being everything must take place at a decisive place and time.[105] Since al-Shabaab took on an identity of its own, after ICU was defeated in 2006,[106] it used excessive force which it needed to achieve its objectives in a swarm-like manner. The terrorist organization started attacking the military bases of the Uganda Peoples Defence Forces and the Burundi National Defence Forces in order to weaken AMISOM and hinder its expansion in and within Somalia. In 2018, al-Shabaab conducted five synchronized attacks on military bases in Somalia's Lower Shabelle region. The first attack occurred at AMISOM's heavily protected Bula Marer camp.[107] Two suicide vehicle bombs were detonated and was immediately followed by an al-Shabaab infantry attack on the camp with rocket propelled grenades and machine guns. Shortly afterwards, AMISOM's bases in Golweyn and Barawe were attacked with mortars and Vehicle-Borne Improvised Explosive Device (VBIED).[108] The fourth and fifth attacks took place in Somali government strongholds

---

[102] Global Security. (n.d). African Union Mission in Somalia. https://www.globalsecurity.org/military/world/int/amisom.htm.

[103] Grigsby, Jr., Wayne W, Fox, Todd, Dabkowski, Matthew F., & Phelps, Andrea N. (2015, September–October). Globally Integrated Operations in the Horn of Africa Through Principles of Mission Command. Military Review, 95(5), 9–18, 51.

[104] Air Marshal David Evans. (2016). War: A Matter of Principles (p. 72). Springer.

[105] Ibid.

[106] Ellis, Stephen, & van Kessel, Ineke. (2009). Movers and Shakers: Social Movements in Africa (p. 104). BRILL.

[107] Center for International Security and Cooperation. Al Shabaab, Mapping Militants. https://cisac.fsi.stanford.edu/mappingmilitants/profiles/al-shabaab#text_block_13374. Stanford.

[108] Maruf, Harun, & Joseph, Dan. (2018, December). No End in Sight for the al-Shabaab Threat to Somalia, 11(11), 17. CTC SENTINEL.

in Qoryoley and Mashallay by al-Shabaab infantry.[109] Mass combat in time and space has to occur simultaneously in order to record destructive and constructive results depending on who is carrying out the offensive so as to overwhelm the target's defensive system before they can react effectively. The five attacks were geared towards preventing AMISOM troops from getting reinforcement and supporting each other. UPDF fought the group fiercely and killed close to 100 al-Shabaab soldiers while losing 8 troops.[110] UPDF also destroyed weapons and explosives used by the terror group and 13 vehicles. The capability of AMISOM to perform such lethal counterstrikes and defensive operations is a crucial component of counterterrorism/counterinsurgency operation. Most Recently, al-Shabaab's capacity to "mass" has been tested by US and AMISOM airstrikes which has made the group vulnerable on the ground yet still focused on conducting attacks to weaken AMISOM and hinder its success.

In Operation Sledge Hammer[111] the principles of surprise, manoeuvre, and offensive were employed by the Kenya Defence Forces (KDF). The principle of surprise means to attack the adversary at a time, at a place, or in an approach for which he is unprepared, thereby placing the enemy on the defensive.[112] Manoeuvre aims to place the adversary in an unfavourable position through the flexible use of combat power.[113] Effective manoeuvre keeps enemies off balance by forcing them to confront new challenges and new threats quicker than they can

---

[109] Maruf, Harun. (2018, April 1). Extremists Attack African Union Base in Southern Somalia. VOA News. https://www.voanews.com/africa/extremists-attack-african-union-base-southern-somalia-0.

[110] Shmuel Yosef Agnon. (2018, April 3). UPDF-AMISOM Contingent Kill Close to 100 Al-Shabaab Militants in Bulo-Marer, Lower Shabelle. https://intelligencebriefs.com/updf-amisom-contingent-kill-close-to-100-al-shabaab-militants-in-bulo-marer-lower-shabelle/.

[111] Raghavan, Sudarsan. (2012, September 28). Kenyan Military Says It Has Driven Al-Shabab Militia from Its Last Stronghold in Somalia. The Washington Post. https://www.washingtonpost.com/world/africa/kenyan-military-drives-al-qaedas-shabab-militia-out-of-somali-port/2012/09/28/e06b2646-095f-11e2-858a-5311df86ab04_story.html.

[112] Johnsen, William T. (1995). The Principles of War in the 21st Century: Strategic Considerations (p. 19). DIANE Publishing; Lt. Cmdr. Christopher E. Van Avery. (n.d). 12 New Principles of Warfare. http://armedforcesjournal.com/12-new-principles-of-warfare/.

[113] Johnsen, William T. (1995). The Principles of War in the 21st Century: Strategic Considerations (p. 33). DIANE Publishing.

deal with them. Operation Sledge Hammer also known as the Battle of Kismayo, AMISOM forces, SNA forces and Ras Kamboni teamed efforts to take control of the Port of Kismayo. It was a complex mission in which KDF forces landed on the Kismayo's northern beach on 28 September 2012 under the cover of darkness.[114] As a team advanced on Kismayo by sea, another group of troops advanced on land from the north and south. Using a snake-like formation, AMISOM troops moved into Kismayo and took strategic positions before al-Shabaab could respond to the surprise attack. It caught residents of Kismayu by surprise. Al-Shabaab had become familiar with land assaults and therefore the amphibious attack was a great deception and clever use of the terrain to AMISOM's advantage.[115]

The oceanic assault was backed by aerial bombing of al-Shabaab targets. There was little opposition, and the port was easily secured with no casualties to the KDF. The micro surprises were critical to tip the al-Shabaab off balance and keep them at a disadvantage. Al-Shabaab militants took flight leaving only pockets of opposition that were overrun as they merely reacted to the heated situation on ground that AMISOM controlled. The undertaking was challenging as it involved synchronizing an attack with naval, ground, and air force with no/limited civilian casualties and even worse blue-on-blue encounters (attacks on someone who is in the same team).[116] The operation was lauded for liberating several coastal towns from al-Shabaab control and being the first operation of its kind by an African military. The plan was to isolate the city's southern airfield, an accessible corridor used by al-Shabaab to transfer their armoury, before seizing other important positions where the al-Shabaab operates. Kismayu was al-Shabaab's base and the port its fiscal engine, providing an approximate $35 million to $50 million annually

---

[114] Zimmerman, Katherine. (2012, October 3). Al Shabaab after Kismayo. https://www.criticalthreats.org/analysis/al-shabaab-after-kismayo; Daily Nation. (2015). Outnumbered Outgunned, and Outwitted: How KDF Took Charge of Kismayu Town. https://www.nation.co.ke/lifestyle/dn2/How-KDF-took-charge-of-Kismayu-town/957860-2748750-btab16z/index.html.

[115] Ibid.

[116] Ibid.

to the terrorist group.[117] Ejection of al-Shabaab was meant to indicate the total annihilation of its power of all the financial and logistical operations.[118]

The Kismayu takeover compelled al-Shabaab to regroup at strategic positions throughout Jubaland and Shebelle Valley.[119] Operation Juba Corridor was therefore launched in July 2015 as a collaborative effort between the 3000 Ethiopian National Defence Forces, Kenya Defence Forces, and supporting units within the Somali National Army with the aim of destroying al-Shabaab strongholds in the Bay, Bakool, and Gedo which were the heart of al-Shabaab's operations.[120] A month prior, al-Shabaab had attacked a Burundian military base in Leego killing 54 soldiers and taking with them military hardware.[121] These regions of Somalia between the Ethiopian and Kenyan borders needed to be secured to prevent overspill of al-Shabaab into their countries. Jubaland forces also assisted in the operation by approaching Baadhere from a different direction from the KDF, taking the al-Shabaab by storm. This offensive took place after US precision attacks which killed 30 al-Shabaab fighters and some commanders.[122] AMISOM troops were also engaged in demining efforts because the explosive devices had been placed along major roads and neighbourhoods connecting communities making it difficult for the Somali population in these regions trade thus reducing economic

[117] Keatinge, Tom. (2014). The Role of Finance in Defeating Al-Shabaab (pp. 18–19). Royal United Services Institute for Defence and Security Studies. https://rusi.org/sites/default/files/201412_whr_214_keatinge_web_0.pdf.

[118] Counter Extremism Project. (n.d). Al-Shabab. https://www.counterextremism.com/threat/al-shabab.

[119] Solomon, Hussein, & Meleagrou-Hitchens, Alexander. (2012). Factors Responsible for Al-Shabab's Losses in Somalia, CTC Sentinel, 5(9), 7–9.

[120] Ambassador Francisco Caetano Madeira. (2016). Operation Jubba Corridor Struck to the Heart of Al-Shabaab's Operations in Gedo, a Vulnerable Province Near Kenya. https://www.theafricareport.com/1082/now-is-not-the-time-to-slacken-our-commitment-to-amisom/.

[121] Lotze, Walter, & Williams, Paul D. (2016, May). The Surge to Stabilize: Lessons for the UN from the AU's Experience in Somalia (p. 15). New York: International Peace Institute.

[122] FRANCE 24. (2015). AU, Somali Troops Drive Al Shabaab Out of Key Base. https://www.france24.com/en/20150722-au-somali-troops-drive-al-shabaab-out-key-base-bardhere.

growth.[123] It cleared the main supply routes to enable delivery of humanitarian aid to the population. After a heavy offensive these towns among others were recovered and placed under their command. Although the operation was considered a great breakthrough in the fight against al-Shabaab, the fighting continued in other areas where the group had not been defeated. The principles of economy of force and surprise were employed with the use of drone strikes. A counterterrorism weapon being used in the same operating environment for the success of a PKO. Surprise prevents an enemy from acquiring an unexpected advantage while economy of force is the judicious employment and distribution of combat power based on primary and secondary enemies.[124] The use of drones and air strikes decreased al-Shabaab's capacity to function in a unified, effective manner and restricts their ability to control regions.[125] It weakens the effectiveness of terrorist/insurgent groups by eliminating the brains, power, and backbone of their operations, that is persons with valuable skills, resources, and connections.[126]

As these principles also apply to al-Shabaab attacks, the organization applied economy of force and surprise constantly. Economy of force[127] was employed in relation to the allocation of minimum combat power to subordinate efforts. This was seen when the group would retreat to rural areas when it was obvious that AMISOM had an upper hand as seen in Operation Sledge Hammer and Juba Corridor. The terrorist group also used surprise, flexibility, and manoeuvre in its terror attacks in Kenya and Uganda. The Uganda twin attack illustrated al-Shabaab's flexibility and ability to strike beyond Somalia's border as well as presence of sleeper cells. The attacks were carried out attacks during the screening

---

[123] AMISOM. Update on Operation Jubba Corridor. https://www.peaceau.org/en/article/update-on-operation-jubba-corridor.

[124] Johnsen, William T. (1995). The Principles of War in the 21st Century: Strategic Considerations (pp. 31, 34). DIANE Publishing.

[125] Jordan, Jenna. (2014, Spring). Attacking the Leader, Missing the Mark: What Terrorist Groups Survive Decapitation Strikes. International Security, 38(4), 7–38; Johnston, Patrick B. (2012, Spring). Does Decapitation Work? Assessing the Effectiveness of Leadership Targeting in Counterinsurgency Campaigns. International Security, 36(4), 47–79.

[126] Jordan, Jenna. (2009). When Heads Roll: Assessing the Effectiveness of Leadership Decapitation. Security Studies, 18(4), 719–755.

[127] Johnsen, William T. (1995). The Principles of War in the 21st Century: Strategic Considerations (p. 13). DIANE Publishing.

of the World Cup killing 74 people.[128] Kenya has had many al-Shabaab attacks. In 2013 al-Shabaab launched the Westgate Mall which left 65 people dead, the Garissa University attack, and a number of attacks at the Manda Bay military base in Lamu, among others.[129] As stated earlier once an attack is launched in adherence to these principles the likelihood of success is high whether it is an insurgent group or peacekeeping mission.

Challenges to Successful Counterterrorism Efforts in AMISOM

Efforts to maintain peacekeeping where there is no peace to keep has led to increased counterterrorism. The inevitable merger is fraught with challenges which in some instances are both structural strategic and operational. Unpacking some of these challenges is critical for further discussions on the route taken by AU in continental peacekeeping operations and some of the structural bottlenecks which ought to be removed for the success of PKOs.

Given the diversity of armed forces from countries represented in AMISOM, tensions within its command structures can manifest in ways that challenge the mission's success in CT. For example, the existence of armed forces drawn from different countries is a great challenge to interoperability of equipment and doctrine.[130] AMISOM troops are deployed following a country-based sectorization approach in which every nation is accountable for a specific geographical region in Somalia. The AMISOM sectorization was organic, as it developed from the increased military personnel, in essence from two TCCs, Uganda and Burundi troops to the inclusion of Kenya, Ethiopia, and Djibouti. The six sectors comprise as follows; sector one which covers Banadir and Lower Shabelle is under Ugandan People's Defence Forces command; in sector two, Kenya Defence Forces safeguard lower and middle Juuba which comprises Dholbey, Tabda, and Afmadow; Ethiopian National Defence Force are in

---

[128] Aljazeera. (2010). Al-Shabab Claims Uganda Bombings Twin Attacks Targeting World Cup Fans in Kampala kill at Least 74 People. https://www.aljazeera.com/news/africa/2010/07/2010711212520826984.html.

[129] International News Safety Institute, Country profile for Kenya. https://newssafety.org/country-profiles/detail/19/kenya/.

[130] Freear, Matt, & de Coning, Cedric. (2013). Lessons from African Union Mission for Somalia for Peace Operations in Mali. International Journal for Security and Development, 2(2)23, 1–11.

charge of sector three which covers Bakool, Bay, and Gedo; Djiboutian forces have been deployed in sector four which encompasses Hiiran and Galgadung[131]; sector five is protected by Burundian Armed Forces and covers Lower Shebelle; sector six involves a multinational approach in which Kenyan, Burundian, and Ethiopian troops have been deployed.[132] The complexity of the incorporation of various national troops, which involves the synchronization of a range of diverse institutional cultures, capabilities, and has not been an easy feat. Tensions associated to strategies employed and priorities among different troop contingents are rife. For example, parallel military operations conducted in AMISOM's operating environment by Ethiopia and Kenya without the approval of the mission.[133] In another case, Kenyans were made second in command of AMISOM. The Burundians strongly felt that they ought to have been given the position as they joined the mission earlier and had suffered more casualties. In an effort to ensure force cohesion as each nation employed significant operational autonomy in their particular sectors, AMISOM established the Military Operations Coordination Committee at chief-of-staff level position.[134]

The challenge posed by country-specific sectorization is the interests of individual TCCs and the absence of a centralized command and control structure. In UN multidimensional operations all TCCs are under a singular command structure. In AMISOM the operational environment is large in comparison to the number of boots on ground however, the force commander has no control over the TCC troops. The Djibouti declaration states that AMISOM TCCs were expected to obey orders of the force commander in order to accomplish synergy of the Mission's efforts against al-Shabaab.[135] The inclusion of this declaration in a high-level

---

[131] AMISOM Military Component. http://amisom-au.org/mission-profile/military-component/.

[132] Williams, Paul D. (2018). Fighting for Peace in Somalia: A History and Analysis of the African Mission in Somalia (p. 16). Oxford University Press.

[133] Wyss, Marco, & Tardy, Thierry. (2014). Peacekeeping in Africa: The Evolving Security Architecture (p. 164). Routledge.

[134] Ibid. (p. 4).

[135] The Permanent Mission of the Republic of Djibouti to the United Nations. (2016). Summit of the Troop and Police Contributing Countries of the African Union Mission in Somalia (AMISOM). Djibouti Declaration. https://www.un.int/djibouti/news/summit-troop-and-police-contributing-countries-african-union-mission-somalia-amisom.

document indicates that the force commander had no control over the AMISOM forces. Such command and control challenges are also experienced in AU force headquarters in Addis Ababa since the African Union cannot determine what the TCC governments ought to do with their troops.[136]

AMISOM has operated as a counterinsurgency operation consisting of an irregularly coordinated block of TCCs because the force commander does not have combat command[137] (i.e., full range of control over the troops and equipment). Instead of possessing complete operational command, and control of the mission, AMISOM's force headquarters in Mogadishu has largely performed a liaising role, although it failed to guarantee effective coordination through the mission's various sectors. On the surface, it seems quite evident that the operational control challenges within the mission can be easily addressed, however, it all boiled down to the mandate and the context of Somalia. As AMISOM's mandate evolved into peace enforcement, it was imperative to have more unilateral operations. It becomes very challenging to fight a war successfully if soldiers from different states are involved at the same time unless they undergo training in the same camps. The closer the theatre of operation is likened to war the more unilateral the operations should be because, for example, the Ugandan military knows its military best so the sectorization approach becomes application albeit with challenges stated above. A potential result of this sectoral approach is that al-Shabaab operates in the borders between the sectors due to AMISOM's weakness in cross-sector and multinational operations.

As mentioned in the paragraph above AMISOM troops have continuously acted unilaterally based on their interests and intelligence they had gathered. In counterterrorism theatres, sharing information with team members is critical. From 2007 Ethiopia, Kenya, and the United States have been undertaking different kinds of military operations in AMISOM's operational environment. These acts were neither under AMISOM's command, nor did these nations always seek out prior authorization, or even synchronize their actions with AMISOM. Ethiopia regularly conducted military operations within Somalia between 2006

---

[136] Lotze, Walter, & Williams, Paul D. (2016). The Surge to Stabilize: Lessons for the UN from the AU's Experience in Somalia. IPI Publications.

[137] Alberts, David S., & Hayes, Richard. (1995). Command Arrangements for Peace Operations. National Defense University Press.

and 2009, and later in 2011. These operations often included thousands of troops on air and on ground. These attacks were not welcomed by Somali nationals and became a magnet to youth joining al-Shabaab. In 2014, Ethiopian troops were deployed as part of AMISOM. Its counterpart Kenya invaded Somalia in 2011–2012 in an operation called Linda Nchi[138] (protect the country) with a troop strength of 6000.[139] Kenya's goal was to stop al-Shabaab attacks in the country by building a buffer zone to the city of Afmadow, which was a known al-Shabaab stronghold. Since the invasion airstrikes in Sectors 2 and 6 have been the norm.[140] During the same period US drone strikes in Somalia increased.[141] US special forces also conducted raids during the same period to date. In 2017 the United States conducted 33 drone strikes,[142] in 2018 an estimated 45 air strikes[143] and in 2019 63 attacks were reported.[144] These unilateral interventions undermine unity of command in counterterrorism operations. If there was a unified counterterrorism strategy, then all troop/police contributing countries would work in concert with the shared goal. The lack of a strategy means each nation conducts operations within its own discretion. This has the potential to harm future missions. As the decisions are made at the strategic level. It is imperative to ensure that all Troop and Police Contributing Countries (T/PCC) have a shared vision of the mandate, ROE as well as purpose of the mission itself.

[138] Williams, Paul. (2019). Fighting for Peace in Somalia: A History and Analysis of the African Union Mission (AMISOM), 2007–2017 (p. 127). Oxford University Press; Anderson, David M., & McKnight, Jacob. (2015). Kenya at War: Al-Shabaab and Its Enemies in Eastern Africa. African Affairs, 114(454), 1–27.

[139] Anderson, David M., & McKnight, Jacob. (2015). Kenya at War: Al-Shabaab and Its Enemies in Eastern Africa. African Affairs, 114(454), 1–27.

[140] Zimmerman, Katherine. (2011, October 24). Timeline: Operation Linda Nchi. https://www.criticalthreats.org/analysis/timeline-operation-linda-nchi.

[141] Williams, Paul D. (2018). Fighting for Peace in Somalia: A History and Analysis of the African Union Mission in Somalia (p. 128). Oxford University Press.

[142] The Bureau of Investigative Journalism's "Drone Warfare" database at https://www.thebureauinvestigates.com/projects/drone-war.

[143] The Bureau of Investigative Journalism. (2018). Somalia: Reported US Actions. Somalia: Reported US Actions. https://www.thebureauinvestigates.com/drone-war/data/somalia-reported-us-actions-2018.

[144] The Bureau of Investigative Journalism. (2019). Somalia: Reported US Actions. https://www.thebureauinvestigates.com/drone-war/data/somalia-reported-us-actions-2019-strike-logs.

Fourthly, there was a disparity between equipment available[145] for counterterrorism operations and the threat posed by the terrorist organization al-Shabaab. Combating terrorism demands more dynamic capabilities for instance: intelligence, military air assets, Quick Reaction Force (QRF), and constructive real-time communication. All these capabilities are tough to negotiate, and in the eventuality of bilateral support there are preconditions that streamline those national contingents who qualify to access them. The AU should be able to assist TCCs with considerable assistance in negotiation, deployment, pre-deployment training, and monitoring and evaluation of the use of these assets. Although the AU has assisted to some degree in facilitating operational readiness of forces using the AMANI II Field Training Exercise, more efforts can be taken. Moreover, in the early years of the operation AMISOM lacked critical enablers and resources such as military helicopters, engineering, transportation, and logistics capabilities that were approved by the UNSC. This is humiliating for a mission that peacekeepers died in thousands because of neglect. It also meant that in the eventuality of a terrorist attack it was difficult to send backup as these assets and the quick reaction force were not under the force commander's control. For instance, AMISOM lacked a QRF to assist the Ugandan, Burundian, and Kenyan contingents who were attacked in their operational bases.[146] At the time of these attacks, AMISOM did not have any military helicopters which could have been used. Especially in remote locations such as El Adde where al-Shabaab launched the worst attack on any peacekeeping mission recorded.[147] The Kenyan operational base was in a remote area which made the peacekeepers vulnerable to attacks from the insurgent group which has substantial freedom of movement.[148] These attacks against AMISOM operational bases were an unpleasant reminder that AMISOM strongly relied on poorly equipped troops to neutralize extremists. In order to prevent such attacks from taking place, AMISOM should

---

[145] Boon, Kristen, Huq, Aziz Z., & Lovelace, Douglas. (2012). U.S. Approaches to Global Security Challenges (p. 494). Oxford University Press; Ploch, Lauren. (2011). Countering Terrorism in East Africa: The U. S. Response (p. 30). DIANE Publishing.

[146] Williams, Paul D. (2016). The Battle at El Adde: The Kenya Defence Forces, Al-Shabaab, and Unanswered Questions, Issue Brief (p. 9). International Peace Institute.

[147] Ibid. (p. 6).

[148] Williams, Paul D. (2019). Lessons for "Partnership Peacekeeping" from the African Union Mission in Somalia (p. 3). IPI Institute.

ensure that an equipment package covers all the requisite equipment for counterterrorism/counterinsurgency operations.

Fifthly, suspicion among the troop contributing countries greatly affected sharing of intelligence among AMISOM troops.[149] Unity of effort cannot be achieved if the contingents are distrustful of each other thereby jeopardizing military operations. As indicated previously, Kenya and Ethiopia which had part of their troops integrated into AMISOM in January 2014 were also frequently blamed of pursuing nefarious political interests in Somalia and utilizing AMISOM to legitimize and mask their activities. Besides illicit trading, specific allegations involved selecting winners in the race to establish the new regional administrations. While in the case of Ethiopia case, behaving as the power behind the throne of the Federal Government of Somalia.[150] This was also witnessed by the remarks of UPDF Brigadier Paul Lokech that his troops had been conducting counterinsurgency operations in Mogadishu[151] while other KDF troops in Kismayo would not leave their bases to collect intelligence and cordon villages.[152] Such experiences indicate that each TCC has been serving its own interests which means that nobody covers or supports each other. It also justifies why an outpost was overrun in the Gedo region, yet the response team had to come from Nairobi, two days later.[153] An unfortunate occurrence yet Ethiopian troops were not far off, but due to poor communication their support was absent. If proper command and control particularly, operational command such an incident would be a fallacy, reinforcement would have been dispatched to protect the soldiers in El Adde.[154] Additionally, KDF forces and SNA soldiers

---

[149] Williams, Paul D. (2016). The Battle at El Adde: The Kenya Defence Forces, al-Shabaab, and Unanswered Questions, Issue Brief (pp. 6–15). International Peace Institute.

[150] Williams, Paul D., & Effectiveness of Peace Operations Network. (n.d). Assessing the Effectiveness of the African Union Mission in Somalia (p. 75). George Washington University.

[151] Mwenda, Andrew M. (2012, August 11). Taking the War Beyond Mogadishu. The Independent. http://www.independent.co.ug/cover-story/6251?task=view.

[152] Verini, James. (2012, December 17). The Last Stand of Somalia's Jihad. Foreign Policy, 4. https://foreignpolicy.com/2012/12/17/the-last-stand-of-somalias-jihad/.

[153] Maruf, Harun, & Joseph, Dan. (2018). Inside Al-Shabaab: The Secret History of Al-Qaeda's Most Powerful Ally (p. 251). Indiana University Press.

[154] Africa Yearbook Volume 13. (2017). Politics, Economy and Society South of the Sahara in 2016 (p. 330). BRILL.

stationed at El Adde had a poor working relationship.[155] It was virtually impossible for AMISOM to defeat al-Shabaab without the support of the local population and an effective set of Somali national security forces, therefore cultivating a good relationship was critical. According to Williams (2016), the attacks that were used in El Adde by al-Shabaab were similar in nature to that of the Burundian and Ugandan bases. The tactics involved vulnerability of the freshly deployed rotations of military personnel; inability to conform to known al-Shabaab strategies such as vehicle-borne improvised explosive devices; inability to deliver timely support to friendly units in distress; poor relationship with Somali security forces and local population; insufficient base defences as well as inability to spot al-Shabaab preparations for the attack.[156] All these factors stated above play out previous attacks and particularly in El Adde. During the attacks, no SNA troops were present. A critical factor that should not be neglected because approximately three hundred SNA soldiers were positioned at the base as part of the personnel Kenya had trained in 2011. A week before the gruesome attack less than thirty SNA troops were in El Adde and some clan elders mentioned that a possible attack was imminent. The Somali National Army was given three options by al-Shabaab namely, to blend with the local population; leave El Adde and move to Garbaharey or Elwak; if not perish/be killed with the Kenyan contingent. A number of the SNA troops heeded the warning given to them by al-Shabaab and the result was an empty SNA base during the time of the attack.[157] The SNA base neighboured the El Adde base which means the contingents at the base should have picked up and acted on the danger signs.

Conclusion

The chapter sought to unpack the changing dynamics of peacekeeping in the AMISOM and the merger of peacekeeping and counterterrorism. PKOs are now being deployed to respond to violent intra-state violence and as such the role of peacekeepers has morphed from observation

---

[155] Williams, Paul D. (2016). The Battle at El Adde: The Kenya Defence Forces, al-Shabaab, and Unanswered Questions (p. 6). International Peace Institute.
[156] Ibid. (pp. 6–9).
[157] Ibid. (p. 7).

and monitoring to secure peace processes with the view of ensuring sustainable peace. AMISOM was an atypical operation compared to other traditional or contemporary PKOs for five reasons: it was tasked to recover territories from al-Shabaab; it was mandated to perform counterterrorism operations; logistical support to the mission was offered by the UN; the mission was mandated to become one of the key protagonists in the conflict so as to protect the TFG in a highly dangerous environment; and Somalia's Eastern African neighbours provided personnel for the mission.[158] The mission therefore lost some credibility in the eyes of some Somalis. It was often viewed as an occupational force and a party to the conflict by Somali nationals and therefore al-Shabaab heavily pursued a strategy of calculated targeting of AMISOM's military, police, and civilian components. It was against this background that the Principles of Peacekeeping and Principles of War were used to assess AMISOM's mandate and operations since its inception. The key argument being that the binaries of peacekeeping and counterterrorism, often seen to be at cross purposes, are no longer polar opposites but rather linked by the constantly evolving threats to the international security system.

The chapter also purposed to sketch out some of the dangers that have accompanied the convergence of peacekeeping and counterterrorism. There is clear evidence that TCCs did not have adequate artillery, armoury, and flexibility to fight al-Shabaab as it changed its tactics continuously. AMISOM would have had an upper hand with four things; firstly, increased agility and flexibility at all levels (strategic, tactical, and operational); secondly satisfactory force enablers and thirdly, less dependence on financial resources and fourthly, good maintenance capabilities to ensure crucial to successful military advances. These lacunas have ramifications beyond the simple understanding of the mission's mandate as this interaction is critical for attaining the mission end-state. The desired end-state was greatly challenged by a high number of civilian deaths obtained through the heavy-handed comeback to al-Shabaab attacks. It is also evident that although AMISOM's mandate did not include an explicit protection of civilians' mandate, local Somalis assumed that the mission would automatically protect them. The African Union therefore must pivot all its peacekeeping missions on a clear strategy for the protection

---

[158] Wondemagegnehu, Dawit Yohannes, & Kebede, Daniel Gebreegziabher. (2017). AMISOM: Charting a New Course for African Union Peace Missions. African Security Review, 26(2), 199–219.

of civilian mandate in order to reduce civilian casualties in its operational environment—because this inexorably wears down the mission's legitimacy, champions blow back to the mission as it pushes people to further support the "enemy," and eventually dents the mission's effectiveness.

The AMISOM case study offers a unique opportunity for the AU to undertake a diagnostic exercise based on recent and current peace support operations, relating to the impact of terrorism on peace support operations, with a view to reposition the AU's role to better support its member states in their security approaches to counterterrorism. There is currently a disparity between equipment and other capabilities deployed for counterterrorism operations and the definite threat of the cancerous nature of terrorism. The merger of peacekeeping and counterterrorism provides a grim reminder that in some cases multilateral peacekeeping operations depend on poorly equipped troops to address acute security challenges. A paradigm shift is therefore requisite to change the future of peacekeeping and counterterrorism on the continent and as it stands AMISOM's military success or lack thereof is still fragile and reversible.

References

Abidde, Sabella, & Abegunrin, Olayiwola. (2018). African Intellectuals and the State of the Continent: Essays in Honor of Professor Sulayman S. Nyang. Cambridge Scholars Publishing.

Adebajo, Adekeye. (2011). UN Peacekeeping in Africa: From the Suez Crisis to the Sudan Conflicts. Lynne Rienner Publishers.

Air Marshal David Evans. (2016). War: A Matter of Principles. Springer.

Africa Yearbook. (2017). Politics, Economy and Society South of the Sahara in 2016 (Vol. 13). BRILL.

African Union. AMISOM Background. http://amisom-au.org/amisom-background/.

African Union. (2002). Protocol Relating to the Establishment of the Peace and Security Council of the African Union. https://au.int/en/treaties/protocol-relating-establishment-peace-and-security-council-african-union.

African Union. (2003). Policy Framework for the Establishment of the African Standby Force and the Military Staff Committee Exp/ASF-MSC/2 (I). https://www.peaceau.org/uploads/asf-policy-framework-en.pdf.

African Union. (2007). Communique of the 69th Meeting of the Peace and Security Council, PSC/PR/Comm(LXIX). https://www.peaceau.org/uploads/communiqueeng-69th.pdf.

African Union, AMISOM. (2014). AMISOM and Somali National Army drive Al Shabaab Out of Six Towns. https://amisom-au.org/2014/03/amisom-and-somali-national-army-drive-al-shabaab-out-of-six-towns/.
Agnon, Shmuel Yosef. (2018, April 3). UPDF-AMISOM Contingent Kill Close to 100 Al-Shabaab Militants in Bulo-Marer. Lower Shabelle. https://intell igencebriefs.com/updf-amisom-contingent-kill-close-to-100-al-shabaab-milita nts-in-bulo-marer-lower-shabelle/.
Alberts, David S., & Hayes, Richard. (1995). Command Arrangements for Peace Operations. National Defense University Press.
Alexander, Orakhelashvili. (2011). Collective Security. Oxford United Press: Oxford.
Aljazeera. (2010). Al-Shabab Claims Uganda Bombings Twin Attacks Targeting World Cup Fans in Kampala Kill at Least 74 people. https://www.aljazeera.com/news/africa/2010/07/2010711212520826984.html.
Ambassador Francisco Caetano Madeira. (2016). Operation Jubba Corridor Struck to the Heart of Al-Shabaab's Operations in Gedo, a Vulnerable Province Near Kenya. https://www.theafricareport.com/1082/now-is-not-the-time-to-slacken-our-commitment-to-amisom/.
AMISOM Civilian Component. http://amisom-au.org/mission-profile/ami som-civilian-component/.
AMISOM Military Component. http://amisom-au.org/mission-profile/mil itary-component/.
AMISOM Police. https://amisom-au.org/mission-profile/amisom-police/.
AMISOM Police. https://amisom-au.org/wp-content/cache/page_enhanced/ amisom-au.org/mission-profile/amisom-police/_index.html_gzip.
AMISOM, Update on Operation Jubba Corridor. https://www.peaceau.org/ en/article/update-on-operation-jubba-corridor.
Anderson, David M. & McKnight, Jacob. (2015). Kenya at war: Al-Shabaab and its enemies in Eastern Africa. African Affairs,114(454), 1–27.
Beadle, A. W. (2012). Protecting Civilians While Fighting a War in Somalia – Drawing Lessons from Afghanistan. NUPI Policy Brief.
Bouchet-Saulnier, Françoise. (2013). The Practical Guide to Humanitarian Law. Rowman & Littlefield Publishers.
Botha, Anneli. (2008). Challenges in Understanding Terrorism in Africa: A Human Security Perspective. African Security Review, 17(2), 28–41.
Boon, Kristen, Huq, Aziz Z., & Lovelace, Douglas. (2012). U.S. Approaches to Global Security Challenges. Oxford University Press.
Bronwyn E. Bruton, & Williams, Paul D. (2014). Report on Counterinsurgency in Somalia: Lessons Learned from the African Union Mission in Somalia. JSOU Report 14–5. https://www.socom.mil/JSOU/JSOUPublications/JSO U145_BrutonWilliams_AMISOM_FINAL.pdf.

Center for International Security and Cooperation. Al Shabaab, mapping militants. https://cisac.fsi.stanford.edu/mappingmilitants/profiles/al-shabaab#text_block_13374.Stanford.
Cellamare, Giovanni, & Ingravallo, Ivan. (2018). Peace Maintenance in Africa: Open Legal Issues. Springer.
Charbonneau, Bruno. (2018, June 28). Counterterrorism and Challenges to Peacekeeping Impartiality. The Global Observatory. https://theglobalobservatory.org/2018/06/counterterrorism-peacekeeping-impartiality/.
Crelinsten, Ronald. (2014) Perspectives on Counterterrorism: From Stovepipes to a Comprehensive Approach. http://www.terrorismanalysts.com/pt/index.php/pot/article/view/321/html.
Davies, Sara E., & True, Jacqui. (2019). The Oxford Handbook of Women, Peace, and Security. Oxford University Press.
De Coning, Cedric, Gelot, Linnéa, & Karlsrud, John. (2013). The Future of African Peace Operations: From the Janjaweed to Boko Haram. Zed Books Ltd.
de Coning, Cedric. (2017). Peace Enforcement in Africa: Doctrinal Distinctions between the African Union and United Nations. Contemporary Security Policy, 38(1), 145–160.
Dersso, Solomon Ayele. (2010). Somalia Dilemmas: Changing Security Dynamics, Limited Policy Options. International Security Studies Paper no. 218, Addis Ababa: Institute for Security Studies. https://issafrica.org/research/papers/somalia-dilemmas-changing-security-dynamics-but-limited-policy-choices.
Ellis, Stephen & van Kessel, Ineke. (2009). Movers and Shakers: Social Movements in Africa, 104. BRILL.
FRANCE 24. (2015). AU, Somali Troops Drive Al Shabaab Out of Key Base. https://www.france24.com/en/20150722-au-somali-troops-drive-al-shabaab-out-key-base-bardhere.
Freear, Matt, & de Coning, Cedric. (2013). Lessons from African Union Mission for Somalia for Peace Operations in Mali. International Journal for Security and Development, 2(2), Art. 23, 1–11.
Garowe Online. (2020). US Trained Forces Operations Kills Al-Shabaab Militants in Somalia, Staff Correspondent. https://www.garoweonline.com/en/news/somalia/us-trained-forces-operation-kills-al-shabaab-militants-in-somalia.
Garowe Online. (2018). US Trained Somalia Danaab Forces Kill Dozens of Al-Shabaab Militants, Staff Correspondent https://www.garoweonline.com/en/news/somalia/us-trained-somalias-danab-forces-kill-dozens-of-al-shabaab-militants.

Gatehouse, Gabriel. (2012, September 24). Kenyan AMISOM Soldier Kills Six Somali Civilians. Nairobi: BBC News. https://www.bbc.com/news/world-africa-19698348.
Geraint, Hughes (2011, May). The Military's Role in Counterterrorism: Examples and Implications for Liberal Democracies, Letort Paper. https://publications.armywarcollege.edu/pubs/2140.pdf.
Global Security African. (n.d). Union Mission in Somalia. https://www.globalsecurity.org/military/world/int/amisom.htm.
Goldbaum, Christina. (2018). A Trumpian War on Terror That Just Keeps Getting Bigger "Drone Strikes May Have a Purpose, But They are No Substitute for a Political Strategy". https://www.theatlantic.com/international/archive/2018/09/drone-somalia-al-shabaab-al-qaeda-terrorist-africa-trump/569680/.
Goldenberg. (2020). US Airstrike Kills Three Al Shabaab Terrorists in Bangeeni, Lower Jubba in Support of Danaab Forces. https://intelligencebriefs.com/us-airstrike-kills-three-al-shabaab-terrorists-in-bangeeni-lower-jubba-in-support-of-danaab-forces/.
Gray, C. S. (2002). Defining and Achieving Decisive Victory. U.S. Army War College.
Gray, Colin S. (2013). War, Peace and International Relations: An Introduction to Strategic History. Routledge.
Grigsby, Jr., Wayne W., Fox, Todd, Dabkowski, Matthew F., & Phelps, Andrea N. (2015). Globally Integrated Operations in the Horn of Africa Through Principles of Mission Command. Military Review, 95(5), 9–18.
Hansen, Stig Jarle. (2013). Al-Shabaab in Somalia: The History and Ideology of a Militant Islamist Group, 2005–2012. Oxford University Press.
Harnisch, Chris. (2010). The Terror Threat from Somalia: The International Ization of Al Shabaab. Critical Threats Project of the American Enterprise Institute. https://www.criticalthreats.org/analysis/the-terror-threat-from-somalia-the-internationalization-of-al-shabaab.
Hassan, Muhsin. (2012). Understanding Drivers of Violent Extremism: The Case of Al-Shabab and Somali Youth. CTC Sentinel, 5(8), 18–20. http://www.ctc.usma.edu/posts/understanding-drivers-of-violent-extremism-the-case-of-al-shabab-andsomali-youth.
Headquarters, Department of the Army. Counterinsurgency Operations. Field Manual – Interim.
Institute for Economics & Peace. Global Terrorism Index 2019: Measuring the Impact of Terrorism. Sydney. http://visionofhumanity.org/app/uploads/2019/11/GTI-2019web.pdf.
International News Safety Institute. (n.d). Country Profile for Kenya. https://newssafety.org/country-profiles/detail/19/kenya/.

John A. United States Army, United States Marine Corps. (2008). The U.S. Army/Marine Corps Counterinsurgency Field Manual. University of Chicago Press.
John, Maszka. (2017). Al-Shabaab and Boko Haram: Guerrilla Insurgency or Strategic Terrorism? World Scientific.
Johnsen, William T. (1995). The Principles of War in the 21st Century: Strategic Considerations. DIANE Publishing.
Johnston, Patrick B. (2012). Does Decapitation Work? Assessing the Effectiveness of Leadership Targeting in Counterinsurgency Campaigns. International Security, 36(4), 47–79.
Jones, Seth. G., Liepman, Andrew., & Chandler, Nathan. (2016). Counter terrorism and Counterinsurgency in Somalia Assessing the Campaign against Al Shabaab. Santa Monica, California: The RAND Corporation. https://www.rand.org/content/dam/rand/pubs/research_reports/RR1500/RR1539/RAND_RR1539.pdf.
Jordan, Jenna (2014). Attacking the Leader, Missing the Mark: What Terrorist Groups Survive Decapitation Strikes. International Security, Vol. 38 (4), 7–38.
Jordan, Jenna. (2009). When Heads Roll: Assessing the Effectiveness of Leadership Decapitation. Security Studies, 18(4), 719–755.
Kaldor, Mary (1999). New and Old Wars: Organized Violence in a Global Era. Stanford University Press.
Keatinge, Tom (2014). The Role of Finance in Defeating Al-Shabaab. Royal United Services Institute for Defence and Security Studies. https://rusi.org/sites/default/files/201412_whr_214_keatinge_web_0.pdf.
Kenkel, Kai Michael. (2013). Five Generations of Peace Operations: From the "Thin Blue Line" to "Painting a Country Blue." Brasiliera Politica Internacionale, 56(1): 122–143.
Lapidus, Ira M. (2014). A History of Islamic Societies Front Cover. Cambridge University Press.
Leurdijk, Dick (2004). NATO's shifting priorities: From peace support operations to counter-terrorism. Tardy, Thierry (Ed). Peace operations after 11 September 2001. London, Frank Cass.
Lotze, Walter, & Kasumba, Yvonne. (2012) AMISOM and the Protection of Civilians in Somalia. Conflict Trends, 2, 17–24.
Lotze, Walter, & Williams, Paul D. (2016). The Surge to Stabilize: Lessons for the UN from the AU's Experience in Somalia. IPI Publications.
Maruf, Harun, & Joseph, Dan. (2018a). Inside Al-Shabaab: The Secret History of Al-Qaeda's Most Powerful Ally (p. 251). Indiana University Press.
Maruf, Harun, & Joseph, Dan. (2018b, December). No End in Sight for the Al-Shabaab Threat to Somalia. 11(11), 17. CTC SENTINEL.

Maruf, Harun. (2018, April 1). Extremists Attack African Union Base in Southern Somalia. VOA News. https://www.voanews.com/africa/extremists-attack-african-union-base-southern-somalia-0.
Mateja, Peter. (2015). Between Doctrine and Practice: The UN Peacekeeping Dilemma. Global Governance: A Review of Multilateralism and International Organizations, 21(3), 351–370.
Menkhaus, Ken. (2012). The Somali Spring. Foreign Policy, September 24, 2012. www.foreignpolicy.com/articles/2012/09/24/the_somali_spring?page=0,1.
Michael Jonsson & Daniel Torbjörnsson. (n.d). Resurgent, Reinvented or Simply Resilient? The Growing Threat of al-Shabaab in Somalia. Studies in African Security. https://www.foi.se/download/18.7fd35d7f166c56ebe0bb3bd/154 2369060470/Resurgent-Reinvented-or-Simply-Resilient_FOI-Memo-5913. pdf.
Miles, Kitts R. (2019). The Strategic Use of Force in Counterinsurgency: Find, Fix, Fight. Rowman & Littlefield.
Mwenda, Andrew M. (2012, August 11). Taking the War beyond Mogadishu. The Independent. http://www.independent.co.ug/cover-story/6251?task=view.
Nacos, Brigitte L. (2016). Terrorism and Counterterrorism. New York: Routledge.
Nagl, John A. (2005). Learning to Eat Soup with a Knife: Counterinsurgency Lessons from Malaya and Vietnam. Chicago: University of Chicago Press.
Ndegwa, Loise W. (2018). An Analysis of the Counterterrorism (CT) and Counterinsurgency (COIN) Operations Employed by African Union Mission in Somalia (AMISOM) to Counter the Threat of Al-Shabaab in Somalia (2007–2016). Cape Town, South Africa: University of Cape Town.
Ndiaye, Michelle (2016). The Relationship between the AU and the RECs/RMs in Relation to Peace and Security in Africa: Subsidiary and Inevitable Common Destiny in The Future of African Peace Operations. From the Janjaweed to Boko Haram. Cédric de Coning, Linnéa Gelot, & John Karlsrud (Eds.) Uppsala, Nordiska Afrikainstutet. http://nai.divaportal.org/smash/get/diva2:913028/FULLTEXT02.pdf.
O'Hanlon, Michael. (2003). Expanding Global Military Capacity for Humanitarian Intervention. Washington DC: Brookings Institution Press.
O'Neill, John Terence, & Rees, Nick. (2005). United Nations Peacekeeping in the Post-Cold War Era. Routledge.
Ononogbu, Olihe Adaeze, & Nwangwu, Chikodiri. (2018). Counter-Insurgency Operations of the African Union and Mitigation of Humanitarian Crisis in Somalia. Mediterranean Journal of Social Sciences, 117–129.

Per M. Norheim-Martinsen, Tore Nyhamar. (2015). International Military Operations in the 21st Century: Global Trends and the Future of Intervention. Routledge.

Paul, Christopher, Clarke, Colin P., & Grill, Beth. (2010). Victory Has a Thousand Fathers: Sources of Success in Counterinsurgency. Rand Corporation.

Philpott, Don. (2019). Is America Safe?: Terrorism, Homeland Security, and Emergency Preparedness. Rowman & Littlefield.

Ploch, Lauren. (2011). Countering Terrorism in East Africa: The U. S. Response. DIANE Publishing.

Raghavan, Sudarsan. (2012, September 28). Kenyan Military Says It Has Driven Al-Shabab Militia from Its Last Stronghold in Somalia. The Washington Post. https://www.washingtonpost.com/world/africa/kenyan-military-drives-al-qaedas-shabab-militia-out-of-somali-port/2012/09/28/e06b2646-095f-11e2-858a-5311df86ab04_story.html.

Rempfer, Kyle. (2019). Lightning Brigade: Training Advanced Infantry—Not Airstrikes—Is Africom's Primary Effort in Somalia. Military Times. https://www.militarytimes.com/news/your-military/2019/03/27/lightning-brigade-training-advanced-infantry-not-airstrikes-is-africoms-primary-effort-in-somalia/.

Security Council Counter Terrorism Committee (2010). United Nations Global Counter-Terrorism Strategy. https://www.un.org/sc/ctc/resources/general-assembly/un-global-counter-terrorism-strategy/.

Shawn Snow. (2019, September 30). US Launches Airstrikes on Al-Shabab in Response to Attack on US Commando Outpost in Somalia. Military Times. https://www.militarytimes.com/news/your-military/2019/09/30/extremists-launch-2-attacks-on-military-targets-in-somalia/.

Solomon, Hussein, & Meleagrou-Hitchens, Alexander. (2012). Factors Responsible for Al-Shabab's Losses in Somalia. CTC Sentinel, 5, 9.

The Bureau of Investigative Journalism's "Drone Warfare" database at https://www.thebureauinvestigates.com/projects/drone-war.

The Bureau of Investigative Journalism. (2018). Somalia: Reported US Actions. Somalia: Reported US Actions. https://www.thebureauinvestigates.com/drone-war/data/somalia-reported-us-actions-2018.

The Bureau of Investigative Journalism. (2019). Somalia: Reported US Actions. https://www.thebureauinvestigates.com/drone-war/data/somalia-reported-us-actions-2019-strike-logs.

The Permanent Mission of the Republic of Djibouti to the United Nations. (2016). Summit of the Troop and Police Contributing Countries of the African Union Mission in Somalia (AMISOM), Djibouti Declaration. https://www.un.int/djibouti/news/summit-troop-and-police-contributing-countries-african-union-mission-somalia-amisom.

Thierry, Tardy. (2007). The UN and the Use of Force: A Marriage Against Nature. Security Dialogue, 38(1), 49–70.
Tsagourias, Nicholas. (2006). Consent, Neutrality/Impartiality and the Use of Force in Peacekeeping Operations: Their Constitutional Dimension. Journal of Conflict & Security Law, 11(3), 465–482.
United Nations. (2000). Report of the Panel on United Nations Peace Operations, A/55/305–S/2000/809. https://www.un.org/ruleoflaw/files/brahimi%20report%20peacekeeping.pdf.
United Nations. (2008a). United Nations Peacekeeping Operations Principles and Guidelines. https://peacekeeping.un.org/sites/default/files/capstone_eng_0.pdf.
United Nations. (2008b). United Nations, Department of Peacekeeping Operations Principles and Guidelines (Capstone Doctrine) New York.
United Nations. (2015). Report of the High-Level Independent Panel on Peace Operations https://peaceoperationsreview.org/wpcontent/uploads/2015/08/HIPPO_Report_1_June_2015.pdf.
United Nations. (2019). Yearbook of the United Nations 2014. United Nations.
United Nations General Assembly and Security Council (UNGASC). (2000). Report of the Panel on United Nations Peace Operations A/55/305-S/2000/809. http://www.un.org/documents/ga/docs/55/a55305.pdf.
United Nations General Assembly A/72/840*. (2018). Activities of the United Nations system in implementing the United Nations Global Counter-Terrorism Strategy. https://undocs.org/pdf?symbol=en/A/72/840.
United Nations High Commissioner of Refugees & Center for Civilians in Conflict (CIVIC). (2011). Civilian Harm in Somalia: Creating an Appropriate Response. https://issuu.com/civiliansinconflict/docs/civic_somalia_2011/67.
United Nations Security Council Resolution 1722. http://unscr.com/en/resolutions/1772.
United Nations Security Council Resolution 1744, S/RES/1744. (2007). http://unscr.com/en/resolutions/1744.
United Nations Security Council. (2007). SC/8960 Security Council Authorizes Six-Month African Union Mission in Somalia, Unanimously Adopting Resolution 1744. (2007). https://www.un.org/press/en/2007/sc8960.doc.htm.
United Nations Security Council. (2009). https://www.un.org/securitycouncil/content/secretary-generals-reports-submitted-security-council-2009.
United Nations Security Council, SC/10550. (2012). Security Council Requests African Union to Increase Troop Level of Somalia Mission to 17,700, Establish Expanded Presence in Keeping with Strategic Concept. https://www.un.org/press/en/2012/sc10550.doc.htm.

United Nations Security Council Resolution. (2013). Resolution 2093. http://unscr.com/en/resolutions/2093.
United Nations Web TV, The United Nations Live & On Demand. (2018). Remarks of António Guterres to the 8407th Meeting of the United Nations Security Council Open Debate on Strengthening Peacekeeping Operations in Africa. http://webtv.un.org/watch/ant%C3%B3nio-guterresun-secretary-general-on-strengthening-peacekeepingoperations-in-africa-security-council-8407thmeeting/5969510237001/.
United States Congress House Committee on Foreign Affairs. (2014, October 3). Al-Shabaab: How Great a Threat? Hearing before the Committee on Foreign Affairs, House of Representatives, One Hundred Thirteenth Congress, First Session. U.S. Government Printing Office. https://www.govinfo.gov/content/pkg/CHRG-113hhrg85104/pdf/CHRG-113hhrg85104.pdf.
UNSC. (2009). United Nations Security Council. Retrieved from. https://www.un.org/securitycouncil/content/secretary-generals-reports-submitted-security-council-2009.
Verini, James (2012, December 17). The Last Stand of Somalia's Jihad. Foreign Policy. https://foreignpolicy.com/2012/12/17/the-last-stand-of-somalias-jihad/.
Williams, Paul D., & Effectiveness of Peace Operations Network. (n.d). Assessing the Effectiveness of the African Union Mission in Somalia. George Washington University.
Williams, Paul D. (2016). The Battle at El Adde: The Kenya Defence Forces, Al-Shabaab, and Unanswered Questions. International Peace Institute.
Williams, Paul D. (2018). Fighting Peace in Somalia: A History and Analysis of the African Union Mission in Somalia 2007–2017. Oxford University Press.
Williams, Paul. (2019). Fighting for Peace in Somalia: A History and Analysis of the African Union Mission (AMISOM), 2007–2017. Oxford University Press.
Williams, Paul D. (2019). Lessons for "Partnership Peacekeeping" from the African Union Mission in Somalia (p. 3). IPI Institute.
Willmot, Haidi, Ralph, Mamiya, Marc, Weller, & Sheeran, Scott (Eds.). (2016). Protection of Civilians. Oxford University Press.
Wilkinson, Paul. (2006). Terrorism Versus Democracy: The Liberal State Response. New York: Routledge.
Wise, Rob. (2011). Al-Shabaab. AQAM Futures Project: Case Studies Series. http://www.operationspaix.net/DATA/DOCUMENT/4039~v~Al_Shabaab.pdf.
Wondemagegnehu, Dawit Yohannes, & Kebede, Daniel Gebreegziabher. (2017). AMISOM: Charting a New Course for African Union Peace Missions. African Security Review, 26(2), 199–219.

Wood, M. (2018). Contemporary U.S. Counter-terrorism Strategy toward Somalia. Cape Town, South Africa: University of Cape Town.
Wyss, Marco, & Tardy, Thierry. (2014). Peacekeeping in Africa: The Evolving Security (p. 164). Architecture. Routledge.
Zimmerman, Katherine. (2011, October 24. Timeline: Operation Linda Nchi. https://www.criticalthreats.org/analysis/timeline-operation-linda-nchi.

CHAPTER 8

Cybersecurity and Online Child Trafficking in Africa: A Critique of the Legal Measures Adopted by African Countries

Mercy Mutheu Muendo

INTRODUCTION

Traditionally in many societies, a child was the most important person in the community, as an emblem of innocence and a symbol of the future and hope of the society. The community raised the child alongside the parents who treasured the child and took great care to know of her physical whereabouts. However, in the current digital age the menace known as child trafficking allows a lurking trafficker to prey on unattended children online. Indeed, this menace that began at the turn of the century has been compounded with the aid of technology. It has spread its tentacles into the internet and a virtual world born of cyber technology. The rampant harvesting grounds can be found in areas with little implementation of child and cybercrime laws. This book chapter seeks to analyse online child trafficking, the legal frameworks used to combat it, and

M. M. Muendo (✉)
School of Law, Daystar University, Nairobi, Kenya
e-mail: mercymuendo@gmail.com

© The Author(s), under exclusive license to Springer Nature
Switzerland AG 2023
J. Adero Ngala et al. (eds.), *Innovations in Peace and Security in Africa*,
https://doi.org/10.1007/978-3-031-39043-2_8

whether they have been effectively implemented. Of keen interest to this analysis are domestic criminal law and international law. This research also examines the legal frameworks that govern online child trafficking and child pornography in Africa; and accordingly addresses whether they are being effectively implemented by the necessary stakeholders.

DEFINING HUMAN CHILD TRAFFICKING

Child trafficking violates the tangible needs and physical rights of children but also their psychological and security rights. Children that have undergone the ills of child trafficking lose their right to dignity as a person and suffer psychological trauma with sometimes long-term mentally crippling effects. They also may suffer from dangerous psychopathy with predatory behaviour, at first as a coping security mechanism then later as a means of coping with an addiction arising from Post Traumatic Stress Disorder (e.g., paedophilia). Additionally, they may become child traffickers themselves since they know the ins and outs of the human trafficking industry if raised in such an environment.

Child sex trafficking is one form of child sexual exploitation. If a child takes part in a sexual act in exchange for some benefit or the promise of such from a perpetrator, the child is a victim of sexual exploitation. Several forms of child sexual exploitation, such as performing sexual activities in exchange for food or accommodation, can occur without the existence of trafficking. Likewise, the sexual exploitation of children through prostitution, while often related to trafficking, may occur without the child having been trafficked. Child pornography can be defined as technology-facilitated child sex trafficking and child sexual exploitation.

The Use of Cyber Technologies to Facilitate Child Trafficking, Child Pornography and Other Sexual Abuse of Minors

Online child trafficking can be summarized as child trafficking that is facilitated by or exclusively takes place in a computer network or internet network,[1] including the actions of sourcing, facilitation and exploitation

---

[1] Witting, S. (2017). Cyber' Trafficking? An Interpretation of the Palermo Protocol in the Digital Era. Voelkerrechtsblog: International Law and International

of the child. The different forms of online child trafficking can be summarized by two class types that entail: sourcing or facilitating the act of child trafficking online; and exploitation of a child online. As contemplated by the Protocol to Prevent Suppress and Punish Trafficking in Persons (2003)[2] (further discussed below), the trafficking crime requires a person to be procured or acquired. Thus, in order to be a subject of child trafficking the child must be presented as the commodity in a transaction. These types of online child trafficking are located in the deception and sourcing stage, such as using the internet to deceive the child to enter into the trafficking relationship. Many traffickers rely on computer networks to conduct their criminal actions in an attempt to evade detection by legal authorities. To that end, online child pornography can also be used to commit the crime of child trafficking.

Child grooming is the deception of a child via seduction or enticing the child to trust the predator and compromise themselves, such as by sending a naked picture to the predator. Once the child is compromised, the predator can use the same action to psychologically torture the child or blackmail them into a forced sexual relationship. Especially in cases of distrust of parents or guardians, the child feels they have no choice but to yield to the predator and thus becomes a victim of online child trafficking.

Online child trafficking also can take place in messaging applications or online chat rooms, which are used to identify, lure, and deceive a child to participate in a physical sexual relationship. Using Facebook or messaging services, parents or guardians can pawn off children to potential employees. Once the employees are in control of these children, they in turn pawn off the child or exchange them via Facebook to other potential employers. Normally these children are trafficked into Arab countries where the same roulette game takes place. The children are exploited and their travel documents confiscated by their employers; this represents a typical modern-day slavery relationship. Sexual predators also look for potential child victims online. They regularly visit "kids only" chatrooms and communicate with children who divulge personal information about themselves. Then when the predators are sure, they have caught the child in their net, they solicit for sex over the internet.

Legal Thought, https://voelkerrechtsblog.org/cyber-trafficking-an-interpretation-of-the-palermo-protocol-in-the-digital-era/.

[2] United Nations Convention Against Transnational Organised Crime, the Protocol to Prevent, Suppress and Punish Trafficking in Persons (2003).

The predators will continue to communicate with the child electronically or through other means. Some of these predators may proceed to lower the child's inhibitions by gradually introducing sexual content into their online conversations and even send pornographic images to the child.[3] When children are shown images of peers engaged in sexual activities, they are manipulated to believe this behaviour is acceptable. This lowers their inhibitions and makes it easier for the predator to take advantage of the child sexually.[4]

A number of child molesters are now using computer technology to organize and maintain and increase the size of their collections of illegal images.[5] Manufactured unlawful images of children are especially valuable on the internet, which provide the predator with a respected status among fellow exploiters and traders of this material. Once this status is achieved, molesters will often begin to trade images of their sexual exploits with children among themselves in encrypted peer-to-peer sharing platforms found on the dark web.[6]

Parameters and Drivers of Human Trafficking in Africa

Human trafficking is a global issue that affects people from virtually every part of the world. A Global survey on human trafficking published by the International Labour Organization (ILO), estimated that 40 million people were reported to be in modern slavery in 2017.[7] The annual revenue from human trafficking has been estimated to be between US$5 and US$42 billion. Statistics also reveal that 7.8 million persons are enslaved in Sub-Saharan Africa and 9.24 million are African nationals, comprising 23% of the total global population in modern slavery.[8] Furthermore, such reports reveal that 8% of the world's sexually exploited

---

[3] Kenya: Human Trafficking and Child Exploitation on the Increase During COVID-19, https://allafrica.com/stories/202006020452.html.

[4] Ibid.

[5] ICE, https://www.ice.gov/.

[6] Judie Kaberia, "Human Trafficking And Child Exploitation On The Increase During COVID-19," Capital FM, 2 June 2020, https://www.capitalfm.co.ke/news/2020/06/human-trafficking-and-child-exploitation-on-the-increase-during-covid-19/.

[7] UNODC. Global Report on Trafficking in Persons. New York: UNODC, 2016.

[8] Human Trafficking Trends in sub-Saharan Africa, http://asec-sldi.org/news/current/human-trafficking-sub-saharan-africa/.

children are from Africa.[9] Such alarming statistics however do not occur in isolation but within key structural conditions. Africa has undergone a number of crises, including high levels of unemployment, poverty, and hunger, leading to internal displacement of people. This systemic political and economic instability contributes to and creates an environment ripe for human trafficking.

Indeed, the parts of Africa that have been heavily impacted by human trafficking are countries hit by unrest and strife. Owing to their social, political and economic environment, Nigeria, Togo, and Benin rank among Africa's top source countries for human traffickers.[10] Other places heavily impacted by human trafficking are countries viewed as transit and destination locales due to geographical and economic conditions favourable to illicit trade, such as port countries like South Africa, Kenya, and Libya.[11] These countries are attractive to human traffickers because of the thriving market for cheap labour and young prostitutes. In the case of transit locales (e.g. Kenya and Libya), the commoditized person awaits their final destination, such as Europe, Malaysia, or the Emirates. Once the trafficked persons reach their destination their travel documents or passports are confiscated by the employer, commencing the modern-day slavery relationship.

Among other factors discussed above, children can become trafficked persons for reasons related to family circumstances. Traffickers pounce on the economic vulnerability of parents or guardians by dangling a strand of hope of a better life for the child in another country, deceiving them into surrendering the child.[12] Other parents decide to sell their children into the slave market due to economic challenges. And, in dysfunctional families with a history of drug or alcohol abuse, children can be viewed as dispensable commodities to fetch extra coins.

---

[9] Carmel, Rickard. Human Trafficking Reports Show Sub-Saharan Africa A Global Player, AfricanLII, University of Cape Town, 18 July 2019. https://africanlii.org/article/20190718/human-trafficking-reports-show-sub-saharan-africa-global-player.

[10] Paul O. Bello, & Adewale A. Olutola. (2020). The Conundrum of Human Trafficking in Africa. In J. Reeves (Ed.), *Modern Slavery and Human Trafficking*. InTech Open.

[11] Ibid.

[12] INTERPOL. (2019). Human Trafficking Hundreds Rescued in West Africa. https://www.interpol.int/en/News-and-Events/News/2019/Human-trafficking-hundreds-rescued-in-West-Africa.

Furthermore, child trafficking appeals to criminal organizations as it is becoming increasingly easy and inexpensive to procure, move and exploit children. One child can generate a profit of several thousand dollars a day and can be abused and sold repeatedly, unlike other forms of illicit trade like drug trafficking. As trafficking often occurs in countries racked by civil strife and war, such contexts have little existence of the rule of law and functioning formal legal systems. As such there is low risk of detection and prosecution of technology-facilitated child sex trafficking, as opposed to the comparatively higher risk associated with traditional forms of trafficking. Trafficked children are also youthful and can be later used for organ harvesting after being sexually exploited.

Complexities of Cybercrimes and Related Challenges to Detection and Enforcement in Africa

Internet-based technologies are becoming the principal machinery by which children are lured, entrapped, and forced into enslavement for sexual purposes. Child sex trafficking is not a new crime; however, the use of technology to facilitate this crime is. As the internet is highly unregulated, provides anonymity, accessibility, and a global reach, the use of cyber technology by traffickers will increase. Child sex traffickers may be strangers, but they can also be family members, friends, guardians, or acquaintances. Nearly half of all identified cases of child trafficking begin with some family member's involvement; and the extent of family involvement in the trafficking of children is four times higher than in cases of adult trafficking. Child traffickers use social media platforms to gain trust and build relationships by showing admiration or desire for the child, posing as a friend, and eventually employing tactics such as manipulation, coercion, and control to lure them away from their homes and loved ones.

Traffickers are criminals that conduct trade and exploitation of human beings. In most cases traffickers may be freelancers or members of organized criminal networks. They recruit and find potential victims from families that are financially challenged or emotionally dysfunctional, or where there is rampant alcohol or drug abuse. Furthermore, a trafficker may be a family member or friend of someone within the community that is highly trusted and thus likely to convince the families that their children are better off being taken to another place. Online child traffickers lure or coerce victims through interactions on social media, game chatrooms, kid chat rooms, message applications, peer-to-peer file sharing sites, and online ads, with the intent to exploit the victims for profit. Utilizing false job adverts on Facebook, or other online media, traffickers lure children by promising fame or money, expressing love or praise, or the promise of economic opportunity in modelling and hotel industries.[13] Additionally, traffickers may trick the victims into sharing explicit private pictures, and in turn blackmail them into doing what the perpetrator wants.

Online child trafficking is attractive to criminal organizations as it is easy and inexpensive to buy, move, and exploit children. There is a low risk of detection and prosecution of technology-facilitated child sex trafficking, compared to the risk associated with traditional forms of trafficking. One child can generate much profit a day for traffickers, and the child can be abused and sold repeatedly. This is unlike other forms of illicit trade like drug trafficking.

The investigation of cybercrime and collection of evidence for a child pornography prosecution through digital forensics can be a complicated and complex issue. This is due to the intangible and evanescence nature of data, especially in a networked environment. The technology renders the process of investigation and evidence collection and presentation extremely vulnerable to defence claims of errors and technical malfunction. Such an error may lead to a mistrial or acquittal because of the inadmissibility of evidence.

To be able to successfully prosecute online child trafficking and pornography, you need to be able to provide proof of the infrastructure and computers (ICTs) that were used for online crime. Also, you need to be able to trace the artificial intelligence and server stream that was used to commit or connect to child pornography. It is difficult to identify the routers and servers that were used because of encryption.

Additionally, prosecutors need to prove that the culprit or accused is a child pornographer or trafficker who are believed to be the perpetrators. In cases where child pornography or trafficking has a multinational dimension, the individual trafficker may be part of a larger organized crime group. Moreover, child trafficking or pornography may be a predicate of another crime for purposes of raising funds or increasing finances,

---

[13] Michael C. Seto, et al. (2018). Production and Active Trading of Child Sexual Exploitation Images Depicting Identified Victims, National Center for Missing and Exploited Children (Thorn-funded), March. https://www.thorn.org/wp-content/uploads/2018/03/Production-and-Active-Trading-of-CSAM_FullReport_FINAL.pdf.

such as terrorism or drug cartels, thus making the crime of child trafficking or pornography a chain crime. In such cases, the perpetrators could include the financier of the organized crime, the purchaser, and the third party or intermediary seller.

A lack of adequate training in national judicial infrastructures—including law enforcement officers, prosecutors, and the judges—will often exacerbate these difficulties. In many African countries, efforts have been made to address these capacity needs, with the establishment of specialized facilities and courses offered by INTERPOL and specialized digital forensic organizations.

INTERNATIONAL AND REGIONAL LEGAL AND REGULATORY FRAMEWORKS

In his address at the opening of the signing conference for the United Nations Convention against Transnational Organized Crime, Kofi Annan, then Secretary General, gave the following sentiments on human trafficking[14]:

> *I believe the trafficking of persons, particularly women and children, for forced and exploitative labour, including for sexual exploitation, is one of the most egregious violations of human rights that the United Nations now confronts. It is widespread and growing. It is rooted in social and economic conditions in the countries from which the victims come, facilitated by practices that discriminate against women and children and is driven by cruel indifference to human suffering on the part of those who exploit the services that the victims are forced to provide. The fate of these most vulnerable people in our world is an affront to human dignity and a challenge to every State, every people and every community.*

These sentiments are echoed in the Protocol to the same United Nations Convention Against Transnational Organised Crime which requires states to enact legislation dealing with human trafficking and in the present case child trafficking.

---

[14] Secretary General Address Palermo 201 (12 December 2000).

Palermo Protocol

Supplementing the United Nations Convention against Transnational Organised Crime, the Protocol to Prevent, Suppress and Punish Trafficking in Persons (hereinafter "Palermo Protocol") clearly addresses protections for child trafficking and the sexual exploitation of children. The Palermo Protocol defines trafficking in persons as[15]—

> the recruitment, transportation, transfer, harbouring or receipt of persons, by means of the threat or use of force or other forms of coercion, of abduction, of fraud, of deception, of the abuse of power or of a position of vulnerability or of the giving or receiving of payments or benefits to achieve the consent of a person having control over another person, for the purpose of exploitation. Exploitation shall include, at a minimum, the exploitation of the prostitution of others or other forms of sexual exploitation, forced labour or services, slavery or practices similar to slavery, servitude or the removal of organs;

Paragraph (c) categorically states that the recruitment, transportation, transfer, harbouring, or receipt of a child for the purpose of exploitation will be considered as trafficking in persons.[16]

The Protocol recognizes child trafficking as a form of human trafficking and crime, and child sex trafficking is one form of child sexual exploitation recognized. A child is any person under the age of 18 and under this provision cannot give consent,[17] which is a legal defence to the crime of exploitation in human trafficking crimes. If a child takes part in a sexual activity in exchange for some benefit or the promise of such from a perpetrator, then the child is a victim of sexual exploitation. Several forms of child sexual exploitation can occur without the existence of trafficking, such as performing sexual activities in exchange for food or accommodation. Likewise, the sexual exploitation of children through prostitution, while often related to trafficking, may occur without the child having been

---

[15] Article 3, Protocol to Prevent, Suppress and Punish Trafficking in Persons Especially Women and Children, supplementing the United Nations Convention against Transnational Organized Crime (2000), United Nations. https://www.ohchr.org/en/instruments-mechanisms/instruments/protocol-prevent-suppress-and-punish-trafficking-persons.

[16] Ibid.

[17] Ibid.

trafficked. Child pornography can be defined as technology-facilitated child sex trafficking and child sexual exploitation.

The Convention on Cybercrime ("Budapest Convention")

As the issue of child trafficking has proved to be a menace to various countries, it has become a transnational issue requiring domestic legal frameworks that addresses the criminal violation of children's rights. Due to lax domestic laws and cultures that encourage child sexual labour, many national jurisdictions have acted as catalysts of child trafficking with pockets that have become notorious for child trafficking.[18] To address these challenges, there have been additional legal frameworks for human trafficking protections. The Convention on Cybercrime ("Budapest Convention") came into force on July 20[19] and categorizes the crime of child pornography as a content-related offence.[20] The Budapest Convention was the first international legal framework to specifically recognize and deal with child pornography as an offence separate from human trafficking and child trafficking. This is in contrast to the Palermo Protocol which only recognizes the crime of human and child trafficking. However, this contrast reveals a necessary link between the two, considering that in order for online child pornography to be facilitated or manifest the crime of child trafficking is involved.

The Budapest Convention outlines elements of the crime of pornography in Article 9(2) as follows[21]—

(2) pornographic material that visually depicts:
(a) minor engaged in sexually explicit conduct;
(b) a person appearing to be a minor engaged in sexually explicit conduct
(c) realistic images representing a minor engaged in sexually explicit conduct.

---

[18] Ferrao Ranjano. (2020). Sale and Sexual Exploitation of Children in the Context of Travel and Tourism in Goa. Journal of Victimology and Victim Justice, 3(1). https://journals.sagepub.com/doi/10.1177/2516606920921152. Last Accessed 9 September 2021.

[19] Convention on Cybercrime (ETS No. 185), 2004. https://www.coe.int/en/web/conventions/full-list?module=treaty-detail&treatynum=185.

[20] Ibid, Article 9 deals specifically with child pornography.

[21] Ibid, Article 9.

(3) A "minor" shall include all persons under 18 years of age. A Party may, however, require a lower age-limit, which shall be not less than 16 years.[22]

Accordingly, for the crime of child pornography to take place, there must be a child involved, and that means that the subject must be below the age of 18 years. The content and images included must portray the child involved or engaged in sexually explicit conduct. However, the content or image is subject to interpretation, with little precedence or consistent interpretation. For example, the United States interprets the section in a content-based way, while the EU interprets it in a statutory liability format relying on the civil jurisdiction interpretation precedence.

Article 9 (1) of the Budapest Convention provides that each Party shall adopt such legislative and other measures as may be necessary to establish criminal offences under its domestic law, when the following conduct is committed intentionally and without right[23]—

(a) producing child pornography for the purpose of its distribution through a computer system;
(b) offering or making available child pornography through a computer system;
(c) distributing or transmitting child pornography through a computer system;
(d) procuring child pornography through a computer system for oneself or for another person;
(e) possessing child pornography in a computer system or on a computer data storage medium.[24]

When we look at the Budapest Convention, it seeks to seal the loophole that used to be exploited by online child traffickers and pornographers claiming that the prosecution did not meet their burden by failing to prove a particular step of the crime. Indeed, when we look at the crime of child pornography, it is broad in range yet specific to the subject matter, which is the sexually explicit image of a minor. Child pornography

---

[22] Article 9 (2) Convention on Cyber Crime.
[23] Ibid, Article 9(1).
[24] Article 9 (2) Convention on Cyber Crime.

is a chain crime whereby each crime element forms part of the crime. However, the steps taken to successfully commit the crime as a form of online child trafficking is a separate crime on its own that needs to be proved by prosecutors. Now when we look at the crime as defined and provided for under Article 9 each step towards the sourcing, facilitation, and exploitation of the minor for sexual purposes has been captured as a separate crime, all together lessening the lumped-up burden of proof prosecutors used to face.

We can now summarize it as the crime of offering to make child pornography available, through production, possession, distribution, transmitting, procuring for self or another, all done through a computer system. The image is digital and is found in a computer system and stored as computer data storage medium.

Consequently, in order for the crime to be adequately prosecuted, one needs to deal with the first requirement of ascertaining that a child or minor is involved, depending on the state's legislation. When we look at the tail end of Article 9 (1), to prove the guilt of the crime of child pornography the perpetrator must be found in possession of the digital image. Guilt can also be shown if the prosecution established that a person distributed the pornographic image through a computer system; so the key will be to determine the means of distribution. This requires finding the exact computer premises and network used, and the same given as evidence for the prosecution to be able to prove the other crime of distribution.

A state is also required to adopt domestic legislation that addresses possession of compromising computer data, such as child pornography, and laws that address the preservation of such data for requisite time periods. The state is to adopt legislation and any other necessary measures to preserve and maintain the integrity of computer data, in order to preserve the evidence that is likely to be relied upon to prosecute child pornography. This is because evidence can be found in various computers, and the primary links and the material contained on the server have to be preserved. The Convention categorically requires member states to adopt legislative and other measures as may be necessary to oblige the custodian or other person who is to preserve the computer data to keep confidential the undertaking of such procedures for the period provided for by domestic law. Furthermore, Articles 17 and 18 of the Budapest Convention are pertinent because they require evidence to be preserved correctly with proper chain of custody maintained. It also highlights clear guidelines to align with global standards during preservation of evidence and digital forensics processing.[25]

Another tool that has been created under the Convention is the provision for inter territorial submission of collected data and the power to compel a service provider to relay pertinent information contained within its possession or control.[26] Such a provision tries to seal any loopholes that arise in a state's legal framework on the collection of evidence or preservation of child pornography evidence that is highly perishable and can easily be wiped out by a stroke of a key. These kind of loopholes make it difficult for prosecution to take place against perpetrators.

The Convention also addresses the issue of privacy and collection of personal information for purposes of prosecution. It lays down guidelines for the collection of subscriber information in the case of a cybercrime, and particularly in our case child pornography creation, possession and distribution. The Convention also lays down guidelines on the procedures to be followed when dealing with subscriber information. This provision seeks to harmonize the process among member states. It describes subscriber information to be collected and relayed as content data. This data is to be used to establish the communication service used, the subscriber's identity, geographical location, and service arrangement. This provision also grants power to the requisite authorities to collect such sensitive information. If the provision was not there, the prosecution would face challenges in the collection of evidence.

The other requirement in order to collect and rely on such data for a child pornography case is that a search and seizure warrant must be issued by the Judiciary. The search and seizure procedure is clearly highlighted under Article 19 of the Convention. The provision serves as a guideline when states consider enacting cybercrime legislation. It harmonizes the process for efficient state cooperation, prosecution, and extradition of online child trafficking and pornography perpetrators.

The Convention also serves as a global guideline and guide for authorities to consider when enacting legislation that deals with content data generated from criminal activities. It takes into consideration the global reach of child pornography and online child trafficking. Thus,

---

[25] Article 18 Convention on Cyber Crime.
[26] Ibid.

it categorically provides that states should have legislation that deals with the collection of content data found in another's territory through the encouragement of interstate authorities and transboundary cooperation. This is with an aim to make it efficient to successfully prosecute perpetrators of online child trafficking and child pornography.[27]

In the likelihood the perpetrator of the cybercrime is located in another country or has left the jurisdiction where the crime took place, Article 24 of the Cybercrime Convention serves as a guideline for states when such a scenario arises, providing for extradition of the accused perpetrator. The state that seeks prosecution for the transboundary crime can request for the perpetrator of child pornography to be extradited for prosecution and sentencing under its legal system.[28]

In summary, the Budapest Convention is an international instrument that serves as a global guide to member states and requires member states to domesticate it. It also serves as a guide to best industry practice to non-member states and can be relied upon as a sign post when it comes to prosecuting and legislating child pornography and online child trafficking. The actual problem of the information and technology age seems to be to deciding precisely how much value should be attached to a given piece of information, especially when that information is stored electronically and digitally. As discussed above the Cybercrime Convention has been relied upon as a guideline for states when enacting laws on child pornography. Article 11 of the Convention requires that each member state adopt and enact legislation to declare child pornography a crime and to put measures in place to criminalize all forms of child pornography. Each country should also put measures into place that ensure that the criminals can be tried and held liable for child pornography,[29] whether through criminal, civil, or administrative means including restriction of movement. In order for the penalties and sanctions to be effective, there must be proportionate and dissuasive criminal or non-criminal sanctions or measures, including monetary sanctions, measures that many countries are lacking. Indeed, in lax jurisdictions one might find that the criminal of child defilement in a particular state would only serve two years imprisonment and a cartel lord would be sentenced to less than five years. Such

---

[27] Article 20 Convention on Cyber Crime.
[28] Article 24 Convention on Cyber Crime.
[29] Article 11, Convention on Cyber Crime.

weak deterrence may lead perpetrators to opt for the criminal activity and as the legal consequences are negligible.

Finally, Under Article 14 of the Cyber Crime Convention member states are required to adopt legislation and other measures as may be necessary to enable its competent authorities to order and obtain the expeditious preservation of specified computer data. This includes traffic data that has been stored on a computer system, in particular where there are grounds to believe that the computer data is particularly vulnerable to loss or modification.[30] Without such provisions for digital forensics and cooperation among state authorities to acquire the data, then the perpetrator will walk away scot-free, as has happened in previous cases.

Thus, African countries rely on the Budapest Convention for implementing legislation, however they also have a regional legal instrument that was passed to deal with cybersecurity, crime, and data protection—known as the African Union Convention on Cyber Security and Data Protection. I shall proceed to analyse the aforementioned legal instrument.

The African Union Convention on Cybersecurity and Data Protection

On 27 June 2014, the African Convention on Cybersecurity and Data Protection (Africa Convention) came into force. The African Convention shares similarities with the Budapest Convention in several key respects. Under the African Convention, Article 1 defines child pornography as:

1. Any visual depiction of sexually explicit conduct, including any photograph, film, video, image, whether made or produced by electronic, mechanical, or other means;
2. Where such visual depiction is digital or computer generated image where a minor is engaging in sexually explicit conduct, or when images of their sexual organs are produced or used for primarily sexual purposes and exploited with or without the child's knowledge; and,
3. Where such visual depiction has been created, adapted, or modified to appear that a minor is engaging in sexually explicit conduct for the purposes of distribution, transmission or possession.

---

[30] Article 14, Convention on Cyber Crime.

The African Convention brings clarity to the description of child pornography. It broadens the scope of the crime to not only include possession of digital images or reels with sexually explicit content featuring minors, but also images depicting minors' sexual organs. Also, other than possession it also deals with the distribution and transmission of such images. However, for these actions to take place a physical location is needed that acts as a warehouse or room to place the child. This is also a key element of the online child trafficking part of the crime. For example, trafficking destinations or transit routes often utilize the porous borders of war torn countries. An example would be Nigeria where girls were abducted from school and captured. Some of these girls were trafficked to other locations and used as sex slaves.

The African Convention broadens the scope of the child pornography crime to include the possession, production, dissemination, and transmission of any sexually explicit images of children. This very broad scope is aimed to cast a wide net and make sure that all manner of ways of perpetrating child pornography are covered. This means it takes into account the fragmentation of the image and how it can be transmitted and hidden in a computer system. If these areas are not legislated upon, retrieval of the image could amount to a violation of privacy of the computer device's owner.[31]

The African Convention also requires state parties to take necessary steps to enact laws that not only deal with production, possession, and dissemination, but also the solicitation and offering of child pornography. By making it a crime this will act as a deterrence to producing and disseminating child pornography. This will also save many children from becoming victims of the predicate crimes of defilement and sexual assault related to the crime of child pornography.[32]

The Convention also requires State Parties to take the necessary legislative and/or regulatory measures to ensure legal procedures and processes are in place that support the search and seizure of computers and digital content. These legal measures will be able to assist in the successful prosecution of child pornography cases, allowing prosecutors to submit digital

---

[31] Article 29 (3)(1), African Union Convention on Cyber Security and Personal Data Protection. https://au.int/sites/default/files/treaties/29560-treaty-0048_-_african_union_convention_on_cyber_security_and_personal_data_protection_e.pdf. Last accessed March 2022.

[32] Article 29 (3) 2, African Convention.

evidence. That is pertinent for the prosecution of child pornography; if states do not have such laws then they end up being safe havens for child pornographers. Because of laxity in children laws, or lax implementation of children laws, some states in Africa have been used by child pornographers and traffickers as safe havens. I will now proceed to explore the aspect of human trafficking in Africa.

Guidance for Prosecuting Child Pornography and Online Trafficking from Other Jurisdictions

While states are generally free to criminalize and punish most behaviour, state actors seeking to punish individuals for the creation, distribution, or possession of images must do so in a way that is consistent with the constitutional law. However, an individual's free speech right is far from absolute. For example, the US Supreme Court has recognized several categorical exceptions to the First Amendment, including exceptions for obscenity and for child pornography. These cases carry legal questions as to whether an image constitutes child pornography, its creation, distribution, and possession. If an image is not child pornography, then those who create, distribute, or possess it may be entitled to First Amendment protection. This will depend on the jurisdiction and how the countries' judiciaries choose to interpret the provisions on child pornography, and to determine whether the images in question comprise child pornography or fall under protected speech.

There are also important legal questions regarding the cybersecurity criminal dimensions of child pornography and trafficking. Don B. Parker (1998) states that in many cases, crimes that legislators would call cybercrimes are familiar legal terrain for elements of a crime, except that a computer network is involved.[33] On the other hand, Mohamed Chawki et al.[34] states that the computer network gives criminals a new way to commit existing crimes. Statutes that prohibit these acts can be applied to people who used a computer to commit them as well as to those who commit them without the use of computer or computer network.

---

[33] Don B. Parker. (1998). Fighting Computer Crime: A New Framework for Protecting Information. ISBN 0471163783. New York: Wiley.

[34] Mohamed Chawki et al (2015). Cybercrime, Digital Forensics and Jurisdiction. London: Springer.

Nula Frei[35] is of the opinion that for online child trafficking to be prosecuted as a crime it has to be committed in what she terms as a "cyber" way. The recruitment or transportation and the offering of the victim is or must be linked to the cyber world; as well as the use of coercion and threat, fraud and deception, known as the means of action. Thus, the exploitation can take place with the aid of a computer system or network.[36] If any of these actions are linked to the cyber world and successfully proved then one can state that online child trafficking has taken place.

In analysing the crimes of child pornography and online trafficking, I will rely on the legal theory developed by Sabine Witting.[37] It requires the following:

1. The interpretation of online child trafficking as the recruitment or the transportation and the offering of the victims;
2. The use of coercion and threat, fraud and deception; and
3. The exploitation can all take place with a computer system or technological tool.

Thus, we can summarize the four elements as: the action, means, purpose, and information technology tool. The first step is to determine whether a minor is involved. Establishing this will depend on domestic laws, as different countries have different legal definitions regarding the age of sexual consent. Some states set the age of majority at 18 years while others are at 16 years.

The other aspect the courts are required to establish is whether the digital image contains a minor *and* is sexually explicit. There is little interpretation of this in Africa; however, the prosecution can borrow from other judicial interpretations in other jurisdictions. For example, in

---

[35] Nula Frei. (2017). On 'Cyber Trafficking' and the Protection of Its Victims, 26 July 2017. Voelkerrechtsblog: International Law and International Legal Thought. https://voelkerrechtsblog.org/de/on-cyber-trafficking-and-the-protection-of-its-victims/.

[36] Ibid.

[37] Sabine Witting. (2017). Cyber' Trafficking? An Interpretation of the Palermo Protocol in the Digital Era, 28 June. Voelkerrechtsblog: International Law and International Legal Thought, https://voelkerrechtsblog.org/cyber-trafficking-an-interpretation-of-the-palermo-protocol-in-the-digital-era/.

a case in the US Federal Court of Appeals, Eight Circuit[38] the defendant, Donna Zauner, took sexually explicit pictures of her underage daughters. She sent them to a man whom she knew had sexually molested children in the past, and ultimately was found guilty of the crime of child pornography.

Another aspect is to balance rights regarding the protection and dignity of the child, on one hand, with the rights of the holders of child pornography, on the other. As for the latter, particularly at issue is the right to possession of obscene content. Again, the Zauner case is instructive as the Court determined that children's rights are to be upheld above those in possession of child pornography. That is, when the image in question is determined to be child pornography, then the law prioritizes the protection of children from sexual exploitation and abuse during the creation of said image(s).

Other remaining aspects are the injury created from the distribution of child pornography, and the trauma that occurs from the child sexual exploitation and abuse. These are related to the twin crimes of possession and distribution of child pornography. As possession of child pornography encourages paedophiles and molesters to continue producing child pornography, the distribution of the image(s) has a compounding traumatic effect, recording for life the sexual abuse of a child. Therefore, the Court in Zauner stated that the only effective way to end the harm was to shut down the distribution network of child pornography.[39]

In Osborne v. Ohio (1990),[40] the US Supreme Court emphasized the creation of harm principles, particularly the prevention of the harm of production and the harm of circulation of child pornography. The Court argued that finding and sanctioning possession as a crime could serve as a deterrence and protect future victims of child sex abuse. This includes deterring against the production of child pornography, but also protection

---

[38] United States v. Zauner, 688 F.3d 426, 428 (8th Cir. 2012).
[39] Ibid, Pg 37.
[40] Osborne v. Ohio, 495 U.S. 103 (1990).

from paedophiles[41] who use child pornography to seduce other children into sexual activity.[42]

Elsewhere, the US Supreme Court is instructive regarding the prosecution of crimes surrounding child pornography. In United States v. Williams (2008), the Court held that the definition of child pornography is limited to images based on the depiction of real children; and that to prove child trafficking there must be proof that the images were created through exploitation or abuse.[43] Furthermore, the Court expounded on the issue of harm in *Williams* regarding solicitation of child pornography. Solicitation propagates child molestation for purposes of creating the sexually explicit image. Therefore, the Court found that criminalizing solicitation is necessary to prevent and deter child pornography consumers.[44]

ASSESSMENT OF NATIONAL ENFORCEMENT AND LEGAL ACTION IN AFRICA

In Africa, INTERPOL and interstate task forces have been mandated with the duty to deal with online child trafficking and the disgusting menace of child pornography. Nonetheless, national and international enforcement efforts have found it challenging to contend with this menace, in part due to lack of political will. There is a glimmer of hope however from recent actions taken by African national Leaders. For example, with the help of INTERPOL Chadian children were rescued in February 2020 from a plane run by Spanish and French citizens attempting to ferry the children out of the country.[45] Since then, INTERPOL has helped countries set up institutions and infrastructure to counter child trafficking. These countries have borrowed from the Child Convention, ILO, and

---

[41] There is a difference between paedophilia and child molesters. Paedophilia is a manifestation of a psychological, sexual attraction to children; while child molesters are adults who act on this type of appeal and may end up sexually abusing children. There are also child molesters who sexually abuse children for monetary reasons.

[42] Ibid, p. 109.

[43] United States v. Williams, 553 U.S. 285 (2008).

[44] Ibid.

[45] Xan Rice, et al. (2007). Child Accuses French Charity of Child Trafficking, 29 October, The Guardian. https://www.theguardian.com/world/2007/oct/29/spain.france.

the Budapest Convention, which specifically speaks to the issue of child pornography. However, lack of adequate training of law enforcement officers, prosecutors, and the judiciary will often increase difficulties in successful prosecution. In many West and East African countries efforts have been made to address this training need, with the establishment of specialized facilities and courses, supplemented by training courses offered by INTERPOL.[46]

Thirty-seven African countries have signed the United Nations Convention on Children Human Rights.[47] However, few countries have signed and ratified both the Budapest and African Convention on Cybersecurity and Data Protection. South Africa enacted The Films and Publications Act, 1996, Amendments: Child Pornography Offences[48] to criminalize all forms of child pornography. The Act defines child pornography to include the following elements[49]:

"any image, however created, or any description of a persons, real or simulated, who is or who is depicted, made to appear, look like, represented or describe as being, under the age of 18 years—

(a) engaged in sexual conduct;
(b) participating in, or assisting another person to participate in, sexual conduct; or
(c) showing or describing the body, or parts of the body, of such a person in a manner or in circumstances which, within context, amounts to sexual exploitation, or in such a manner that it is capable of being used for the purposes of sexual exploitation."

---

[46] INTERPOL Supporting East Africa Police Tackle Cross Border Crime. https://www.interpol.int/en/News-and-Events/News/2019/INTERPOL-supporting-East-Africa-police-tackle-rising-cross-border-crime.

[47] Convention on the Rights of Children, United Nations General Assembly resolution 44/25, 1989. https://www.ohchr.org/en/instruments-mechanisms/instruments/convention-rights-child.

[48] Films and Publications Act, 1996, Act No. 65, South Afirca. http://www.saflii.org/za/legis/consol_act/fapa1996220/.

[49] Ibid., Section 8.1.

Section 24B deals with the criminalization of child pornography by defining guilt of the offence as[50]:

(1) "Any person who—
(a) unlawfully possesses;
(b) creates, produces or in any way contributes to, or assists in the creation or production of;
(c) imports or in any way takes steps to procure, obtain or access or in any way knowingly assists in, or facilitates the importation, procurement, obtaining or accessing of; or
(d) knowingly makes available, exports, broadcasts or in any way distributes or caused to be made available, exported, broadcast or distributed or assists in making available, exporting, broadcasting or distributing, any film, game or publication which contains depiction, descriptions or scenes of child pornography or which advocates, advertises, encourages or promotes child pornography or the sexual exploitation of children [...]
(3) "Any person who any person who processes, facilitated or attempts to process or facilitate a financial transaction, knowing that such transaction will facilitate access to the distribution or possession of, child pornography will be found guilty of an offence."

The South African judiciary in the Beale case found the accused guilty of the crime of possession of child pornography, with a ten year sentence handed down on appeal. The court emphasized the right of child to dignity and respect. It made the following sentiments that have been echoed in other South African decisions:

We accept that the appellant was not convicted of manufacturing child pornography or of molesting children, but the argument that an accused 'only' possessed disturbing and disgusting images as a mitigating factor, ignores the reality that possession of the prohibited material creates a trading platform or market for this illegal 'industry'. Every image contained in child pornography reflects abhorrent prohibited sexual conduct, often including violence, involving children. Every child pornography image reflects the sexual violation and the impairment of the dignity of a child, every time that image is

---

[50] Ibid., Section 24B.

viewed. As argued, children, including babies and toddlers, are the unidentified, voiceless victims of child pornography. It cannot be disputed that these victims will bear the emotional scars of their abuse for life.[51]

On the issue of Extradition Order, the same was successfully granted in the South African Carolissen Case[52] The U.S. Department of Homeland Security (HSI) investigated a child pornography network. The investigation revealed that in the years between 2010 and 2012, the accused sexually abused a young girl in South Africa and produced images of the abuse. In September and October 2014, the accused sent these images, as well as other child pornography images depicting additional minors engaged in sexually explicit conduct, to undercover HSI agents in Maine via the internet. The Court charged the accused with the offences of distributing child pornography for which the United States sought extradition under the extradition treaty.

A child trafficking source country, Nigeria signed the Budapest Convention and enacted implementing legislation through the Cyber Crime Act of 2015. Section 23 criminalizes all forms of child pornography, stating as follows[53]:

"Any person who intentionally uses any computer system or network in or for

(a) producing child pornography;
(b) offering or making available child pornography;
(c) distributing or transmitting child pornography;
(d) procuring child pornography for oneself or for another person;
(e) possessing child pornography in a computer system or on a computer data storage medium: commits an offence under this Act and shall be liable on conviction to a fine or imprisonment of ten years."

---

[51] Beale v S, A283/2018 [2019]ZAWCHC. http://www.saflii.org/za/cases/ZAWCHC/2019/47.html.

[52] Carolissen v Director of Public Prosecution, A 531/2015 [2016], ZAWCHC. http://www.saflii.org/za/cases/ZAWCHC/2016/50.html.

[53] Cybercrimes (Prohibition, Prevention, Etc) Act, 2015, Nigeria.

Subsection (3) further states that any person who, intentionally proposes, grooms or solicits, through any computer system or network, to meet a child for[54]:

(a) engaging in sexual activities with the child;
(b) engaging in sexual activities with the child where—
  (i) use is made of coercion, inducement, force or threats;
  (ii) abuse is made of a recognized position of trust, authority or influence over the child, including within the family; or Child pornography and related offences.
  (iii) abuse is made of a particularly vulnerable situation of the child, mental or physical disability or a situation of dependence;
(c) recruiting, inducing, coercing, exposing, or causing a child to participate in pornographic performances or profiting from or otherwise exploiting a child for such purposes; commits an offence under this Act and shall be liable on conviction to pay a fine or imprisonment for a term of 15 years for the former and 10 years for the latter.

However, there is little successful prosecution that has taken place in Nigeria for child pornography. Among the few cases prosecuted, a Nigerian was found guilty of possession of child pornography in Ireland. He had left his phone for repair and the technician found child pornography on the device. Further investigation revealed two more videos in his laptop. The Nigerian was also found guilty of pornography in the United States. However, he fled to Canada before the sentence was imposed.[55]

A source and transit country, Kenya signed the African Convention on Cyber Security and enacted the Computer Misuse and Cybercrimes Act, with a provision criminalizing child pornography. Section 24 defines "child pornography" to include data which, whether visual or audio, depicts[56]—

---

[54] Ibid.

[55] Fiona Ferguson, Court Hears Child Porn Video was Discovered on Phone of Father of Two After It was Left in for Repair," 25 July 2019, Irish Examiner. https://www.irishexaminer.com/breakingnews/ireland/court-hears-child-porn-video-was-discovered-on-phone-of-fatherof-two-after-it-was-left-in-for-repair-939451.html.

[56] The Computer Misuse and Cybercrimes Act, Kenya (2018) https://nc4.go.ke/the-computer-misuse-and-cybercrimes-act/.

(a) a child engaged in sexually explicit conduct;
(b) a person who appears to be a child engaged in sexually explicit conduct; or
(c) realistic images representing a child engaged in sexually explicit conduct.

In a case involving child pornography, Mr Maweu was arrested in Kenya in 2015, and extradited to and tried in the United States, ultimately being convicted with a life sentence. He had been a member of the notorious Dream Board Website that was serving millions from all over the world.[57] In July 2020, German national Thomas Sheller was charged for child pornography and sodomizing four teenagers aged between 10 and 13 years in Kisumu and Nairobi.[58]

As national jurisdictions in Africa struggle to erect robust legal and regulatory architecture for monitoring and prosecuting child pornography and child trafficking, these extraordinary security threats continue apace. For example, in 2019 more than 150 trafficked children between the ages of 11 to 16 were rescued in Nigeria at the border with Benin as well as in Mali. The victims originated from Benin, Burkina Faso, Niger, Nigeria, and Togo. Some had been forced into prostitution and forced labour. The children in Mali were tricked into capture by traffickers through promises of hotelier jobs in Malaysia.[59] As no child deserves to be forced into slavery and prostitution, or denied a full psychologically and physically healthy life, jurisdictions in Africa must urgently take up the challenges to protecting Africa's children and find innovative, locally adapted solutions.

---

[57] "Kenyan child pornography producer sentenced to life in prison for participation in Dreamboard child sexual exploitation website." Press Release, 29 September 2015, United States Attorney's Office, Western District of Louisiana. https://www.justice.gov/usao-wdla/pr/kenyan-child-pornography-producer-sentenced-life-prison-participation-dreamboard-child.

[58] Faith N. (2020). German Man Charged with Sodomy, Child Trafficking Detained until July 1. The Star, 19 June. https://www.the-star.co.ke/news/2020-06-19-german-man-charged-with-sodomy-child-trafficking-detained-until-july-1/.

[59] Bukola, A. (2019). Interpol: 157 Children Rescued from West Africa Trafficking Ring, CNN, 25 April. https://edition.cnn.com/2019/04/25/africa/dozens-of-human-trafficking-rescued-africa-intl/index.html.

Conclusion

Child trafficking is an international threat that violates the tangible needs and physical rights of children, as well as their psychological and security rights. In Africa, trafficking and its related menace of child pornography is an endemic problem that must be addressed, especially considering that 8% of the world's sexually exploited children are from the continent. Moreover, key structural conditions in Africa exacerbate this problem such as high levels of unemployment, poverty, hunger, and internal and transnational displacement of populations. Such political and economic instability contributes to and creates an insecure environment ripe for human trafficking. This chapter assessed the legal frameworks established to contend with online child trafficking in Africa. While there have been some successes, there are ongoing challenges in the effectiveness of legal measures in creating a secure cyber environment for children. Key among these challenges, and opportunities for needed reform, are highlighted as follows. First, African states must address deficiencies of legal regimes within their borders. This includes laxity in national laws protecting children, which allows child pornographers and traffickers to exploit such jurisdictions as safe havens. Additionally, the legal and regulatory architecture for prosecuting child trafficking and pornography needs further development to address lack of clarity in legal questions, such as determining whether an image constitutes child pornography and the nature of its creation, distribution, and possession—elements of the crime needed for successful prosecution. Second, weak capacity in judicial infrastructures contributes to inadequate enforcement of national laws for child trafficking. For example, shortcomings in the investigatory process and evidence collection can make cases vulnerable to defence claims of errors and technical malfunction; and inadequate training of judicial officers—law enforcement, prosecutors and judges—exacerbate these weaknesses. Third, while there are a number of signatories to the United Nations Convention on Children Human Rights, more African states need to sign and ratify other international and regional conventions on the protection of children, such as the Budapest Convention and the African Convention on Cybersecurity and Data Protection. Indeed, as the menaces of online child trafficking and pornography persist, African leaders and citizenries cannot delay action to protect our children, the most cherished and vulnerable segment of African societies.

REFERENCES

Adebayo, B. (2019). Interpol: 157 Children Rescued from West Africa Trafficking Ring, CNN, 25 April. https://edition.cnn.com/2019/04/25/africa/dozens-of-human-trafficking-rescued-africa-intl/index.html.

African Sisters Education Collaborative. (2021). Human Trafficking Trends in Sub-Saharan Africa, 5 January. http://asec-sldi.org/news/current/human-trafficking-sub-saharan-africa/.

African Union Convention on Cyber Security and Personal Data Protection.

Beale v S, A283/2018. (2019). ZAWCHC. http://www.saflii.org/za/cases/ZAWCHC/2019/47.html.

Bello, P. O., & Adewale A. O. (2020). The Conundrum of Human Trafficking in Africa. In Jane Reeves (Ed.), *Modern Slavery and Human Trafficking*. InTech Open.

Carmel, R. (2019). Human Trafficking Reports Show Sub-Saharan Africa A Global Player, AfricanLII, University of Cape Town, 18 July. https://africanlii.org/article/20190718/human-trafficking-reports-show-sub-saharan-africa-global-player.

Carolissen v Director of Public Prosecution, A 531/2015. (2016). ZAWCHC, http://www.saflii.org/za/cases/ZAWCHC/2016/50.html.

Chawki, M., Darwish, A., Khan, M. A., & Tyagi, S. (2015). Cybercrime, Digital Forensics and Jurisdiction. London: Springer.

Convention on Cybercrime (ETS No. 185). (2004). https://www.coe.int/en/web/conventions/full-list?module=treaty-detail&treatynum=185.

Convention on the Rights of Children, United Nations General Assembly resolution 44/25 (1989). https://www.ohchr.org/en/instruments-mechanisms/instruments/convention-rights-child.

Cybercrimes (Prohibition, Prevention, Etc) Act (2015), Nigeria.

European Union Treaty No. 185. https://www.coe.int/en/web/conventions/full-list/-/conventions/treaty/185.

Ferguson, F. (2019). Court Hears Child Porn Video was Discovered on Phone of Father of Two After It was Left in for Repair, 25 July. Irish Examiner. https://www.irishexaminer.com/breakingnews/ireland/court-hears-child-porn-video-was-discovered-on-phone-of-fatherof-two-after-it-was-left-in-for-repair-939451.html.

Films and Publications Act, 1996. Act No. 65 of 1996, South Africa. http://www.saflii.org/za/legis/consol_act/fapa1996220/.

Frei, N. (2017). On 'Cyber Trafficking' and the Protection of Its Victims," 26 July. Voelkerrechtsblog: International Law and International Legal Thought. https://voelkerrechtsblog.org/de/on-cyber-trafficking-and-the-protection-of-its-victims/.

INTERPOL. (2019). Human Trafficking Hundreds Rescued in West Africa. https://www.interpol.int/en/News-and-Events/News/2019/Human-trafficking-hundreds-rescued-in-West-Africa.

INTERPOL supporting East Africa Police Tackle Cross Border Crime. https://www.interpol.int/en/News-and-Events/News/2019/INTERPOL-supporting-East-Africa-police-tackle-rising-cross-border-crime.

Kaberia, J. (2020). Human Trafficking and Child Exploitation on the Increase During COVID-19, Capital FM, 2 June. https://www.capitalfm.co.ke/news/2020/06/human-trafficking-and-child-exploitation-on-the-increase-during-covid-19/.

Kenya: Human Trafficking and Child Exploitation on the Increase During COVID-19. https://allafrica.com/stories/202006020452.html.

Nyasuguta, F. (2020). German Man Charged with Sodomy, Child Trafficking Detained until July 1. The Star, 19 June. https://www.the-star.co.ke/news/2020-06-19-german-man-charged-with-sodomy-child-trafficking-detained-until-july-1/.

Osborne v. Ohio, 495 U.S. 103 (1990).

Parker, D. B. (1998). Fighting Computer Crime: A New Framework for Protecting Information. ISBN 0471163783. New York: Wiley.

Protocol to Prevent, Suppress and Punish Trafficking in Persons Especially Women and Children, Supplementing the United Nations Convention against Transnational Organized Crime. (2000). United Nations. https://www.ohchr.org/en/instruments-mechanisms/instruments/protocol-prevent-suppress-and-punish-trafficking-persons.

Ranjano, F. (2020). Sale and Sexual Exploitation of Children in the context of Travel and Tourism in Goa. Journal of Victimology and Victim Justice, 3(1).

Rice, X., Dale, F., & Alasdair, S. (2007). Child Accuses French Charity of Child trafficking, The Guardian. 29 October. https://www.theguardian.com/world/2007/oct/29/spain.france.

Secretary General Address Palermo 201 (12th December 2000).

Seto, M. C., Buckman, C., Dwyer, R. G., & Quayle, E. (2018). Production and Active Trading of Child Sexual Exploitation Images Depicting Identified Victims. National Center for Missing and Exploited Children (Thorn-funded), March. https://www.thorn.org/wp-content/uploads/2018/03/Production-and-Active-Trading-of-CSAM_FullReport_FINAL.pdf.

The Computer Misuse and Cybercrimes Act, Kenya. (2018). https://nc4.go.ke/the-computer-misuse-and-cybercrimes-act/.

United Nations Convention against Transnational Organised Crime, the Protocol to Prevent, Suppress and Punish Trafficking in Persons (2003).

United States Attorney's Office, Western District of Louisiana. (2015). Kenyan child pornography producer sentenced to life in prison for participation in Dreamboard child sexual exploitation website. Press Release,

29 September. https://www.justice.gov/usao-wdla/pr/kenyan-child-pornography-producer-sentenced-life-prison-participationdreamboard-child.
United States v. Williams, 553 U.S. 285 (2008).
United States v. Zauner, 688 F.3d 426, 428 (8th Cir. 2012).
US Immigration and Customs Enforcement. https://www.ice.gov/.
Witting, S. (2017). Cyber' trafficking? An interpretation of the Palermo Protocol in the digital era, 28 June. Voelkerrechtsblog: International Law and International Legal Thought. https://voelkerrechtsblog.org/cyber-trafficking-aninterpretation-of-the-palermo-protocol-in-the-digital-era/.

Postscript

Understanding how we create peace in any given context is complex because it involves many institutions, people, and communities having to deal with a range of violence and conflicts. We know that peace is created by those who live in the midst of the violent conflicts. We need their knowledge of how to create new structures and develop a contextual understanding of what long-term peace and security looks like. The authors in this book are both experts in their field and are from Africa which means they bring a deep local knowledge with them and apply that to their research. They are building a new understanding that helps us see that local issues of PTSD and domestic violence and international concerns about climate change and cybersecurity are all part of building peace and security in Africa.

It was such a pleasure to be at the workshop at which these papers were first presented in Nairobi. The authors not only bring expertise but also a great commitment to understanding and building peace in Africa, and of supporting one another. I am excited by the range of topics that participants have chosen because it shows that the violence people experience in their lives, and the community responses to it, are as important as the global issues that are addressed internationally and experienced locally such as terrorism. This book is an important contribution to learning about peace and security in Africa because we're hearing from those who bring their expertise as Africans. I look forward to hearing more from all of these authors as their research, theories, and insights build the field of peace and security in Africa by Africans.

Dr. Rachel Julian
Professor of Peace Studies
Leeds Beckett University

Index

A
African experiences, 2
African leaders, 6, 23, 116, 226
African Peace and Security Architecture (APSA), 10, 21, 25
African scholars, 2
African Union (AU), 2, 10, 149, 151, 153, 157, 160, 161, 168, 171, 173, 178, 182, 184, 189
African Union Mission in Somalia (AMISOM), 5, 6, 10, 152–154, 156–164, 166–168, 170–190
Alcohol abuse, 5, 77, 137–141, 143–145, 205

C
Child trafficking, 6, 201–203, 206–210, 212–214, 216, 218, 220, 223, 225, 226
Civic engagement, 4, 22
Climate crisis, 1
Collaboration, 2, 4, 17, 20–23, 26
Communities, 2–6, 10–13, 16, 17, 19, 20, 22–27, 38–43, 47, 48, 50–57, 64, 65, 67, 70–74, 77, 78, 81–86, 88, 90, 91, 93, 94, 96–99, 111, 114, 115, 127, 129, 138, 140, 142, 171, 180, 201, 206
Conflict, 3–5, 7–30, 41, 44, 47, 48, 52, 63–69, 71–74, 80–82, 84, 85, 89, 90, 93, 94, 111, 112, 116, 117, 123, 124, 126–129, 149, 150, 153, 163, 165, 166, 170, 189
Conflict-related sexual violence (CRSV), 4, 5, 63–74, 76–79, 81, 82, 85–91, 93, 95, 96, 98–101
Conflict resolution, 4, 13, 14, 17, 22, 28, 41, 43, 49, 54, 56, 150
Conflict transformation, 12, 52, 57, 58
Coping mechanisms, 64, 66–68, 75, 76, 78, 80, 82–87, 96–101, 144
Coping strategies, 5, 64, 67, 68, 74, 76, 81–85, 87, 98, 100

© The Editor(s) (if applicable) and The Author(s), under exclusive license to Springer Nature Switzerland AG 2023
J. Adero Ngala et al. (eds.), *Innovations in Peace and Security in Africa*, https://doi.org/10.1007/978-3-031-39043-2

INDEX

Counterterrorism, 5, 151, 152, 154, 156, 164, 165, 167, 169–175, 178, 181, 182, 184–190
COVID-19 pandemic, 1, 2
Cybersecurity, 4, 6, 215, 217

E
ECOWAS, 23
Elections, 17, 18, 28, 89–91, 100, 120, 150, 158
Emotional trauma, 5
Employment, 45, 98, 145, 181
Empowerment, 4, 5, 20, 54, 56, 118, 119, 145
Endemic threat, 4
Extremism, 14, 17, 19

F
Failed system, 35

H
Human security, 26, 40, 46, 49, 51, 53, 57

I
Impoverishment, 140, 145
Innovation, 2–4, 8, 9, 11–14, 16, 17, 20–22, 24–28
Insecurity, 3, 5, 14, 35, 36, 39–41, 43, 44, 46–51, 53, 56, 58, 88, 93, 96, 150
Institutions, 2, 9, 14, 17, 18, 41, 42, 45, 49, 71, 89, 145, 149, 150, 152, 159, 170–172, 174, 220
Interdisciplinarity, 2
International institutions, 2

J
Judicial infrastructures, 6, 208, 226

K
Kagame, Paul, 116–123, 125
Kenya, 2, 4, 5, 22–24, 35–44, 46–50, 54–56, 64, 66, 67, 73, 74, 78, 79, 81, 84, 87–99, 101, 125, 137, 138, 140, 143–145, 155–158, 175, 181–185, 187, 188, 205, 224, 225
Kiambu County, 138, 144

L
Leadership, 4, 112, 113, 115–118, 122, 123, 126, 128, 129
Legal frameworks, 6, 201, 210, 213, 226
Legitimacy, 6, 27, 116, 152, 154, 159, 160, 166, 190
Long-term consequences, 4, 52, 64, 66

M
Migration, 17, 18, 47, 48, 51

N
National institutions, 1, 174

P
Peacebuilding, 3, 4, 11, 12, 50–52, 54, 55, 57, 58, 82, 127, 150, 160
Peacekeeping, 5, 11, 17, 23, 149–154, 159–162, 164–168, 170–173, 182, 186, 188–190
Peace technologies, 4
Perspectives, 2, 3, 13, 14, 53–55, 57, 169
Policy, 1, 4, 5, 11, 12, 20, 21, 49, 63, 65, 68, 72, 81, 94, 100, 113, 128, 138, 145, 157

INDEX 235

Policy-making, 4
Political system, 4, 117, 127
Post-traumatic Growth Theory
  (PTG), 66, 78–80, 116, 120–122
Post-traumatic stress disorder (PTSD),
  5, 73, 79, 83, 92, 93, 112,
  137–145, 202
Practitioners, 2, 94
Productivity, 5, 39, 95
Psychological impacts, 4, 111, 112,
  126
Psychological trauma, 92, 113, 114,
  126, 202

R
Rehabilitation programs, 138
Rural communities, 4, 39, 42–44,
  49–58
Rwanda, 5, 22, 64, 69, 71, 86, 99,
  117–121, 123, 149

S
Self-organisation, 4, 56
Sexual violence, 63–73, 78–82,
  84–95, 97
Socio-economic security, 5
Survivors, 2, 5, 64–68, 70, 73, 74,
  77–89, 91–101, 114, 118, 121,
  122, 124
Survivors' experiences, 63
Sustainable peace, 5, 9, 27, 43, 50,
  52, 53, 55, 56, 126, 128, 189
Systems thinking, 35

T
Technological advances, 1, 27
Threats, 1, 2, 7, 19, 23, 75, 99, 114,
  125, 154, 161, 162, 174, 178,
  189, 225
Trauma, 4, 5, 65, 66, 72, 74, 75,
  79–81, 83–87, 92, 97, 112–118,
  120–123, 125–129, 140–142,
  144, 219

U
United Nations (UN), 2, 10, 25,
  63–65, 68, 69, 81, 149–154,
  157, 159–161, 164–167,
  169–171, 175, 183, 189
Utopian dream, 2

V
Violence, 1–5, 7–10, 12, 17, 18, 22,
  24–26, 35, 39–41, 43, 46–51,
  53, 55–58, 64, 66, 67, 71, 73,
  74, 80, 81, 88–90, 92, 95–101,
  114, 116, 124–129, 139, 141,
  142, 144, 150, 163, 164, 170,
  188

Y
Youth, 5, 26, 37, 40, 43–45, 47, 52,
  56, 57, 85, 111, 137, 138, 140,
  143–145, 156, 164, 167, 168,
  185
Youth populations, 5

Printed in the United States
by Baker & Taylor Publisher Services